Outlaw Ballplayers

ALSO BY R. G. (HANK) UTLEY AND SCOTT VERNER

*The Independent Carolina Baseball League,
1936–1938: Baseball Outlaws*
(McFarland, 1999; softcover 2005)

ALSO BY TIM PEELER

*Waiting for Godot's First Pitch:
More Poems from Baseball*
(McFarland, 2001)

Touching All the Bases: Poems from Baseball
(McFarland, 2000)

Outlaw Ballplayers

*Interviews and Profiles from the
Independent Carolina Baseball League*

R.G. (Hank) Utley and Tim Peeler
with Aaron Peeler

McFarland & Company, Inc., Publishers
Jefferson, North Carolina, and London

LIBRARY OF CONGRESS CATALOGUING-IN-PUBLICATION DATA

Utley, R.G., 1924–
 Outlaw ballplayers : interviews and profiles from the Independent Carolina Baseball League / R.G. (Hank) Utley and Tim Peeler with Aaron Peeler.
     p.   cm.
 Includes bibliographical references and index.

 ISBN 0-7864-2614-4 (softcover : 50# alkaline paper)

 1. Carolina League (Baseball league)—Interviews.
I. Peeler, 1957–   II. Peeler, Aaron.   III. Title.
GV875.C37U855   2006
796.357'6409756 — dc22   2006011858
[B]

British Library cataloguing data are available

©2006 R.G. Utley, Tim Peeler and Aaron Peeler. All rights reserved

No part of this book may be reproduced or transmitted in any form or by any means, electronic or mechanical, including photocopying or recording, or by any information storage and retrieval system, without permission in writing from the publisher.

On the cover: Edwin Pitts of the Albany Senators and prison bars of Sing Sing *(Hank Utley);* Ivey Weavers team, 1953 *(courtesy Harold Lail)*

Manufactured in the United States of America

McFarland & Company, Inc., Publishers
 Box 611, Jefferson, North Carolina 28640
  www.mcfarlandpub.com

To my parents, Jack and Ruby Utley, and my wife, Jean Utley.
— R.G. (Hank) Utley

To Mark Bolick, vice-president of the Carolina League, and to my mother, Ethel Sloop Peeler, Kannapolis native.
— Tim Peeler

One after one the old guys
tell me, "We sure did have fun,"
came straight from tailing rip saws,
from stacking cartons of beer
from teaching high school PE,
from driving a linen truck,
straight to the field changing in
the cabs of Ford pickups or
in the cement block ball field johns,
the clack of cleats across the
dugout slab, a coke, an oatmeal
cake, and the adrenaline to
face a forty-something ex-
minor league pitcher, bent to
prove the eminent gas of
his game — cigarettes between
the machinery of innings.
Nearing or past eighty, their
eyes glisten as we scan through
dog eared photos, players, lean
and hawk-faced in stadiums
preserved by the bright trance of
camera. Their voices
narrate — this kid was from New York,
this guy always lost his glove —
this one made it to the show.
I listen wistfully — they speak excitedly
of memories plowed deep,
now words rising in these fertile rows.

—Tim Peeler

Acknowledgements

I cannot say enough about the original work of R.G. (Hank) Utley and Scott Verner. On this project we are also grateful for the help provided by the venerable baseball researcher John F. Pardon of Crugers, New York, who gathered often obscure player records. Mr. Pardon, a founding member of SABR(the Society for American Baseball Research), insisted that we toe the line of accuracy, a hard duty for folks raised in the storytelling South. Mr. Pardon, who wrote for the *Asheville Citizen-Times* from 1966–1971, knows well our condition. I am also grateful to Myrtice Carr whose timely assistance with the Alabama Pitts chapter shed new light on old mysteries. In addition, I must express my gratitude to several family members: my wife, Penny, who allowed me the room to deal with this latest obsession; my late father, the Rev. J.L. Peeler, a very caring man who introduced me early to the game; and my son Thomas, who obliged my every technical request.

— Tim Peeler

I wish to acknowledge and thank Scott Verner once again for the excellent job of editing the nearly 2,000 pages of commentary, interview, and statistics that went into *The Independent Carolina Baseball League, 1936–1938* (McFarland, 1999). With so much material to draw from, and despite the comprehensiveness of that first volume, much that might have been published — including some of the best stories — were necessarily left out. And so I want to thank Tim Peeler for putting together my unpublished research. This second volume brings into focus the men (and women) whose talents, grit, and defiance made the Carolina League memorable. Finally, I'd like to thank the Public Library of Charlotte and Mecklenburg County for housing my papers in the Robinson-Spangler Carolina Room.

— Hank Utley

Table of Contents

Epigraph — vi
Acknowledgments — viii
Preface by Tim Peeler — 1
Introduction — 3

1. The Judge: Clement Manley Llewellyn — 7
2. The Preacher: Glenn Allen "Razz" Miller — 14
3. The Slugger: Norman Woodnut Small — 21
4. Cause Célèbre: Edwin Collins "Alabama" Pitts — 33
5. The Showman: Charles M. "Struttin' Bud" Shaney — 53
6. The Manager: Bobby Hipps — 60
7. A Gang of Two — 66
    The Forgotten: Richard Grey Clarke — 66
    The Scout: Edwin "Cy" Williams — 69
8. The Brain: Richard Broadus Culler — 71
9. The Wives — 81
    Winnie Taylor — 81
    Edna Carrier — 84
10. The Star: Lawrence Columbus "Crash" Davis — 86
11. The Pro: Lee Raven "Buck" Ross — 97
12. The Phenom: George Barley — 103
13. The Truth: Ulmont Baker — 111
14. Umpires — 117
15. The Canadian Tornado: Vince Barton — 120

16. Mr. Henry: William Henry Whitley	125
17. Home Boys	133
Who's on First?: Frank Hopkins	133
Brother: Marvin Watts	135
The Sandlapper: Houston Hines	139
18. Rebels	144
The Pitcher: Tracey Hitchner	144
The Tramp Athlete: Robert Merritt "Pat" Shores	149
The Batboy: Harold Lail	154
Appendix A: Pitts Family History by Myrtice Ann Carr	161
Appendix B: Henry Whitley's Team Record Book	169
Appendix C: Selected Batting and Pitching Statistics	171
Appendix D: The Carolina Victory League	177
Bibliography	193
Index	195

Preface
by Tim Peeler

Hank Utley and Scott Verner published their exquisite account of the rise and fall of the Depression-era outlaw Carolina League in 1999. After my first book of baseball poems (*Touching All the Bases*, McFarland, 1999) came out, I was lucky enough to meet them at a literary festival in Charlotte, NC. I later shared a book signing with Mr. Utley and quickly became a fan of both him and his passion for research and history.

In 2004, along with Brian McLawhorn, I authored a history of local baseball in Catawba County, NC. Hickory, NC, my hometown, offered a rich history of baseball on the professional as well as amateur levels. Included in that history was the three-year run of the Hickory Rebels outlaw Carolina League club. Mr. Utley met our request for assistance on this chapter with an unparalleled zeal and generosity.

When I approached him earlier this year about this project, his response was no less enthusiastic. Soon the Utley files began to arrive, and I was astounded by the quality of his research and his ability to recognize the humanity and the vitality of this story. Far from being leftovers from his prior book, these profiles and interviews affix another layer of meaning to an already important story. Here you will find the actual words not just of the players, but also those of the sportswriters, an owner, a business manager, a batboy, and the unique perspective of the Depression-era baseball wife. Our subjects range from a successful Lutheran minister who could make more money playing the game to a "notorious" ex-convict whose national celebrity came with a heavy price. Players interviewed in their twilight years recall with great clarity the unpredictable adventure of outlaw baseball and reveal as well the raw energy and independent spirit that made them great competitors.

Here the reader will meet outstanding pitchers George Barley, Buck Ross and Bud Shaney, prolific sluggers Vince Barton and Norman Small, and superior fielders Richard Broadus Culler and Glenn "Razz" Miller, among others. The reader will travel to the out of the way nooks of the rural South, places like Watts Crossroads and Rockwell, Landis and Cooleemee. Most often it is in the theater of the bucolic South where baseball was a way of life that these stories, filled with wisdom, joy, and sadness, begin. Hopefully, with our faithful attention to memory and history, they will live on for a while.

Introduction

The Independent Carolina Baseball League 1936–1938: Baseball Outlaws was published in 1999. The book has been well-received by baseball fans and historians. It has become a definitive history of the dreams, trials, and tribulations of textile executives, civic leaders, and professional baseball players during the period of the Great Depression, labeled the "desperate years" by author James D. Horan.

In writing the story of outlaw baseball with my good friend, Scott Verner, of the *Charlotte Observer,* our goal was to identify how and why this league came to be, how it grew and how it died in three short years. The Carolina League never challenged the infamous "reserve clause" of organized professional baseball. It simply ignored it, and encouraged dissatisfied professional baseball players to jump valid contracts, change their names to protect their identities from organized baseball and thereby allow themselves the opportunity of earning a living by playing a game that they loved.

Those were desperate years for the entire nation. In the early 1930s, half of organized professional baseball's minor leagues went broke and ceased operations. Yet they maintained ownership of all their players, who could not play anywhere else in organized baseball unless the new team purchased the player's contract from the defunct team. Twenty-five percent of the nation was unemployed. Professional players sometimes picked up extra money by playing one or two games as a ringer for the hundreds of semi-pro teams all over the country.

In order to complete my first book, it was necessary to edit dozens of down-to-earth human interest stories to a few lines apiece. This book in effect has the purpose of identifying the dreams of many ballplayers, some in their own words, and to explain how and why they became "outlaws."

Some were young college players on their way to the major leagues. One, a man who became a noted Christian minister, was a baseball outlaw because he could not make a living in the church. Several players became successful businessmen after their baseball careers ended. And many others held on to their dreams as their baseball years dwindled down to a precious few. The environment of the outlaw league is best described in these news articles from 1936.

> Today is opening day, you know. It's a new baseball picture for Charlotte and this section. Not organized professional baseball ... but something which may prove just as entertaining and diverting. Certainly, it's a noble experiment, and most engaging.
>
> Charlotte is in the Carolina League. The league abides by the rules and general plan of organized professional baseball. The ball they hit is standard and bears the league president's signature. The carefully chosen umpires are uniformed, draw regular salaries, and work under strict supervision. The only difference is the players are not strictly chattels as in organized professional baseball. They can leave on a moment's notice and go to an organized professional league, but they cannot jump from one club to another in this circuit.*
>
> By June, the Carolina League had the attention of organized baseball:
>
> Presence of players on the ineligible list of organized baseball on the rosters of clubs in the Carolina League, an independent organization, has brought forth a warning from President W.G. Bramham of the National Association of Professional Baseball Leagues, calling the attention of all players and clubs in the National Association to conditions which exist in this outlaw league.
>
> "This Carolina League," Bramham said, "composed of Concord, Kannapolis, Mooresville, Shelby, Hickory, Forest City, Charlotte, and Valdese is harboring and playing players under contract or reserve with organized ball. All such

Carolina League Managers — Five of the original managers from the outlaw Carolina League. Standing left to right: Stumpy Culbreth, Hickory Rebels; Blackie Carter, Charlotte Hornets. Sitting: Mack Arnette, Shelby Cee Cees; Ginger Watts, Kannapolis Towelers; Maurice Frew, Forest City Owls (Hank Utley).

*Charlotte Observer, May 18, 1936, from an editorial by Jake Wade.

1941 Philadelphia A's — After the Carolina League disbanded in 1938, many of the players went on to establish themselves at higher levels of organized ball. The 1941 Philadelphia Athletics included former Kannapolis Toweler star shortstop Fred Chapman (front row, last on right) as well as former Kannapolis Toweler pitcher Lee (Buck) Ross (back row, fourth from right) and Gastonia native Larry "Crash" Davis (back row, fifth from right). Manager Connie Mack is at center, in the suit (courtesy Fred Chapman).

players are placed on the ineligible list, and all players and clubs in organized ball are notified that the playing with or against ineligibles, or with or against clubs playing or harboring ineligible players, will bring about the ineligibility of any and all players who fail to observe this warning." President Bramham declared the law would be rigidly invoked in dealing with players under jurisdiction of the national association who competed with or against organizations harboring ineligibles.*

---

*National Association of Professional Baseball Leagues news release. Concord Tribune, June 16, 1936.

1

The Judge: Clement Manley Llewellyn

Born: August 1, 1895, Dobson, North Carolina; died: November 26, 1969, Concord, North Carolina

In 1922 at the age of 26, Manley Llewellyn climbed the mound at the Polo Grounds, then the home field for the Yankees, and offered up batting practice pitches to the immortal Babe Ruth. He could hardly have imagined then what twists and turns his life would take and how long he would be involved with America's Pastime. Llewellyn made his professional debut that summer, a rarity in that he went directly from the college game to the major leagues. Contrary to his wishes, the Yankees would provide him little more than the proverbial cup of coffee. His official record shows that he pitched one scoreless inning. After his debut, Llewellyn's career as a player was all downhill. By 1926, he was playing semi-professional textile ball in Kannapolis, North Carolina, a small mill town that was owned by Cannon Mills.

Most people would have quit the game for good, but Llewellyn's failure as a player never stopped him from finding other ways to impact the game. For years he would be the center of the baseball world in neighboring Concord, serving much as Henry Whitley did in Kannapolis as a kind of Mr. Baseball, managing, promoting, and most importantly procuring players that provided the town with the competitive edge that its residents so desired. Eventually, he would make the leap to the legitimate minor league professional ranks where he served as league president at the Class B and D levels.

Judge Lew, as he later came to be called, was born the son of an important attorney in the northwestern piedmont town of Dobson, North Carolina, in 1895. He grew up playing baseball like most of the boys of his time. He did well at the game and continued to play after high school at the Oak Ridge Military Academy. By 1915 he had earned an academic scholarship to attend the state's oldest university, the University of North Carolina at Chapel Hill.

1922 Yankees pitchers — From left: front row, Bob Shawkey, Joe Bush; back row, Lefty O'Doul, Waite Hoyt, Manley Llewellyn, Sam Jones, George Murray (courtesy Robert C. Llewellyn III).

Having arrived at Carolina, Lew quickly established himself as both an outstanding pitcher and hitter as well as a team leader. His academic and athletic careers were temporarily sidelined when the United States became involved in World War I. Llewellyn withdrew from school in order to work in a Virginia munitions plant. Later he joined the Navy, but the war ended before he saw military action.

When he returned to Chapel Hill in 1919, Lew had determined that he would, like his father, enter the field of law. He also returned to the game he loved. That spring he was charged with two losses as a pitcher. They would be the last of his Carolina career. He finished his college career with a 23–2 record, and in his senior year was credited with 11 of the team's 17 victories. The Chapel Hill nine, led by Llewellyn and future major leaguer Ernest "Mule" Shirley, won three straight state championships between the years of 1920 and 1922.

Despite his age, Lew's exploits on the diamond drew attention from many major league scouts. This included the defending American League champion New York Yankees. Llewellyn signed for a bonus of $500, and records indicate that he received a monthly salary of $400, both enormous amounts for a rookie of that time. As soon as he completed his senior year at Carolina, he reported to New York. In a 1948 interview, Llewellyn recalled his introduction to the major league version of the game:

1. The Judge

I was told to report direct to the New York office. I got off the train about seven o'clock in the morning, early in May, 1922, and I got to the Yankee office before it opened. They told me to report for practice that day. I got out to the ballpark, and they gave me a uniform. Right away, they put me on the mound for batting practice, and I wasn't doing too badly when a big guy steps up to the left side of the plate. He's swinging a big bat, and I know it's Babe Ruth. It was the first time I had ever seen him, and a knot comes up in my throat. I thought I would choke. I couldn't get the ball over the plate, three or four balls. Finally I got them in to him, but I was scared to death.

But I became Babe's favorite batting practice pitcher. I had good control, and I would send them right off the thigh on the inside corner. He used to hit four out of five pitches out of the ball park. In the Polo Grounds, he could knock them over the short right field corner with one hand. Babe would wait for my turn to pitch batting practice, or hurry to bat if I was about ready to quit. It was a grand experience for a rookie.

Llewellyn made what turned out to be his only appearance on June 18, 1922. In the game which featured future Hall of Fame pitchers Waite Hoyt and Stan Coveleski, Yankee manager Miller Huggins used Lew in a cleanup role in the eighth inning of a game which the Yankees lost 9–2. He gave up one hit but allowed no runs or walks. A month and a half later after he had sustained several broken ribs in a pre-game accident, he was sent down to the Class AA Buffalo Bisons of the International League. The Yankees recalled him to the parent club September 12, but he failed to make another appearance.

In January of 1923, the Yankees sold Llewellyn to the Atlanta Crackers of the Southern Association. His ribs were still bothering him, however, and he only appeared in three games, winning none and losing two. At the end of the year he dropped another rung on the minor league ladder when he was sent to the Class B Greenville Spinners of the South Atlantic League. In 1924, he finally got to play a full season of professional ball, winning 15 and losing 10 in 31 appearances while pitching for a weak team.

Before the next season, Llewellyn began a new chapter in his life. At the age of 29 on April 13, 1925, he married Ruth Pitchford of Oxford, North Carolina. That year he won ten while losing 11 on a Spinners ball club that staggered to a 60–68 sixth place finish. A July 1 *Greenville News* report summed up his season:

> Manley Llewellyn, the tall North Carolina lawyer who plays ball in the summer for pleasure, seemed to hit his stride in Knoxville Saturday, when he blanked the Smokies 2–0. He has pitched good ball all season, but just at the wrong time, somebody would pole out a home run and take the game. In one game, Lew allowed only four hits while the Spinners collected about ten but lost the game by a one run margin.

Later in August, a *News* report after a disappointing 3–1 loss was captioned, "Tar Heel lawyer allows seven hits and fans seven to take a bitter defeat."

The following year the Spinners organization decided to make a change in an attempt to make their team more competitive. They hired well-known minor league player-manager Frank Walker. In order to improve the team, space would have to be made for talented young players. Llewellyn made his only appearance that year for the Spinners on May 2, pitching well in a 3–2 victory over Columbia. Ten days later his playing days in Greenville came to an end. When Greenville tried to sell him to the Hattiesburg Pine-toppers of the Cotton States League, he refused. At thirty years of age, sore-armed and likely frustrated, Llewellyn had reached the bottom of the ladder at the Class D level. He was released.

At this point, he looked around for a place to locate a law practice. Since passing the bar in 1921 he had practiced law in his hometown of Dobson during the off-season. While he searched for a new home, he heard about a semi-pro team in Cabarrus County that was looking for good players to finish out their season. The *Concord Tribune* reported on August 14 that Manley Llewellyn, star pitcher from the University of North Carolina and former New York Yankee, was now the first baseman for the Kannapolis Towelers. During seven games, he batted .450 for Kannapolis and was paid well for his services. Lew and Ruth lived in a rooming house in Kannapolis and were considering the town as their new home. The folks in nearby county seat of Concord had other plans. His full time practice would do better in a larger town. Besides he was not ready to quit the game he loved. Concord hired him to manage and play for their team with the intention that he build a team that could defeat Henry Whitley's Kannapolis nine. The textile ball of this era was a fast uncontrolled brand with rabid fans and unpredictable, sometimes violent, situations. Llewellyn thrived in these adverse conditions. He applied his strong leadership abilities to managing his quirky players and learned quickly the art of raiding regional minor league teams to gain an edge in big games. The result for Concord was the chance to play Kannapolis in a season-ending championship series.

Preparations for the games went beyond ordinary practice. When C.E. Stewart, a Concord theater owner, heard that Kannapolis was bringing in outlaw players, he proceeded to do the same and began to scout both the South Atlantic and Piedmont Leagues for potential players. Llewellyn in the meantime contacted Frank Walker, the Greenville manager who had released him, about borrowing some players. It was to be the first wholesale use of outlaw players in an area game. It was the kind of contest that required a combination of game expertise, promotion, and recruitment that both Llewellyn and Whitley would bring to the independent Carolina League nine years later. *Charlotte Observer* sportswriter Jack Wade noted the escalation in his column:

1. The Judge

Concord and Kannapolis had set the sky the limit for the final games. So rapidly did the managers of the two clubs change players that we doubt seriously if they knew all the players they were giving tremendous salaries. The clubs quit semi-professional ball and began to scout the South Atlantic, Piedmont and Virginia Leagues. They succeeded in getting the men, but the prices came high. Two more weeks of such procedure and we daresay that most of the fans in both places would have had to mortgage house and lot to pay salaries to the ball players.

Rumors circulated that the umpires had been paid off by both teams. Finally, the Concord mayor declared the game day a holiday so that all the citizens could attend. When the afternoon of September 8 arrived, Webb Field was packed. The crowd estimate, including people in trees and on surrounding hillsides, was around 7000. Marvin Watts, who would later be a star infielder in the Carolina League, watched the game from a tree. Watts, who would later play before 6000 fans in Kannapolis, insisted that it was the biggest crowd he had ever seen in Cabarrus County.

The rivalry between the two towns was outrageous. There were rumors that fans from both Concord and Kannapolis were armed with knives and guns. It was also a great social occasion with most folks wearing their Sunday best. The arguing began before the game over ground rules and what would be expected of the crowd which edged against each foul line. After Kannapolis had taken a 2–0 lead in the top of the first, Concord rallied in the bottom of the frame, apparently tying the score. When the umpires disallowed the second run, fans from both sides headed toward home plate. Just as the fight was about to begin, a terrific downpour of rain erupted from the sky. The crowd stampeded from the field through ankle deep water only to find that a few blocks away, the streets were dry. The next day, an emergency meeting was held between the managers of the two teams. Llewellyn and his counterpart, Rube Wilson, reached an agreement that the series would not be played. The antagonism between the fans and players of the two teams was simply too great to take a second chance on a riot.

In 1928 Llewellyn began another chapter of his life. He successfully ran for the office of Concord city judge. Judge Lew became a popular man on the bench, known for his sense of humor and his firm but judicious handling of cases. As a result he was easily reelected at the end of each term.

While serving on the judicial bench, Llewellyn continued to serve on the baseball bench as well. He managed the 1928 and 1929 Concord semipro team to great success. The 1929 team included two players who would make it all the way to the major league. They were Ray Prim and Buck Marrow. When the 1929 season concluded, the thirty-four-year-old judge retired as a field manager. He served rather in the front office where he could more easily influence the behind-the-scenes action.

The fierce rivalries between area towns elevated the level of ball and created a demand for highly-paid quality players. Even as the country worked its way through the toughest times of the Great Depression, a fully professional league named the Carolina League was formed in 1936. The league operated independently of the National Association of Professional Baseball Leagues, the same organization that soon labeled it an outlaw league. The practice of bringing in professional players from organized ball was elevated to a new level. What Llewellyn had begun in 1927 became accepted practice. Judge Lew stayed involved with the Concord Weavers during the outlaw years of 1936–38 as a member of their board of directors. While Lew remained behind the scenes at this point, the team's success and style certainly had his stamp. The exchange of players was a fast and furious process. One observer noted that over 100 different men suited up for the Kannapolis Towelers during the 1937 season.

By the end of the 1938 season, the Carolina League had run its course. High salaries and pressure from organized baseball took their toll. Ironically, it was at a January 1939 meeting that Manley Llewellyn proposed a new Class D League that would bring the outlaw league cities into the fold of organized baseball. When his proposal was accepted, the outlaw league was in effect dissolved and the NC State League was formed. By the next year the league suffered a financial scandal. When the team owners determined that the league president was at fault, they approached Judge Lew about the job. While maintaining his law practice, he began to serve as the NC State League president. He kept this position for six years, and at one time maintained the practice of viewing at least one inning of every opening day game. At the end of the 1942 season, war restrictions and a lack of players forced the league to suspend play. Though professional ball ceased during 1943, area fans still remained loyal to the game. In order to satisfy them and to boost the wartime morale, Llewellyn took it upon himself to form a semi-pro league which became known as the Carolina Victory League. The league was comprised of teams from four of the NC State League towns. The players were a wild mix of men who were either too old or too young to serve in the war. Play took on the rambunctious nature of the old Carolina League, and was often interrupted by fights and disputes.

At the end of World War II, play was resumed in the NC State League. Llewellyn resumed his position as president in 1945. The following year representatives from larger cities in western North Carolina and eastern Tennessee formed the Class B Tri-State League. Again in the search for an experienced baseball man, they set their sights on Manley Llewellyn. During 1946, Judge Lew practiced law, served as a county judge and as the president of two minor leagues. This situation lasted for only one season. At the end of 1946, Llewellyn gave up the Class D NC State League and concentrated

1. The Judge 13

Judge Lew continued his work as a minor league executive after World War II. Here he meets with representatives for potential teams in the new Tri-State League in 1946. Left to right: Calvin Griffith, Charlotte; Clyde Short, Shelby; Llewellyn; and Jay Jenkins, Wilmington (courtesy *Charlotte Observer*).

his efforts on expanding the Class B Tri-State. Under his guidance that league prospered, adding two new cities in 1947. After the 1950 season, Judge Lew turned over the reins of the Tri-State League, officially retiring from the game of baseball. Unofficially, however, he continued to influence baseball affairs in the area. Because of his experience as a player, manager, and executive, his opinions were often sought after. Llewellyn never retired from his primary job. He practiced law and presided over the Cabarrus County Domestic Relations Court until his death in 1969.

While his chosen profession was the field of law, Llewellyn's lifelong vocation was the field of baseball. Although his once promising career as a player may not have turned out like he wanted, Judge Lew was never discouraged by his setbacks. As a player, he got that rare taste of the major leagues, something that thousands of minor league players only dream of. Llewellyn's greatest achievements were gained through his decisions and guidance that helped shape the careers of countless players, umpires, and baseball executives. Using his baseball contacts, (it was once estimated that he knew half of the major league scouts) Lew often went out of his way to help local men secure college scholarships and professional contracts. Because of his undying love for the game of baseball, Manley Llewellyn left a lasting mark on the game and on the people he met along the way. Note: See Appendix D, page 177, for story of the 1943 Carolina Victory League.

2

The Preacher: Glenn Allen "Razz" Miller

Born: November 7, 1909, Rockwell, North Carolina; died: May 13, 1981, Rockwell, North Carolina

> "The name 'Razz' came out of a high school play at the Rockwell High School where he played ball and graduated. He played a character in some high school play called Rastus and the students started shortening it to Razz and somehow the name stuck. His real name was Glenn. Of course, all the ballplayers called him 'Preacher.'"
> — Hollis Miller, son of Razz Miller

"Razz" Miller was a country boy. Throughout his life, he reflected the character of one who had experienced hard work on a farm, strong family love, and immediately after college graduation, the financial devastation of the Great Depression. He was a gifted athlete and an ardent lover of his hunting dogs.

Soon after graduating from Rockwell High School in 1926, he was plowing a muddy field on his family's farm, barefooted, when he was approached by a coach from Lenoir-Rhyne College, a private Lutheran school in Hickory, NC. The coach had been directed to the field by Razz's father, Cal Miller. Because of the muddy condition of the field, Razz insisted that the stranger stay at the edge of the field. From there the coach introduced himself and asked Razz if he was interested in going to college and playing ball. Razz replied that his father was very interested in his going to college and that he liked to play ball.

So, in the fall of 1926, this Rowan County country boy entered Lenoir-Rhyne College. At L-R, he displayed tremendous athletic ability, becoming a three-sport letterman — football, basketball, and baseball. Miller once sustained a broken leg while playing football, and this injury influenced his approach to baseball. Razz was fast on his feet, with a proven ability to steal bases (his 14 stolen bases tied Broadus Culler for the Carolina league lead in 1937), yet he refused to slide and take a chance on reinjuring the leg. Buck Glover, a teammate and first baseman for the 1942 Concord Weavers of the Class D NC State League, said Razz was the only player that he knew of who had a clause in his contract that said he did not have to slide, yet he stole more than his share of bases.

Razz Miller's college years can best be described by the caption printed under his photograph in the school's annual: "To study little, to worry less is my idea of happiness."

While at Lenoir-Rhyne, Miller played on winning baseball teams all four years for Coach Dick Gurley. Those seasons included two victories over North Carolina State and one over Wake Forest. His best season as a Mountain Bear was 1930 when the team went 12–4. Razz shared the diamond with other outstanding players like Shine Rumple, Jack Kiser, Cloyd Hager, and one of the school's finest ever, Lloyd Little.

After getting his BA in the spring of 1930, Miller started teaching at the local Landis, NC, High School and playing baseball with various semi-pro teams. The Great Depression had helped eliminate semi-pro teams in the

Glenn "Razz" Miller was a well-respected member of the Lutheran clergy. He was also a speedy outfielder and star for the Kannapolis Towelers in the Carolina League. He is pictured here in his baseball playing days at his alma mater, Lenoir-Rhyne College (courtesy Mrs. Razz Miller) (courtesy Lenoir-Rhyne College).

textile towns, but nearly every mill village had a team and offered ample opportunity for an extra player to play in a single big game.

While working as a teacher and a coach at Landis High School, Razz lived with the Rev. C.P. Fisher, Sr. (Jr. later became a minister also.) According to Razz's son, the Rev. Hollis Miller, Razz had given serious thought to entering the ministry earlier, but he loved teaching and coaching and being free to play ball during the summer. This meant money year-round, something that not everybody had during this time. The time that Miller spent with the Rev. Fisher and his wife greatly affected him and would later influence his decision to answer the call of the ministry.

Miller entered the Lutheran Theological Seminary and graduated in 1934. Beginning in June 1934, he served for two years at Calvary Lutheran Church in Concord. He continued, however, with the approval of his church, to play semi-pro ball a couple of times a week. He resigned from the ministry in May 1936.

According to his son, Hollis, his love of coaching, teaching, and playing ball, coupled with the financial difficulties that were pervasive in small Depression-era churches led him to decide that he "may not be cut out for the ordained ministry."

Two incidents during this time period may help explain Razz's decision to give up the ministry.

Fred Chapman of Kannapolis, NC, played semi-pro baseball with Razz. Chapman was later signed by the Washington Senators and was assigned to Albany, NY, of the International League. He later played three years for the Philadelphia Athletics and finally many years in the minor leagues.

Chapman told the story of looking back at the team bench during one of the numerous fights that broke out during the semi-pro games. Razz was sitting there with his head hanging between his legs. Chapman, knowing that Miller never participated in any of the fights, walked back to the bench and asked, "Razz, what's wrong?"

Razz replied, "Fred, I've either got to quit playing ball or quit preaching. I can't go on like this—not backing up my teammates."

The second incident occurred when the Landis Cardinals of the 1934 Carolina Textile semi-pro league offered Razz $15 per game to play when he was making only $50 a month at his church. Playing three to four games a week meant more money than preaching for a month. (The average textile worker was making only $10–12 a week if he was fortunate enough to get a full week's work during the Depression) Although the church gave Miller permission to play as long as it did not interfere with his church work, the pressure and responsibility of two jobs that did not necessarily complement each other were too much, especially for a man of Razz Miller's character.

2. The Preacher

Incidentally, an analysis of semi-pro records shows that the 1935 Landis Cardinals were one of the best semi-pro teams to ever play in the Piedmont textile towns. They finished with a 49–24 record and won both the league pennant and playoff. Razz Miller played well enough to be named the league's all-star center fielder.

In 1936, despite the efforts of the National Association of Professional Baseball Leagues, eight Piedmont North Carolina textile towns formed an independent, full six games per week baseball league. Professional players in organized baseball from all over the country flocked to Piedmont, North Carolina, in search of baseball jobs that included off-season mill work. Their eagerness was spurred as well by a nationwide unemployment rate that ran from 20 to 25 percent. This league would last for three years through 1938.

In May 1936, after resigning from the ministry, Razz Miller joined the Kannapolis Towelers in the 1936 independent Carolina League. For the next three off-seasons he would work at Cannon Mills. The outlaw league was challenging, but it was also a financial blessing for Miller. As his son Hollis noted, "About that outlaw league, Dad never did go into too much detail but that it was a very fast brand of ball and a lot of players in that league had just come out of the majors or the high minor leagues because of the way the teams got some of their players, but Dad said they were good. He said you had to be a good player to make one of the teams and to stay with it. The league was very competitive and my dad, even though he was a preacher, was a competitor. I don't know whether the baseball rules went out the window or not, but I had the feeling that you had to be a man to play in it. I don't know what governed that league. He did work in the mill some, but I remember him saying he could pull down enough money in the summer — it was good pay in that day and time — so he didn't have to work in the winter."

In terms of baseball, the outlaw years were good for Miller. He batted over .300 each year and held the reputation as one of the best outfielders in the league. For his team, the Kannapolis Towelers, 1937 was their big year when they won the league pennant by three games over their archrivals, the Concord Weavers.

After the Carolina League collapsed at the end of the 1938 season, Razz Miller finally joined organized professional baseball. He played for the 1939 Martinsville (VA) Manufacturers in the Class D Bi-State League.

Before the 1939 season ended in Martinsville, VA, Miller began a second job. He returned to teaching and coaching at Southmont High School in Lexington, NC. Razz would travel to games each night and return to teach the next morning. It was during this 1939–40 school year that he met Ruth Hollis, English and French teacher at Southmont. Little did they know at the time that they would become man and wife on May 25, 1941.

Ruth Hollis was the daughter of a Baptist minister. When people asked Razz how he talked the daughter of a Baptist minister into marrying a man that was not only a coach and a teacher but also an ordained Lutheran minister, he replied jokingly and with a glint in his eye, "It took a Lutheran to save her." Ruth Hollis Miller was born May 27, 1917 and died April 19, 2006.

After completing that first school year at Southmont, Miller signed with the 1940 Kannapolis Towelers in the Class D NC State League. He ended the season, however, with the Thomasville Tommies in the same league. Undoubtedly, this move was necessary in order to locate within several miles of his teaching and coaching job.

Following the 1940–41 school year, Miller, in anticipation of a career in public education, completed the requirements for a school principal's certificate at Catawba College in Salisbury. That was also the summer that he and Ruth were married. The wedding was delayed for a few weeks when Razz caught the measles from one of his students. They returned to teach the following fall. In their minds, they were to complete their lives teaching, a profession they both truly loved.

Then on December 7, Pearl Harbor was attacked, an event that would ultimately change their lives as it would the lives of many young couples. At the end of the 1941–42 school year, the wartime draft was beginning to take young men from their homes all over America, and this included young professional baseball players and school teachers.

Razz had turned thirty-two years of age on November 7, 1941, and the draft had not reached men his age yet. He returned to Class D professional baseball with the Concord Weavers in the 1942 NC State League. This was to be the last year of the NC State League until the summer of 1945. Although she was pregnant with their first child, Ruth attended as many games as possible that summer. She recalled that on one particularly bad night Razz rushed to dress after the game and was still chewing tobacco when he got into the car. This was the only instance in their lives together that she was around Razz when he was chewing. Needless to say, the aroma of the tobacco and Razz's constant spitting out the window did not help Ruth in her condition.

Miller returned to teaching and coaching at Southmont High for the 1942–43 year. His first child, Hollis, was born in December of that year.

In 1943 the wartime draft was catching up even to men of Razz's age. He reported and to his surprise was classified as an ordained minister and placed in the chaplain pool for future callup. Razz knew, of course, that he was an ordained minister, but he also knew that he had not preached in seven years. He had also just completed four years in the North Carolina education system. To a man like Razz Miller, this was both puzzling and troublesome. He would later realize that this was the first step toward being

2. The Preacher

called again to the ministry. During that soul-searching summer of 1943, Miller had his last fling in semi-pro baseball. A Carolina Victory League had been organized with four teams—Salisbury, Landis, Concord, and Charlotte. Razz joined the Concord Weavers on June 5, 1943, but played only a few games before taking on the responsibilities of principal of Southmont High. He began scrambling to find teachers then for the 1943–44 school year.

Miller's role as principal was short-lived. In November, after just five months in the position, a church committee from the St. Stephens–Mt. Olive Lutheran Parish approached him about becoming minister for their rural parish in Cabarrus County.

Despite the love and satisfaction Razz and Ruth felt for their careers in education, they were now confronted by a pivotal decision. Razz's surprise draft classification as ordained minister followed by this new call to preach God's word caused them to re-evaluate the purpose of their work and lives. Would this be the final step of being once again called to carry the message of God to their neighbors in Rowan and Cabarrus counties? They were perplexed as Ruth said, "I knew I married a teacher, coach and baseball player, but I knew Razz Miller. For four years I had watched Razz, how he related to students and adults, how his concern and love for all he met made our lives and the lives of others richer. This was truly his calling."

Glenn Allen "Razz" Miller served as the minister to the St. Stephens–Mt. Olive Lutheran Parish in Cabarrus County from 1944 to 1950. In 1950, he was called to Trinity Lutheran Church in Vale, NC, where he remained for nine years. In 1959, St. Peter's Lutheran Church in southeastern Rowan County, where parishioners had known Razz Miller as a farm boy, athlete, school teacher and coach called him back to minister to them. He retired from St. Peter's in 1974.

Razz Miller was a complex man who assumed many roles during his life. Besides teaching, coaching, preaching, and playing ball, he was an avid hunter and outdoorsman. As his son Hollis said,

> My dad was a man's man. He had the preacher side of him. He was a religious and spiritual man but not a pious Christian but one who had deep faith in God. Blended in all that was a teacher, coach, an athlete. Also he was a big hunter. He loved to fox hunt until later in life when he couldn't stay out at night like you have to or stay up at night. He also did other kinds of hunting: quail hunting, bird hunting, rabbit, squirrel, possum, just about all of it.
>
> In our home, growing up, there were all kinds of trophies that Dad's dogs had won for hunting at different field trials all over the states of North and South Carolina. My mother was from Tennessee—he had trophies from there too. He judged a lot of dog shows in North Carolina and Tennessee. Dad always kept fox hounds and beagles, always had a pack of dogs. And even to his death in 1981, at the age of 71, there were dogs to feed and take care of. He loved his dogs. He loved baseball and hunting, outside his family and his church.

A final story that shows how his loves often competed for his attention begins with him preaching one Sunday morning. Everyone in the congregation began to hear the howl of hounds chasing their prey. Of course, Razz heard the dogs also, and the more he heard the dogs, the faster he preached. "One of the shortest sermons I ever heard," declared Frank Hopkins. Immediately after the close of the service, Razz jumped into a car with several other members to join the chase.

Razz Miller died May 13, 1981, in Rockwell, NC. On that date, after praying with his wife for the Roman Catholic pope who had been shot that day, Razz went out to attend to his hunting dogs. He died of heart failure in the dog pen, among his beloved animals.

3

The Slugger: Norman Woodnut Small

Born: November 13, 1913, Glen Cove, New York; died: December 25, 1995, Mooresville, North Carolina

Norman Woodnut Small was a professional baseball player. His career spanned twenty years from 1934 to 1953, with two years absent for military service. Small became a legendary power hitter mostly in the Class D Minor Leagues in the Piedmont area of North Carolina. Small led his league in home runs seven times. He led his league in runs batted in four times. He led his league in doubles twice, hits once, and runs once. His career batting average was a hefty .320, and he finished with 336 home runs, but he never made it to the big leagues.

Norman Small was born November 13, 1913, in Glen Cove, New York. He died in his adopted home of Mooresville, NC, on Christmas Day in 1995. His wife, Sara Sherrill Small, whom he married in the Durham Bulls ballpark, died the previous August.

From his early youth, Norman Small was destined to be a baseball player. He batted and threw right handed and grew to be a muscular 5–10, 176-pounder. His father, Harry Small kept a family scrapbook that shows Norman at age eighteen as a hard throwing pitching phenom. That year he struck out 105 in 54 innings while pitching for Friend Academy at Locust Valley. He also hit an eye-popping .592.

During the summer of 1932, Small appeared in 44 games for an independent team, striking out 195 in 145 innings and batting an impressive .473. As a nineteen-year-old in the summer of 1933, Norman pitched five shutouts while posting a 10–3 record for a local Port Washington team. His hitting dropped off to a mere .303.

During the following winter, Norman Small convinced his father that he wanted to be a professional ballplayer. Harry Small wanted to improve his son's chances, so he checked the *Sporting News* and found an advertisement for one of the earliest nationally-known baseball schools—Ray Doan's Baseball School in Hot Springs, Arkansas. In early 1934, Norman became acquainted with the bane of minor league baseball life—the long bus ride. As he described it:

> My father put me on a Greyhound bus in New York and it took me four days and five nights to reach Hot Springs. If you remember anything about the Greyhound buses of the '30s, you know they stopped at every cow path along the road and then took three-four hour layovers in the bigger towns.
>
> When I arrived in Hot Springs there were more than 150 worn-out, starry-eyed young ball players. Most of the major league teams had scouts there and Joe Schultz, scout for the St. Louis Cardinals, picked me out after three-four days. I was sent to their Martinsville, VA, team in the Class D B-State League. Competition was tough. Branch Rickey, general manager of the St. Louis Cardinals, was creating the famous Cardinal farm system that would grow young ballplayers for his major league team. He had over 300 players there, all trying to find a place in the Cardinal organization. Branch Rickey had a good brain. He was smart. He could watch you work out one time and a month later recall your strengths and weaknesses.

Small made the 1934 Martinsville roster and after losing his first start, he won ten straight. Great success seemed to wait in the near future. On July 4, 1934, in a double-header against Fieldale—one game in the morning and one in the afternoon—Norman Small's pitching dream was shattered.

> I was scheduled to report to the Cardinals' Class B team in Asheville in the Piedmont League after I pitched that morning. About the middle of the game, it started raining. During the rain delay, being a naïve young kid, I took off my sweatshirt and uniform shirt to cool off. Today, a minor league manager would be watching over a young pitcher and not permit that.
>
> When the game resumed, I reared back and cut loose with a fastball. My shoulder had stiffened up and I tore some ligaments or muscles in my shoulder and I couldn't throw overhanded for some time. Even as a pitcher, I could hit, so I began playing some in the outfield.

Small finished that season with a .301 batting average. Small summarized his career-changing injury by saying: "Back in those days there were two or three ballplayers waiting to take your job if you got hurt or quit producing. Fortunately, the Cardinals recognized I could hit."

The adjustment, however, did not prove to be as easy as it first seemed. "In 1935," he continued, "I started the season in Asheville and hit a grand slam home run in the opening game. After that, the season became a nightmare and I ended up back in Martinsville." Small hit .244 in 47 games in Martinsville and was released by the Cardinals.

In 1935, Small dropped out of professional baseball temporarily. Marvin Lentz, a 1934 teammate in Martinsville, became manager of a Landis,

3. The Slugger

NC, semipro team in a one stoplight town, subsidized by the one textile plant in the municipality, Corriher Mill.

Small noted that "Marvin offered me more money than I was offered by Martinsville, so I joined him, playing three or four games a week and working part time in the shipping department at the mill. I started tearing that league (Carolina Textile league) up. Landis, in 1935, had been in the Carolina Textile League, but in 1936 when the larger towns, those with two and three stoplights, started playing six games a week with unlimited salaries and unlimited professional players, Corriher couldn't afford the move to a faster and better baseball league.

In 1935 in Landis, Norman Small found the going pretty easy. "I was hitting home runs, doubles and driving in runs right and left. Joe Cambria, scout for the Washington Senators, saw me hit three home runs in one game and wanted to sign me up immediately. He checked to see that I had my release from the Cardinals team in Martinsville. Before Cambria found me in Landis, I had several letters from the Albany club of the International League, of which Cambria was president and treasurer."

A letter dated March 6, 1936, and mailed to Small's home at 32 Prospect Ave., Glen Cove, Long Island, New York, read as follows:

> We would be very glad to have you work out with the Albany club this season. Manager (Al) Mamaux will give you a fair trial to see just what you can do, and if he recommends, we will offer you a contract. As you know, we also have clubs in Class A and Class D in addition to Albany.

The letter was signed, Jeanette Parkinson, Secretary. Another one followed on March 10. In this one, they offered him a tryout at any time, but noted that it would be better to wait till April 12 when Manager Mamaux has had time to look at the many players who are signed to contracts.

On May 20, 1936, Small received a letter of interest from the Louisville, KY, baseball club of the Class AA American Association that stated, "You have been recommended to us as worthy of a trial by the Louisville club. Kindly furnish us with your lowest terms, together with your baseball history. Signed: William Neal, Vice President and General Manager."

Small finally signed with Albany's Class A team in Harrisburg–York, PA, a member of the New York–Penn League. His contract called for $200 a month, but it was made more lucrative by a $250 bonus if he hit .300 for the season.

Small's time away from the game had lasted less than a month. But this part of his career ended after only two games. His father's scrapbook contains a telegram dated May 26, 1936, that reads: "Got hit in eye with ball last night and had to leave game — wanted to suspend me without pay — no go — I got release along with manager and a few others — three fellows from Albany and Washington coming down — anyway don't stand chance — going back to North Carolina — I'll write — Love — Norman."

It should be noted that the York team moved to Trenton, NJ, on July 2. Like many other teams at the time, they were in financial trouble due to the Great Depression.

In 1936, when Small returned to Landis, NC, for his textile job and to play in the Carolina Textile League, he found that Mooresville, another small textile town, had left the Carolina Textile League to join the burgeoning outlaw Carolina League, playing six games a week with far more extensive travel. Immediately, Norman called Jim Poole, a former major league player (1925–27 with the Philadelphia Athletics) and now the manager and first baseman for the Mooresville Moors. Poole knew about Small's ability and told him to stay where he was, not to leave his room, and not to talk to anyone. Poole promised to send someone to pick him up right away, only a twelve mile trip. He also promised more games — six per week — more money, no mill work during the season, but a job after the season with Mooresville Mills.

All within a two-week period, Norman Small moved from a semi-pro team in Landis, NC, to a Class A team in Harrisburg–York, PA, to an outlaw team in Mooresville, NC, where unknown to him at the time, he had found a permanent home.

Just because Small had joined the Mooresville squad did not mean that professional baseball had dropped its quest for his services. On June 11, he received a telegram from Oliver French of the Asheville, NC, Tourists of the Class B Piedmont League: "Norman Small, care the Mooresville Baseball Club — please call me collect six two one six collect." On June 17, Small received another telegram addressed: "Mr. Small, Baseball Player — Mooresville, North Carolina — wire WU lowest terms to play with Augusta — signed Troy Agnew." Augusta was a member of the Class B South Atlantic (Sally) League.

Small was, however, tired of dealing with the financially troubled minor league teams of organized professional baseball. Nevertheless, he received one last letter that year from the Albany, NY, baseball club. It was dated June 12, several weeks after he had received his release from Albany's farm team in York: "The National Association offices will not approve your contract signed May 26th with our Harrisburg/York Club of the NY-Penn League. They do not approve of the stipulation which promised you a bonus of $250 if you hit .300 for the season. Duplicate contract is herewith attached, made out just like the original one, only excluding the above-mentioned clause. Please sign in spaces checked for your signature and return in enclosed envelope so everything will be in order. Thanking you for your prompt attention. Yours very truly, Jeanette Parkinson, Secretary."

3. The Slugger

Was this a case of locking the barn door after the horse was loose, or was it a subtle attempt to get Norman Small's name on another contract?

Small did not return this contract.

In the outlaw Carolina League, the legend of Norman Small the slugger began to develop. By midseason, he had hit 10 home runs in 127 at-bats, an excellent home run ratio. He was hitting .315 with eight doubles and 29 RBIs. Unfortunately, no season ending statistics are available for the 1936 Carolina League season. However, it must be noted again that the Carolina League was a hitters league. Old pro Jim Poole had 13 home runs in 158 at-bats with a blazing .399 average at midseason. Despite the efforts of Small and Poole, the Moors were not very successful. The club had moved from Salisbury early in the season with a 2–6 record and was not as stable as some other league teams. Their final record of 35–64 left them in seventh place with only the Shelby Cee-Cees below them.

In 1937 the Mooresville club left the outlaw league to become a part of the new professional Class D NC State League. Concerned over the success of the Carolina League, the NAPBL had scrambled to start this league in towns located near each of the outlaw league towns. The ability of the Carolina clubs to lure players away from professional minor league, and in some cases, major league contracts had not gone unnoticed. However, with the money being shopped around by the Carolina League clubs and the

Bride-to-be Sara Sherrill and Norman Small are pictured prior to their wedding (courtesy Norman Small).

promise of off-season employment during the Great Depression, the players could hardly be blamed for jumping their contracts.

Small's career as a minor league player would continue all the way to 1953, but the next important event to occur on the ball field for him would be his marriage to his Mooresville sweetheart, Sara Sherrill.

In 1937, after playing only 35 games in the new NC State League, Small had hit 12 home runs in 148 at-bats and had driven in 51 runs with a .392 batting average. His success had caught the eye of the Cincinnati Reds affiliate Durham Bulls team. On June 12, the Bulls paid the Mooresville Moors $2500 for Small's contract. Newspapers reported that this was one of the highest prices ever paid by a Class B team for a Class D ballplayer's contract. Small did not hit as well, .274 in 88 games with only two home runs. The highlight of his season occurred on Sunday afternoon, August 29, at 2:30 at the Durham Athletic Park.

Even before Mooresville sold his contract to Durham, Small and Mooresville native Sara Sherrill had decided that they wanted to be married on a ball field. Such was their love for the game. When asked by Paul Florence, president of the Durham Bulls, why he and Sara were determined to be married in a ballpark, Small replied, "Well, I've chosen baseball as my career. My whole life is wrapped up in the game, and my greatest desire is to succeed. I want my wife to feel the same way about it. I want her to feel that she is an important part of my baseball career. I feel that to be married in the park, before a game, will make an everlasting impression on her. And after all, it isn't the place in which a fellow gets married that counts, it is the girl he gets."

The bride to be, Sara Sherrill, a Lenoir-Rhyne College (Hickory, NC) graduate and then a secretary, stated, "Oh, I realize that it may strike a number of folks as being odd, but baseball is Norman's profession. He and I are both proud of the game. He loves to play it and I enjoy it immensely. It's a clean, terribly exciting and fascinating job. Then too, everyone likes to have his friends attend his wedding. Well, our friends are the players, but more of our friends are the fans" (*Durham Herald*, August 27, 1937).

In 1992 Sara recalled, "When we got married in the Durham Bulls ballpark, they gave us a lot of gifts, a string of pearls to wear with my wedding dress, a brand new 1937 Plymouth automobile and furniture. We had enough furniture for a three-room apartment. And cigarettes—you know they made 'em in Durham. We got cigarettes by the hundreds. We had to get a truck to the ballpark to get all those gifts away.

Norman got three hits, knocked in two runs and we won 11–2. Everybody in the ballpark started hollering, 'you should have gotten married a whole lot earlier.'"

Small explained his hitting that day. It was the end of the season, and

Souvenir Wedding Program

Miss Sherrill, daughter of Mr. and Mrs. K. A. Sherrill, was born at Mooresville, N. C. where she received her early education in the public schools, and later completed her college course at Lenoir-Rhyne.

Norman Small is the only son of Mr. and Mrs. H. A. Small of Glen Cove, N. Y. He attended public school at Glen Cove. He graduated from Friends Academy prior to his entry into professional baseball.

Hugo Germino and his Orchestra

Pictured is the program from the Durham Bulls game where Norman Small and Sara Sherrill were married (courtesy Norman Small).

the game meant nothing to the Asheville Tourists, who were on top of the league. Durham was in the second division. The pitcher for Asheville that day was Al Sherer, Small's former roommate in Martinsville. The catcher, Sam Narron, was also a former teammate at Martinsville.

As Small told the story, "Sam would say, 'Here comes a fastball, here comes a curveball.' He was calling all the pitches for me. Every time I got on base Al would look at me and holler, 'How in the hell did you hit that ball?' Al put on a good act. He knew what was happening."

Small spent the '38 and '39 seasons moving between Durham in the Piedmont League, Waterloo in the Three I League, Columbia in the South Atlantic League, and Meridian in the Southeastern League.

After those journeys, he moved back to Mooresville to play in the Class D NC State League in 1940. The next three years Small played for the Moors. It was at this point that he began to hit with earnest and with great power. For the three years he compiled a total of 75 home runs, led the league twice in homers and twice in RBIs. The slugger also hit for average: .346, .332, and in 1942 a career best .372. As a result of his success, Norman found himself back up north in the International League at Jersey City. In his 53 games at this much higher level, the going got tough for Small. He managed to connect for only four homers in his 158 at-bats and a dismal, for him, .250 average. It didn't matter because at the age of thirty, Small, like many of his fellow country men spent the next two years in the service of the U.S. military.

Small gives a highlight of his wartime experience here in his own words.

Norman Small sent this photograph to his mother in 1937.

We ended up between Pilsen and Prague in Czechoslovakia. We ended as far east as any

3. The Slugger

American foot soldiers. We could hear the Russians with our walkie-talkies. We started taking prisoners. One afternoon I saw something like 20,000 walking down the autobahn with a Jeep in front of them and only one Jeep behind them. They were walking 20–25 abreast. That autobahn was a big wide road anyway. The prisoners were just giving up.

Then we came home and took jungle training to go and make the invasion of Japan. I got a 21 day furlough. When the "bomb" went off, that suited me fine. I thought we were going to get out, but no, they shanghaied our division — the 97th Division — over to Japan for occupation for about eight months. We had fellows with enough points to get out, but they didn't let 'em out. I remember we shipped out of Seattle, but before then, going across the Great Salt Lake flats, somebody got in the records and threw a bunch of 'em out on the flats. The next thing you knew we had MPs standing with a machine gun at the ends of each railroad car and wouldn't let us on the car platforms at all, afraid we'd just jump train. The guy that threw the records out thought we wouldn't have to go to Japan, but they wired Washington and got new ones and all of us had to go to Japan.

We went down to the Mariana Islands first and then to the Philippines. From there we went to Japan and got there three or four days later. We had the job of destroying Japanese planes. The hanger was full of bombs and cars. One of our mechanics got to tinkering with one of those old cars. There was straw all over the bombs. An old truck backfired while our mechanic was working on it, caught the hay on fire, and we ran like hell. We got behind a building 500–600 yards away, and that thing blew up.

We had American planes flying over in five minutes wondering what the hell was going on. It rocked the whole countryside. That hole was over 100 feet wide and about 25 feet deep. They court-martialed the mechanic, but he finally got back to the company.

In 1946 Norman Small was back stateside and picked up his minor league career right where he left off. He played the next five years for Mooresville in the Class D NC State League. Small led the league in home runs all five of those years. One of the highlights of those years was playing with a local boy from Huntersville, NC, who quickly became one of the league's best pitchers. Hoyt Wilhelm began his long and distinguished Hall of Fame career with the support of Norman Small's booming bat. Small had perhaps the best batting year of his career in 1949 when he slammed 41 home runs in 456 at-bats and contributed 152 RBIs with a .344 batting average.

Small had another excellent year for Mooresville in 1950. Playing in only 98 games at the age of 36, he led the league again in home runs with 32 and still managed to drive in 104 runs. Northwest of Mooresville in the foothills town of Hickory, a local boy had returned from a decade-long struggle to make it through the minor league system. D.C. "Pud" Miller, in his role as player-manager, had finished just behind Small in the home run race. Miller had first teamed with Small in 1940 at Mooresville, when he was a young pitcher, just out of high school, trying to get started in pro ball. After World War II, Miller became a position player in order to take advantage of his tremendous batting ability. Playing in the West Texas League for Wichita Falls and Lamesa, he had hit over fifty home runs twice. In 1947, he drove in an astounding 196 runs. He had advanced as far as triple A ball with the San Francisco Seals but never quite made it through to the big time.

In early 1951, Norman Small considered quitting the game. Instead, he joined Pud Miller to create a legendary power combination that would rejuvenate interest in the Hickory Rebels ball club and provide its fans with a memorable home run race.

The local newspaper, the *Hickory Daily Record*, began to build up the arrival of Small even before the season started. The April 16 edition contains this classic bit of sports hype:

> When the Hickory Rebels trot out onto the field Wednesday to open their season in the NC State League, there'll be one man among them that has almost become a legend of the league. He's 38 year-old [actually 37] Norman "Butch" Small of Mooresville.
>
> The square-built, heavy-muscled slugger owns a lifetime average of near .350 [actually .320], has smacked over 300 homers [269], and has averaged over 100 RBIs over a period of eleven seasons.

The year before the Rebels fans had seen their team slump to a 38–73 record, and as a result attendance had slumped as well to just under 37,000 for the year. These guys could use all the hype they could get, and the addition of Norman Small seemed like the perfect prescription to cure their ills. The team struggled at first, losing six of their first seven games before they came alive as reported by Lawrence Smith in the April 27 *Record*:

> There should be great rejoicing among Hickory Rebel fans today. The Rebs won their second game of the season Thursday night, but what seems even more important, a Reb hurler [Hal Griggs, who later played four seasons with the Washington Senators] has gone the full route, and left fielder Norman Small has started his home run campaign.

This first home run was coincidentally against his old team, the Mooresville Moors, in their park.

By June 21 the battle between the two sluggers had heated up. That day's issue of the Record ran a picture of Small and Miller sitting on the bench, crossing their bats. This campy shot was accompanied by the following caption:

> Hard slugging manager Pud Miller (left) closed his eyes and gritted his teeth this week as he crossed bats with center fielder Norman "Butch" Small. "Mister"

3. The Slugger

Small meanwhile hunched up his shoulders and tried his best to look like as big a slugger as the Hickory manager. Through Monday night's games Miller had a .436 batting average and Small was second in the league at .428. Miller was also leading Small in home runs 19–16. Pud, being a native of Hickory, gets frequent inquiries from his friends as to whether he's going to let Small beat him out in the home run race as he did last year, but Hickory fans are mighty glad the former Mooresville player is on the Rebel roster.

The slugging contest between the teammates continued, along with the competitive play of the team. The August 3 *Record* reported the following: "Center fielder Norman Small kicked up his heels in the familiar haunts of the Mooresville park Thursday night and slammed his 28th home run of the current season." Meanwhile, Miller was reported to be only six home runs short of the NC State league record of 41, set by Norman Small in 1948. The August 8 *Record* carried another picture of Small along with this caption:

> Norman "Butch" Small has more than lived up to the expectations of his play with the Hickory Rebels this summer and Tuesday night he smashed his 30th home run of the season at College Field. Butch, who was supposedly quitting the game after many brilliant years has shown excellence as of old at the plate and in his center field post.

By the end of the season, Miller had prevailed in each category, had in fact, as reported in the September 15 issue, won the league triple crown. He finished with 40 home runs, 136 RBIs and a .425 average. The batting average was good enough to win him the silver bat as the highest in all the minor leagues. Small, who played in all 126 games, put up impressive numbers as well. He finished with 37 homers, 127 RBIs and a .340 batting average. Ironically, two players who once had aspirations to be great pitchers ended up in a contest to see who could do the most damage with his bat.

Although they were beaten in the playoffs by Statesville,

Slugger Norman Small was a career minor leaguer who hit more than 300 home runs, playing many years for his adopted home town of Mooresville for the Class D Moors (courtesy Norman Small).

the Rebels improved their record to 72–54 and finished second. As with today's games, the home runs were a big draw. The Rebels increased their attendance by 17,000 with their second highest recorded figure: 53,662.

Small started the following season as the player-manager for the Rebels, but when the team failed to win, they brought Miller back to replace him. Small finished the season in the Carolina League, playing for Raleigh and then played one final season for Mooresville. Even in the twilight of his career, he was no pushover at the plate. Small racked up 12 home runs and 68 RBIs in 112 games for Raleigh. Playing his final season in his adopted hometown, Small managed only 14 HRs, but he drove in 87 runs in only 95 games and finished with an impressive .340 batting average.

Norman Small's accomplishments as a ballplayer earned him recognition from the Society for American Baseball Research that named him among the top 100 all-time minor league players. However, an article dated May 11, 1993, in the *Durham Herald Sun* best sums up his situation.

> There won't be another Norman Small ... or another Earl Richmond or another Eddie Neville.
>
> The era that produced them is gone.
>
> Baseball has changed since Small and his accomplices toiled as career Minor Leaguers. Nowadays, the minors exist only to develop talent for the Major Leagues. Players either prove their worth and move up to "The Show," or they are gone to make way for more young prospects.
>
> It's not likely anybody will again do what Small did between 1934 and 1953 — play for twenty years in the minors without reaching the major leagues.

4

Cause Célèbre: Edwin Collins "Alabama" Pitts

Born: November 22, 1909, Opelika, Alabama; died: June 7, 1941, Valdese, North Carolina

Edwin Collins "Alabama" Pitts was born November 22, 1909, in Opelika, Alabama. His father, Edwin Sr., was a U.S. cavalryman who died when the boy was five months old. His mother, Erma Mills Pitts, nicknamed him "Alabama" to avoid confusion with his father who had been born on the Georgia side of the state line. After Edwin Sr.'s death, Erma lived with her sister Vera Rudd's family on their farm. There she met her second husband, Robert E. Rudd. She and her sister were married to the two oldest Rudd brothers. On February 14, 1914, Mildred Eileen Rudd, Pitts' half sister, was born. Even though Edwin never got to spend much time with her, he adored his sister. It is not known why, but Erma and Robert were divorced. Myrtice Carr, a second cousin to Edwin, speculates that it may have been because she wanted to go to work as a secretary. At any rate, Rudd's parents obtained custody of Mildred while Erma kept Edwin. There are several stories that tell of her attempts to kidnap her daughter from her former in-laws.

Little is known about Erma or about Pitts as a young man. At some point they left the southeast and moved to Peoria, Illinois. Ms. Carr noted that she was highly skilled as a typist and was likely able to find secretarial work. More recent information has revealed that she became a telephone operator, a position much in demand which would have allowed her to support herself anywhere in the country. No sandlot or school athletic records are available. Given his gift for athletics, one can only assume that the young Pitts was successful on the school playground. Little is known as well about his schooling. Robert Gold states that he attended one year of high school (Gold). While he could not have attained much formal education, it is likely that he inherited some of the sharp intellect which his mother was known to possess. Edwin, however, did not have the advantages that allowed his sister to finish school, get a college degree and become a teacher. It would seem that he was on his own, for at the age of fifteen, some time after his parents' divorce, Pitts joined the Navy. He served his three year term, was honorably discharged, and ended up in New York City, broke and unemployed.

According to a story that undoubtedly originated with Pitts, he was convinced by an acquaintance to rob a grocery store. In this version he claims that it was simply because he was hungry, and that the amount of their take was only ten dollars. The amount was rather $76.25, a large sum for that day. Official court records show that it was Pitts who entered a Daniel Reeves Grocery Store with a gun that day. His accomplice, James Murphy, waited outside, serving as a lookout as he had before. Their getaway plan, however, was not the brightest one. Murphy hailed a cab and waited for Pitts who exited the store with gun and money and the proprietor in pursuit. The cab was stopped just up the street, and the two young men were arrested.

Pitts' crimes should not be made light of as they tended to be by the media a few years later. He was implicated in five other robberies and had probably used a gun in them as well. Later he would admit that he was a young thug at the time and that the arrest and prison time had a positive effect on him. The public defender who was provided for him urged Pitts to write a letter to the judge, begging for leniency. It does not seem possible that he could have written these words on his own:

> Dear Sir:
> I am Edwin Collins Pitts who will be sentenced before you Tuesday, March 18. Your Honor, I am guilty twice over and now fully realize the seriousness of the crimes I committed punishable by long years of penal servitude. Sir, I know that one can not be drove or made to commit the crime by persons or circumstances, but Sir, if one should fall, and Sir, both against the state and the church, the way is often paved by both of the mentioned elements. It would be tiresome to you and useless to me to go into details of why I have broken these laws. The madness and folly of youth had much to do with it, ably aided by false pride, broken illusions, and shattered ideals.
> I was nineteen years of age and in an unsettled state of mind caused by personal family troubles at the time I committed the crimes. Your Honor, my object in writing this letter to you is to beg that you be as merciful as possible with me. Sir, if you should see fit for your court to show me mercy, I will try in every way to be worthy of your kindness and goodness.
> Respectfully and Humbly,
> Edwin Collins Pitts

The judge was not moved by his plea and sentenced him to an eight to sixteen year sentence in Sing Sing Prison, the legendary facility located

35 miles north of New York City in Ossining, NY. Because he had used a gun while committing the crime, five of those years were mandatory. Murphy, his accomplice, was sent to a reformatory and told to avoid characters like Pitts. The judge did note in his statement that there were circumstances in the young man's life that might have contributed to his recklessness. He mentioned the erratic behavior of his mother who had left her job in Peoria, Illinois, and come to New York to be with her son. No mention is made of his wife though records show that Pitts was married in 1928. Certainly, the pressure of providing for a wife and dealing with an obsessive mother had some effect on his choices.

During his time at Sing Sing Prison, Pitts was fortunate to come under the influence of Warden Lewis E. Lawes, a progressive administrator and champion of prisoner rehabilitation. Lawes had arrived at Sing Sing in 1919 and immediately began to reform the prison and to institute new, more humane methods of punishment. Joseph Overfield notes that Lawes oversaw "a massive and long overdue plan of modernization, while also instituting a well-rounded athletic program, including outside games. Prison teams of various sports, including football, basketball, and baseball were started, with qualified coaches ... put in charge of each sport." Although some politicians complained that Lawes was pampering the prisoners, he was given a great deal of latitude because he kept a "quiet prison" (Gold).

Pitts, who was labeled a model prisoner, made the most of these opportunities.

Edwin Collins "Alabama" Pitts was a multi-sports phenom in Sing Sing Prison. Here he is pictured in a football pose. Pitts played briefly for the Philadelphia Eagles after his release from Sing Sing (courtesy Philadelphia A's Historical Web site).

He played for the Black Sheep, a football team coached by former Notre Dame star John Law. Law, the son of a bricklayer, and a member of a lower class immigrant family, had been a star football player at the Hamilton Institute. He had gone on to captain the Notre Dame football team and spent five years there as a disciple of the great Knute Rockne. His association with Notre Dame and Rockne, who was killed in a 1931 plane crash, had made him a celebrity. The fact that Lawes was able to bring such a man to Sing Sing Prison as his athletic director shows what an effective pubic relations man he was. Law became his connection to the sports world and provided a high profile image for their programs.

Pitts soon became a sensation, even attracting attention from the New York newspapers. On September 8, 1932, the *New York Times* carried a story that proclaimed Pitts to be a star, and Coach Law noted that he had "all the ear marks of a great halfback." Law had a tremendous effect on Pitts and gave him the kind of coaching attention that he would never receive outside of prison. He thought that Pitts made a mistake when he decided to dedicate himself to baseball. Law always thought he was better-suited for football.

Besides being an outstanding football and basketball player as well as a track athlete, Pitts demonstrated high level baseball skills. He was an especially strong fielder and gained notice in the *New York Times* after an exhibition game with the Yankees in September of 1933. The *Times* account stated that "Alabama Pitts, Sing Sing's star football player, demonstrated that he is equally at home on the diamond." Pitts finished his Sing Sing baseball career with a .500 batting average in 21 games. He also hit eight home runs.

Pitts' cooperation and athletic prowess soon paid off. Warden Lawes made arrangements to reduce his prison sentence by three years. He was to be released in June of 1935. Pitts' accomplishments as an athlete had garnered national attention by late 1934 as evidenced by a *Los Angeles Times* article, discussing his release which called him "the most prominent jailbird athlete in America." Pitts received tryouts from at least two professional football teams while still in prison. But his big break came when Joe Cambria, the owner of the Albany Senators of the International League, took an interest in his services. Cambria asked his manager, the famous second baseman, Johnny Evers, to sign Pitts before his release. With Warden Lawes' consent, Pitts signed a contract on May 22, 1935, for $200 a month. This seemingly innocuous act would soon create such an enormous amount of attention that its recipient would never be the same.

It all started with an Associated Press release dated June 6, 1935. The *Charlotte Observer* ran the story on June 7:

> Alabama Pitts tucked an unconditional release from the Sing Sing Prison Baseball Club in his pocket today, and reported to the Albany Senators in the midst of a controversy over his professional eligibility.

4. Cause Célèbre

As he left the shadows of the prison, the star of Sing Sing athletic teams cupped an ear to the high howl of debate over the question. "Is an ex-convict eligible to play professional baseball?"

The Albany Club signed "Alabama" last month, but when the action was revealed a few days ago, President W.G. Bramham of the National Association of Professional Baseball Leagues set down his foot the first time and started a controversy that immediately brought nationally prominent persons to Pitts' support.

In fact, he said, "No," twice, the last time to Warden Lawes at Sing Sing, who appealed to him.

In a telegram to Lawes, Bramham said, "It is not a question of the individual, Edwin Pitts, but his case presents this question; shall the ranks of organized baseball be opened to ex-convicts? I construe it my duty to answer in the negative. If my judgment is erroneous, I am glad the Executive Committee and the high Commissioner [K.M. Landis, former federal judge] have the power to reverse me." Bramham was obviously under tremendous public pressure. Pitts had public support on his side as well as the support of baseball players such as Dizzy Dean who came forward on behalf of his cause. It is also important to note that International League president Charles H. Knapp first refused to approve the contract. Bramham's move was only one to support his subordinate.

Alabama Pitts leaves Sing Sing Prison on June 6, 1935, accompanied by his mother, Erma Rudd (Hank Utley).

For two weeks, no news item commanded more of the nation's attention. One would have to go back to the kidnapping of the Lindbergh baby in 1932 to find an event that so galvanized this country.

Pitts was not deterred by his initial rejection. As the *Charlotte Observer* reported, "Pitts was a shade on the optimistic side when he arrived in Albany. 'I'm raring to go. I tell you now that I won't make anybody regret giving me an opportunity.' Pitts added, 'In a way, I don't blame Bramham. If he thinks I may do something wrong, I suppose he is right. After all, baseball is a business.'" Pitts could not have been too worried about finding a position on a sports team. He had other offers. The House of David, a touring team in both baseball and basketball and another pro baseball team in Dayton, OH, had wired him job offers. The Philadelphia Eagles, a professional football team was looking to sign him for the fall season.

On June 8, the *Observer* reported that the three man executive committee of the National Association had announced that they would hold a hearing within a few days. The committee had the authority to overrule Bramham. In the meantime, Warden Lawes, in Ossining, NY, announced that he had received hundreds of messages supporting Pitts in his effort to play professional baseball. Among the messages were telegrams from Lou Little, nationally known Columbia University football coach; Judge J.P. Egan of Pittsburgh, and Harry Von Kersburg, Sam Darthy, and H.T. Clinton, all college football referees who officiated some at Sing Sing.

While waiting for the committee's decision, Pitts attended an Albany game and received a tremendous ovation. According to the Associated Press release, "Pitts, barred at least temporarily from active play by the Minor League boss, was given a wild ovation, similar to those accorded Babe Ruth when introduced to some 3,000 Albany fans who braved wintry weather." Between games of a double-header with the Buffalo Bisons, Pitts put on a batting exhibition. National newsreel and newspaper photographers were on hand when Manager A.J. Mamaux pitched to Pitts.

It should be noted that the Albany club was off to a miserable start which had affected attendance figures, so Johnny Evers' efforts were possibly not purely baseball oriented. As Pitts had said, "After all, baseball is a business." Evers was encouraged when Warren Giles, the National League president, telegraphed him and told him that he would personally advise him of the committee's decision.

The June 11 issue of the *Charlotte Observer* includes his announcement:

While we are in sympathy with the program which gives to paroled convicts an opportunity to rehabilitate themselves in society, we are of the opinion that the interests of the man will be served by offering that opportunity in some field where his activities will not be constantly subjected to public scrutiny and comment as they would be in baseball. The decision applies to baseball generally in the future.

This article continues, "With tears in his eyes, Pitts asked the meaning of the decision, saying, 'You mean that if they let me play, every ex-inmate will want to play.'" He then announced that he would appeal to Commissioner Landis and added, "You don't think I'm trying to get into baseball for the money? I love the game." Evers also announced that he

4. Cause Célèbre

would appeal to the highest authority in baseball. He threatened to sever all ties with baseball if nothing could be done and denied allegations that he had signed Pitts in order to take advantage of his celebrity. Evers added that he would seek an outright pardon for Pitts from New York governor Hubert H. Lehman when Lehman returned from a trip to Bermuda.

Within days, editorialists all over America had taken up the cause of Alabama Pitts. Typical of these was Jake Wade's *Charlotte Observer* column of June 12, 1935:

> I've been down to see a picture called "Les Miserables." I first heard the story many, many years ago and as a little boy I was profoundly impressed.... While watching a very faithfully interpreted Jean Valjean go through hell and back, if you will pardon my French, I couldn't help but think of Alabama Pitts and wonder if Judge W.G. Bramham (President of the National Association of Minor Professional Baseball) had seen this picture. Erving Stone, the smart young manager of the Imperial Theater, tells me he sent Judge Bramham a couple of ducats with a special invitation, so maybe he has or will, not that it will make any difference. Judge Bramham is a very firm and opinionated man, and all the Jean Valjean pictures or stories in the world probably won't change his opinion that Alabama Pitts should not be permitted to play baseball in the minor leagues, being a paroled prisoner ... maybe that is not stating it quite right, since Judge Bramham has explained that it is no personal opinion at all, but merely baseball law or custom.
>
> Still there have been fellows, who have come out of jail and played professional baseball, and I could name one in a hurry we all know, but won't because maybe the law or custom applies to him and he has been overlooked and he might lose his job, which I should hate to see ... a lot of people or maybe I should say some agree with Judge Bramham and his associate high knockers in baseball that Alabama Pitts should be banned from the National Pastime. For instance, Johnny Nee, the scout, said he thought it would be a bad move to let him play because when he got to kicking them around [error] the fans would put on a demonstration ... and personally I don't think Johnny Evers is moved by an humanitarian spirit in offering Pitts a job at Albany, but merely wants him as an attraction ... but that is beside the point and I can't for the life of me see where Pitts could harm baseball, while it might make a man of him ... and today that he can't play is putting in cold words and fact what we dislike to believe, that a man who has been to jail and paid society for his wrong, hasn't a chance when released..., if other businesses, along with baseball, adopt this rule, we may as well tear down our jails and build only electric chairs, scaffolds and gas rooms.

Atypical of the editorials was this one found in the June 13 issue of *The Sporting News*, a magazine that served as a mouthpiece for Organized Baseball:

> Baseball yields to no enterprise in its democracy. Its ranks are filled with the highly and lowly born, with college bred and with the graduates of Kerry

Patch and the Ghetto. None of its players ever has been asked to produce a pedigree, a diploma or a birth certificate. They are accepted on faith and it must be admitted that as a whole, they have proved gentlemen, both on and off the field; in fact, their ranking in character is well above the average.

Therefore, the game cannot be charged with drawing a line of demarcation or of discrimination when it refused to permit a prison inmate, just released, to join its ranks and be ballyhooed as a player who had made good behind penitentiary walls. To do otherwise would be unfair, both to the man and the game. Both would be put on the spot and an exceedingly delicate spot at that.

The game, after all, is a quasi public affair. The spot light is constantly directed on it and its members must constantly parade before the powerful glare of publicity. As a sport, it is a living experiment of fair play — helping the other fellow and not knocking an individual when he is down. But the game also has certain ideals that must be maintained and which can only be upheld by those in its ranks.

Therefore, we believe that President W.G. Bramham and members of his Executive Committee of the National Association took the only course open to them when they advised the Albany club of the International League not to go through with its intention of signing a recent inmate of Sing Sing. The special position of baseball before the public seems to make the stand imperative. It would seem to be better to let this man first re-establish himself in a less prominent position and then if his playing ability warrants, allow him to enter the game not as a ballyhooed freak, but as a ball player whose past record, as in the case of all others, will not be questioned. The rosters are always open to the performer who can make good on his own ability and not on a manufactured reputation.

Fortunately for Pitts, when the commissioner of Major League Baseball, Judge Kenesaw Mountain Landis ruled on the matter, he sided with the ex-convict. The nationwide interest in this story is indicated by its June 18 front page placement in the *Charlotte Observer*. The headline which ran above the paper's masthead proclaimed, "Judge Landis rules 'Alabama Pitts May Play Baseball.'" The United Press article noted that the ruling contained a stipulation that Pitts not be allowed to play in exhibition games to avoid notoriety. In his statement, Landis first showed support for Bramham and his initial ruling, justifying his subordinate before overruling him. After a lengthy preamble, Landis commented on the official court record of Pitts' sentence:

> The record shows that it was Pitts who went into the grocery store in Brooklyn and held up a lone clerk with a gun. His accomplice who was one year older than Pitts was unarmed and remained outside the store as a lookout. His accomplice, the record shows, had no previous record, but Pitts had been in five other similar robberies. That record, however, is not important in this case. Many reputable people approached me in Pitts' behalf. The opinion of many of those people is one that there has been a complete reformation in Pitts' character. This fact and the fact barring him from baseball would perhaps have a destroying effect on his entire career provide the reasons for my action.

The reactions to the decision were widespread and positive. Charles H. Knapp, president of the International League said, "I'm very glad Pitts is going to get a chance to play and I hope he makes good." Pitts spoke to legendary *New York Mirror* sportswriter Dan Parker: "The judge has finally earned his salary. His decision is the best boost in the world. I'm just raring to go. Judge Landis' ruling to let me play ball makes me the happiest man in the world. I won't do anything to make him regret it. Whenever I get there, whether it's tonight or Thursday or next week, I am going to do everything I can to make my baseball career a success." Pitts appeared to be humbled by his opportunity. "I hope that someday I'll be able to play in the majors. When I was down there [Sing Sing], I batted .500 and we played against some pretty good teams. I don't know whether I'll be able to hit like that against International League pitching, but you can bet I am going to try my hardest. I know I did wrong and I am thankful that I was sent to prison for that wrong. It was the turning point in my life just as this decision may be also." Pitts went further to mention that Hal Roach had offered him a job in Hollywood and that he would have accepted it if the decision had gone the other way.

Everything seemed to be going Alabama Pitts' way. Even the *Sporting News* adopted a more forgiving attitude toward him. While they had once argued that his presence would tarnish the game, they offered their revised opinion in the June 20 editorial entitled, "It's Up to Pitts Now": "The supreme authority in baseball has spoken and given Pitts a clean bill of health, deciding that he is entitled to consideration on his merits as a player. The final umpire — the public — has yet to pass judgment, but should be willing to give him the chance for which he has appealed and in which plea he was joined by many fans. The future alone can determine the ultimate disposition of this cause celebre." Pitts could ask for no more than this chance. It would be eleven years before anyone else would challenge the baseball establishment status quo. In 1946, Brooklyn Dodger general manager Branch Rickey would sign a young African American named Jackie Robinson to a minor league contract with Montreal.

Pitts finally got his chance three days later in a Sunday afternoon double-header. The *Sporting News* reported that 7,752 people attended the spectacle. Details of the game indicate that Pitts led off the first inning with a ground out to the Syracuse shortstop. In the third he reached first on shortstop Neimiec's error, and flied out to right in the fifth. Pitts' first hit came in the seventh on a line drive. He later scored in a two run rally that chased Syracuse pitcher Fred Fussell. In the ninth inning he drove in his first run with another single. Pitts went hitless in the second game, and Albany lost both ends of the double-header. The report praised his ability in the field: "In the opening game, he ran 40 to 45 feet on soggy turf to catch hard hit balls that looked like certain doubles."

Despite Judge Landis's ruling which stated that Pitts could not be used in extra games or exploited for his notoriety, it became apparent that the Albany club hoped to use his presence to increase gate receipts at all regularly scheduled league games. The *Sporting News* reported, "Johnny Evers, general manager of the Albany club, has stated that Pitts will remain with the Senators the remainder of the season, regardless of whether he makes good or not but the skeptics, who have seen a flock of Cambria's players come and go this season, declare that Pitts will be going the rounds of other clubs with Albany connections (lower minor leagues) if he doesn't make the grade in Albany."

Evers obviously intended to milk Pitts' notoriety for all it was worth. He even requested and received a special ruling from the Canadian government permitting Pitts to play in Montreal and Toronto. The Dominion law against entry of persons charged with "moral turpitude" was lifted, and Pitts was free to travel with his teammates.

Among Pitts' teammates in 1935 when he arrived at Albany was Hack Wilson, caught up in the hopeless tailspin of his life after hitting 56 home runs for the Chicago Cubs in 1930. Three days after the decision to allow Pitts to play, Albany sold Wilson to Portland of the Pacific Coast League in order to clear room for Pitts. Wilson retired from the game rather than play for the teetotaling Portland manager. Another teammate was Fred Chapman, a 20-year-old youngster who the Senators had signed off the semi-pro Kannapolis Towelers team that year.

Chapman, still living in Kannapolis in 1992, recalled that Pitts received a friendly

Edwin Pitts began his professional baseball career with the Albany Senators, where he played for the legendary Johnny Evers. Another memorable but tragic character, Hack Wilson, was optioned out to make room on the roster for Pitts (Hank Utley).

4. Cause Célèbre

welcome in all the International League ballparks that season. This was probably due to the ballyhoo built up by the press about his entry into organized ball as well as his obvious ability to draw crowds. Pitts' entrance into the outlaw Carolina League one year later was anything but friendly. Ulmont Baker, the Concord Weavers' third baseman in 1938, remembered that as late as 1938, two years after he began playing in the outlaw league, he was the subject of fan abuse that was absolutely brutal in every game he played. Chapman also indicated that Pitts was very fast and a good fielding outfielder, but "like a lot of us rookies, he didn't hit too well."

It didn't take long to figure out that Pitts was in over his head in the International League. Even Pitts began to realize his need for playing time at a lower classification.

The July 25 edition of the *Sporting News* reported the following:

> Edwin (Alabama) Pitts told Rochester (NY) scribes last week that he felt he would improve if the Albany Senators would farm him to a club in lower classification for the remainder of the season. Manager Mamaux of Albany asserts that Pitts will remain with the team, because there is no better defensive man on the squad. Pitts had been idle due to injuries. He first injured his shoulder in sliding, then jammed the middle finger of his throwing hand on a fly ball.

The August 1 issue of the *Sporting News* made another reference to Pitts' lack of success at the plate. The story mentioned that before the July 25 game Albany held some track events. "The famous Edwin (Alabama) Pitts showed he could run, even if he isn't much of a hitter." During the event, he circled the bases in a team-best 14.4 seconds.

Speculation about his future with the Albany club was heavy. Yet, in the August 8 *Sporting News*, team president Cambria denied that Pitts and his "puny batting average" would be farmed out the following year. He insisted that "next year Pitts will be a regular with the Albany club." Since he had left Sing Sing, Pitts was batting less than .225.

Although injuries could not be the blame for all of Pitts' problems at the plate, it was reported again in the August 29 *Sporting News* that Pitts had blood poisoning from a self-inflicted knife wound. Because of numerous injuries during the 1935 season, Pitts played in only 43 games. He managed to get 27 hits and 30 total bases in 116 at bats. His only extra-base hits were three doubles, and he produced nine RBIs while finishing with a .233 average.

As the season ended, it seemed that everyone wanted to get in on the Alabama Pitts phenomenon. A vaudeville act was planned along with manager Al Mamaux, but the idea was nixed when Warden Lawes voiced his disapproval. On September 12, the *Sporting News* announced that Pitts had signed a contract to play football with the Philadelphia Eagles. He had in

Pitts helped win a semi-pro championship playing basketball for the Pilot Fashion company squad. He is pictured on the top row at the far left. The other players could not be identified (Hank Utley).

fact signed a contract on September 9 for $1500 to play in four exhibition and four regular season games. Pitts played in only three games and was soon released by the Eagles. He then played in games for the New Rochelle and Stapleton football teams in New York, before a short stint with a traveling professional basketball team called the Alabama Pitts All-Stars. It was a busy off-season in which Pitts maximized the earning potential that his notoriety had gained for him. Given all this activity, 1935 had to be the financial peak of his sports career. It was during December of this year that he went to spend time with relatives in Alabama and bought his half-sister Mildred a car. He also took her to the Blue-Gray All-Star football game.

At the beginning of the 1936 season, Pitts was reassigned along with Fred Chapman to the York, PA, team in the Class A New York–Penn League, another team under Cambria's ownership. At the end of June, the team relocated to Trenton, NJ. The move was blamed on poor patronage, but it was actually the second move of the season for the franchise. The previous season it was located in Harrisburg, PA, but had been moved because the Harrisburg ballpark had been destroyed by spring floods.

Pitts' batting average stayed below .250 for his time in the NY-Penn

4. Cause Célèbre

League. The May 14 *Sporting News* reported that in an effort to shake his past notoriety he had requested that he be addressed as Ed or Edwin rather than as Alabama. At one point he was suspended for 15 days because of a wrist injury and his slow start at the plate.

Pitts began to hit a little better after the team moved to Trenton. Records show he had seven hits in his first four games of July. He peaked with a 3 for 5 showing on July 6. His final records in the NY-Penn League show him with a .224 average that included 35 hits and 21 RBIs. He had two home runs, two stolen bases and had struck out only 16 times in 156 at bats. Then, inexplicably, Pitts showed up in Charlotte, NC, on July 12 as a member of the Charlotte Hornets an outlaw Carolina League team. He had, in fact, been signed by the Hornets to replace Vince Barton, the Canadian slugger who had contractual obligations to the Chicago Cubs, but as it worked out ended up with another outlaw team, the Kannapolis Towelers.

Just a little over a year had passed since Pitts had broken into organized baseball. Now he found himself in a league that played a wide open brand of ball. Pitts seemed relieved to be out of the New York area spotlight. He told the *Charlotte Observer* that he wasn't "happy up there." He said the club had been losing money, and that they wanted to use him as "a circus freak, which didn't appeal to" him.

Pitts went 3 for 5 in his debut on July 13. His production included a triple, and the *Observer* reported that "Pitts brought the crowd to its feet in the ninth with his hair line catch of Heavener's line drive. He cut a flip in the slippery ground after the catch." There was heavy rain that day, but the record crowd of 3000 demanded that the game be played. Charlotte won the game over Concord 10–3.

The Carolina League was a hitters league, and Alabama Pitts found it to be much more to his liking. Just six days after he joined the Charlotte Hornets, the July 19 *Observer* ran an article describing his success: "Pitts Peps Up Hornet Gang Smacks Agate at .411 Clip":

> The Alabama Streak has put power, punch, and magnetism into Frank Packard's Boisterous Bees; whatever it is, those Charlotte Hornet are winning ball games and knocking at the front door of the fast Carolina baseball circuit.
> Edwin (Alabama) Pitts stepped into the Hornets lineup on July 13 (a lucky date) and since that time has been posting that date at a sensational clip and doing a bang up job in the outfield."
> The paper reported as well that the local fans had adopted him as a hero and that he received a huge hand each time he came to the plate. Pitts enjoyed playing in Charlotte, remarking to another player that "these folks are just too swell."

There were no league batting averages published during the first season of the outlaw Carolina League. But a sample of game reports shows that

Pitts continued his torrid hitting. On July 23 he went 2 for 3, both home runs; on July 24 he had 3 for 5. On August 1 Pitts was 4 for 6 and 3 for 5 on August 4. In the August 9 game, he was 3 for 4 at the plate and won the game by stealing home in the bottom of the 9. On August 11, he was 4 for 4, and on August 14, he got two hits and knocked in the game's only run.

In the five game playoff series with Valdese, he had eleven hits. Despite his heroics the Hornets lost their playoff to the smallest town in the league. It should be noted that the series was not played without incident. In the first game, which Charlotte won 4–3, Valdese protested, claiming that Charlotte pitcher "Struttin' Bud" Shaney was cutting the ball. In the second game, played in Valdese, Pitts and Whitey Maxey were ejected for protesting a sixth inning call at the plate. A riot broke out in the grandstand, and when the Charlotte team refused the take the field for the seventh inning, umpire Rube Brandon declared the game a forfeit. Valdese continued its winning ways, defeating the regular season champion Concord team in four of six games to win the first Carolina League playoff championship.

Although complete records are not available, Pitts clearly put up his best numbers during his half season with the Hornets. It seemed that he had found his place in the game. But it was not to be so. The Charlotte franchise elected to withdraw from the Carolina League in 1937, returning to the Class B Piedmont League. Pitts decided to stay in the outlaw league and signed with the Gastonia Spinners.

The success of the Carolina League had not gone unnoticed during its initial season. After players continued to jump professional contracts, Judge Bramham declared it an outlaw league, meaning that its players would be prohibited from participating in organized professional baseball leagues. It was ironic that one of the league stars was Alabama Pitts who had fought so hard to play on an NAPBL team just two years before. The money was so good, and the promise of off-season jobs during the Depression so attractive that players continued to break contracts, some of them playing under assumed names. Pitts, with his notoriety, would hardly have been able to hide his presence.

The 1937 season began with great promise for Sing Sing's greatest athlete. Unlike the first season, statistics are more readily available for this one, and they show that Pitts was batting .311 on June 3. However, during a team meeting in the old National Bank Building, Pitts got into a fight with manager Frank "What a Man" Packard. He was released and then signed by the Valdese Textiles. He had a fine season for Valdese and finished the year with a combined batting average of .333, 14 home runs and 73 RBIs, a huge total for just 321 at-bats. His 97 runs led the league, but the Valdese team managed only a 49–49 record and finished in the middle of the league standings. They were then swept by the Concord Weavers in the first round of the playoffs.

4. Cause Célèbre

After the 1937 season, Pitts settled down in the North Carolina foothills town of Valdese. He became a knitter and worked for Pilot Full Fashion Hosiery Mills. While working there, he met Mary Walker, a young woman from Fallston, NC, a small town just north of Shelby. Mary was born on May 13, 1921, the daughter of Curtis and Callie London Walker, both of whom had died by March of 1937.

A brief article posted in the April 15, 1937, *New York Times* notes that Pitts had been granted a divorce by New York Supreme Court justice Raymond C. Aldrich from his first wife, Kathryn Cruse Pitts of Brooklyn. Ms. Pitts was accused of misconduct while Mr. Pitts was serving his prison sentence. According to the article, they had been married in 1928.

Mary and Edwin were married in 1938, and she became pregnant with their daughter that year. Patricia Ann was born January 17, 1939, and though Mary was 18 at the time, the birth certificate lists her a year older.

Pitts played one more year in the outlaw league, this one for the Lenoir Finishers. Although the Lenoir team won the pennant by five and a half games over Hickory, Pitts did not have as strong a season. He hit 10 home runs and drove in 58 runs, but his batting average fell to .268, not so great when you consider that the Lenoir team average was .312. Despite their regular season success, Lenoir was swept in the playoffs. The last Carolina League playoff ended in a bizarre series in which Hickory, under protest, failed to show up for the fifth and deciding game.

The outlaw league folded after the 1938 season, and Alabama Pitts settled into his small-town life. It has been noted that he made many friends and became a part of the community. He was, however, still connected to sports. He led the Pilot Mills basketball team to a championship in 1938, and records show that he coached the Valdese High School baseball team in 1939. The April 27, 1939, *Sporting News* carried a brief one paragraph article entitled, "Sing-Sing Graduate: Alabama Pitts coaching the Valdese High School baseball team." There is no record of Pitts having played professional ball during 1939. He did play on some local semi-pro teams and may have been one of the players that was forced to sit out for a year because of his participation in the Carolina League.

In 1939, Hickory had been granted a franchise in the Class D Tar Heel League. Pitts joined the Rebels for the 1940 season. One of his teammates on that team was Struttin' Bud Shaney. Pitts, who still lived twenty miles away in Valdese, roomed with Al Kubski and Johnny Carr in Hickory. They remember him for his toughness as a player and for his being a loner. Carr noted that "he'd have been in the big leagues if he could've hit the curve ball." Kubski indicated that Pitts could do everything but throw.

Both players remembered Pitts as a ladies man. "He had a way with the girls," Kubski said. "He'd look around, and he always managed to have

The contract record for Alabama Pitts (National Baseball Hall of Fame Library ad Museum, Cooperstown, New York).

the girls around him." They also remembered him as a fierce competitor who wore nothing under his uniform — no sweatshirt, no jockstrap. "I remember one time he slid into second and he got a strawberry as big as my head. And I asked him, 'What are you gonna do with that?' Well, he goes into the toilet and took out a roll of paper, and slaps it on the thing, and let it absorb. When he pulled it up it was all bloody and all, and he threw it away and slapped another wad on it." Carr said that he remembers him sliding on the wound the next day as if it wasn't there (Clark).

In all his conversations with Pitts, Carr noted that an important piece of information never came up. He never mentioned that he had a wife and daughter. Kubski defended him, however, saying that "he really didn't say much about anything" (Clark).

Harold Lail of Longview, NC, was the batboy for the Rebels from 1938 through the early forties. He remembers Pitts as one of his favorite players. When some of the other players picked on Lail, Pitts was quick to defend him. Lail's most important memory of Pitts was the day that the player approached him and asked if he would like to have a uniform for his sandlot games. Lail, who had lost his father, was quick to answer yes. For the rest of that summer Lail showed up for his games proudly wearing a Sing Sing Prison baseball uniform.

4. Cause Célèbre

Pitts had his best year in official professional baseball, batting .303 in 64 games, scoring 48 runs and driving in 39. Nevertheless, he was released by the club on August 1. One can only speculate as to why. Perhaps his age made him a liability. Hickory had signed him not only as a player, but also as a means to bolster attendance. It could be that he had made himself too available in the area and had lost his drawing power at the gate. Nevertheless, one could assume that Pitts had become disenchanted with organized ball and did not sign with a team the following season.

In 1941 Pitts went back to work at the mill, playing sporadically in semi-pro games. On June 5, a House of David touring team came to Morganton, a town ten miles west of Valdese. Pitts played center field for the touring team. A local newspaper article reported that he played well in the field and hit a home run. The next night he played in a game for the Valdese semi-pro team. Details of his performance are not available.

Later that night after the game, Pitts and two of his teammates, Horace Tron and Reid Suttle, went to a well known roadhouse, a combination dance hall and service station, located beside the swimming pool. In "The Sad Tale of Alabama Pitts" Michael Clark describes what happened:

> Around 3 AM, Pitts, apparently quite drunk, attempted to dance with a young lady, Miss Mildred Deal, of Valdese. She had come to the club in the company of Miss Kate Smith, and the two young ladies were escorted by cousins Roy and Newland LeFevers. Newland LeFevers was dancing with Miss Deal when Pitts decided to cut in.

The *News Herald* reported "Some difference was heard in reports as to actual details as to whether Pitts was starting to hit LeFevers with his fist." Regardless of the nature of the dispute, LeFevers slashed Pitts with a knife, leaving a four-inch gash under his right armpit that severed an artery. After the incident, Suttle attacked Roy LeFevers, but Newland quickly escaped the scene and hid out for seven days.

Hickory Daily Record reporter Wake Bridges included Suttle's account of the incident in his front page June 7 article:

> Suttle said that Pitts was slashed only once, the blade of the knife laying the muscle of the right arm open and severing the large artery.
> He added that he and Horace Tron ripped off Pitts' belt and made a tourniquet and succeeded partly in stopping the flow of blood.
> Pitts helped with and directed the placing of the tourniquet.
> "His calmness was admirable," Suttle commented, adding, "He met it like a soldier."
> Suttle said when the cutting took place he heard loud voices and then heard the splatter of blood on the floor of the tavern.
> "I know that sounds fantastic," he exclaimed, "but it's the truth. I actually heard the blood start splattering on the floor."

Suttle, a fellow worker of Pitts at the Pilot Full Fashioned Hosiery mill in Valdese asserted that Pitts strictly observed the terms of his parole from prison because "that was an ax hanging over his head."

After attempting to stop the bleeding with a tourniquet, the teammates rushed Pitts to the Valdese General Hospital where the newspaper reported, "he bled as much as it is possible for a person to bleed." According to the *News Herald*, Pitts told the hospital staff that "there was no fight and he was cut when he attempted to break in on a dancing couple" (Clark).

Two hours later, as preparations were being made to give him a blood transfusion (Suttle was to have supplied the blood), Edwin "Alabama" Pitts died at the age of thirty-one.

Newland LeFevers remained at large for seven days before turning himself in. Although he was represented by Frank Patton, one of the most respected lawyers in the state, he was convicted of murder. However, he was granted an unconditional pardon by Governor Broughton, who was convinced that LeFevers acted out of self-defense and that Pitts, who was quite drunk, had forcibly grabbed Miss Deal and threatened LeFevers with violence.

The funeral for Alabama Pitts was conducted on June 8, 1941, and is described here by Michael Clark:

> The man who stepped from the spotlight of the sports world to become a hosiery mill worker in the Waldensian city four years previous drew an estimated 5,000 people to pass by his casket in the small Valdese funeral home. A brief service was conducted by Rev. MI Harris of Valdese First Baptist Church, and then the body, followed by a procession of 50 cars, traveled to Friendship United Methodist Church in Fallston, a small community twenty or so miles south of Morganton in Cleveland County. He was buried beside Mary's father, mother and sister Ruby. The funeral was conducted by the Rev. Sylvan S. Poet of the Waldensian Presbyterian Church, and his pall bearers were the Valdese teammates with whom he'd shared a field only a few hours before his death: Will Bumgarner, Reid Suttle, Claude Owens, Harold Pruitt, TP Baker and Louis Vinay. His half-sister, Miss Mildred Rudd, and a cousin, Mrs. Lewis Green, both of Opelika, AL, were in attendance.

Clark also notes that "before their next game, against Morganton, the Valdese players lined up, heads bare, eyes filled with tears, in a silent salute to their centerfielder."

Newspapers from around the country told the story of the tragedy of Alabama Pitts. The *New York Times* carried this story in the June 7 issue:

> Sing Sing Prison, which never saw a faster halfback on its gridiron, a more skillful fielder on its diamond, a better all-around man in its track and field events, was saddened by the news today of Alabama Pitts' death.
>
> A graduate of the Class of '35, Pitts went into the world with the support of

Warden Lewis E. Lawes and the confidence of the other prisoners who liked his athletic and social qualities and considered him, of all the celebrated personages turned out by that institution, "most likely to succeed."

"I'm deeply distressed to learn of his death," Warden Lawes said when informed of the stabbing. "Pitts had an excellent record here as he had in the Navy before he came to Sing Sing."

In the June 12 issue of the *Sporting News*, Pitts was mentioned in the "necrology" column. In their coverage, the "Bible of baseball" failed to mention his years of service in the outlaw league. The Pitts story has similarly been a forgotten commodity in baseball lore. However, his successful battle with the baseball powers paved the way for other ex-prisoners like Ron LeFlore and Gates Brown who both played for the Detroit Tigers after serving time.

Of all the great characters that arrived to play in the outlaw Carolina League, Edwin "Alabama" Pitts remains the most enigmatic. For every answer provided by a study of his life, a question remains. Much of his life is open to speculation. Why, in 1940, did he rent a Hickory apartment during the ball season when his home was only fifteen miles away? Why did he never tell his teammates he had a wife and daughter just down the road? Why was he released by Winston-Salem in 1937? Why did Hickory release him when he was having a great season? Why did he not make another attempt at pro football?

Perhaps the most mysterious and therefore emblematic element of his life is something as simple as his birth date. In this profile we have used the birth date that appears on his Burke County death certificate, November 22, 1909. This date is substantiated by each age reference in his story. However, several Internet sites list his birth as March 1, 1910, or March 1910. This record also fits with age references and possibly comes from baseball records. Total Football provides a record because of his time with the Philadelphia team. That date is 1908. Strangest of all is the date on his Cleveland County headstone: December 18, 1906. Information recently made available has provided an answer to the inaccuracy of the headstone. According to Myrtice Carr, Pitts' second cousin, the grave did not originally have a headstone. An improvement project sponsored by the two churches that shared the graveyard was responsible for this addition. Apparently, they did the best they could with what information they had. This also explains why his first name is misspelled as Edwins on the stone.

Other information obtained from Ms. Carr may explain the secretive nature of Alabama Pitts' existence. During all of his days, from his meteoric rise as Sing Sing's greatest athlete to his lesser-known ones as an outlaw ball player, his mother was always around. She was an obsessive-compulsive and possibly schizophrenic. According to Ms. Carr, she showed signs of instability much earlier in her life. One thing that is certain is that Pitts did an amazing job of maintaining his family secret. In all the comments made by his various teammates, there is never a mention of his mother.

Her condition had worsened in the late 30s to the point where Edwin had her committed to Broughton Hospital, a state-run mental institution, in nearby Morganton. She apparently remained there until the early 50s when she died. Erma is buried on the hospital grounds.

Finally there is this entertaining anecdote from John Church, who was the official scorekeeper for the Valdese Textiles and later retired from the U.S. Postal Service.

In the Great Depression of the 30s it was not unusual for friends of the deceased to make a "love gift" towards the funeral expenses. One of the most used "love gifts" was to dig the grave and thereby save some expenses for the family of the deceased.

A group of Pitts' friends proceeded to the cemetery just outside of Lawndale on Sunday morning, June 8, 1941. They started early. The cemetery was very close to the church. As the morning sun rose higher and higher in the sky, it became unbearably hot.

Pitts' friends had come prepared with spirits of the liquid variety. As the church services began that Sunday morning, the members (being without air conditioning) opened the church windows wide.

The grave diggers' spirit was rising with the heat. In a short time shouts came from the church windows to quiet down, plus suggestions that the friends of Pitts were digging their way to hell laced the hot muggy atmosphere. One of Pitts' friends looked at another and said, "I bet ol' Alabama is smiling." Note: A Pitts family history by Alabama first cousin, Myrtice Ann Carr, can be found in Appendix A, page 161.

5

The Showman: Charles M. "Struttin' Bud" Shaney

Born: January 9, 1900, New Albany, Indiana

Charles M. Shaney was born in the Midwest but grew up in Southern California where the climate allowed him to play baseball for most of the year. Shaney served in the Navy during World War I, stationed on a hospital ship off the coast of Siberia. When the war ended, he returned to the states and began his lengthy professional baseball career.

By the time Charles M. "Struttin' Bud" Shaney reached the outlaw Carolina League in 1936, he was a journeyman ballplayer in the truest sense. He had pitched fourteen years of minor league ball on teams from California to New York. Shaney had learned every possible trick and possessed an array of junk ball pitches, some more legal than others. When he was young, a broken leg failed to heal properly, causing him to walk with a swagger, hence the colorful nickname that was so appropriate for the brand of ball played in the Carolina League. The Carolina League would be remembered not just for its high level of play, but also for its elevated level of entertainment.

Shaney had reached the triple A level in Milwaukee in 1924 and 1925, but was stricken with malaria and jaundice during spring training of 1925 in Florida and lost not just forty-five pounds but also his one big chance to make it in the big leagues. In an interview late in life, he said, "I know I could have won in the majors, but I never got a chance." Instead, at the age of twenty-five, Shaney was sent south to the mountain resort town of Asheville, NC. The Milwaukee ball club's business manager had heard of a man with yellow jaundice who had gone to Asheville and been cured within a year's time. He insisted that Shaney try this remedy. When Bud arrived in Buncombe County, he was told to join the Asheville club. Despite his physical problems he had an outstanding debut against the archrival Charlotte team after which the Asheville team bought his contract from

Milwaukee. Shaney proceeded to win 85 games over the next five years in Asheville.

Of his years in Asheville, 1928 was probably his best and the team's best. Historians rank the 1928 Tourists as perhaps the best ever. The team, which batted .304, sent six players to the major leagues and might have sent more had there been room. In a 1970 interview Shaney stated, "No Asheville club before or since could match the 1928 club. It was a great club, not just a good one. If that club was in the American League or the National League today, with all of its capabilities, it would be a first division team." Shaney posted a 21–11 record with a career-best 2.59 ERA.

Despite his success he did not move up the minor league ladder. His age, in fact, hamstrung his advancement at this time of his career. It was no surprise then that after a 24 win season for the Piedmont League Charlotte team in 1931, he was right back in Charlotte the following year. Shaney was a victim of his time as much as anything. America was still a baseball country, and many was the boy that shared Bud's dream. There were far fewer major league franchises as well, diminishing the chances of realizing that dream. Although the game was very popular at the time, the huge expansion of minor league ball would not occur until the late '30s. As Shaney noted, "Making the major leagues was a tough proposition back then. In fact, it was tough just getting a job playing professional baseball."

It was also a rough game as Bud notes in this reminiscence: "Baseball was as tough a game as a man could play. Everybody sharpened his spikes like Ty Cobb, and most came sliding into second with their spikes flashing." To further elaborate he relates the most vivid memory of his playing career, when Pete Mann was killed by a Tom Farrell pitch: "Farrell threw one inside to Mann and Pete didn't get out of the way. The ball drilled him in the rib cage on the left side and he went down like an ox. I was the first man to him and cradled his head in my lap. A shudder ran through him and he became still. A doctor came out of the stands and examined him and said, 'Boys, he's dead.'" Farrell, who had to be restrained later from jumping out a hotel window, was ruined by the incident. Bud Shaney was an active minor league ball player for twenty years.

When Shaney showed up to pitch for the Charlotte Hornets in 1936, he may have been past hope for his greatest dream, but he could still pitch and had about him a remarkable flamboyance. His knowledge, ability, and knack for entertainment made him an instant star. He was about to become a legend. Shaney, more than any other player, personified the skills, the experience, the cunning, the ingenuity, and the craftiness that made the Carolina League a fan's delight. He was, however, no delight for opposing players who claimed that he cheated. He had a strange relationship with the opposition who cursed him, and yet fell under the spell of his charisma.

5. The Showman

In 1936, pitching for the Charlotte Hornets, he won an incredible 17 straight games. Shaney lost while pitching in relief against the Forest City Owls on May 14. The winning streak then began and lasted until late July. All his games were played at home, a situation that aroused the suspicions of opposing players and sportswriters. On June 20, the winning streak at nine, Dick Montague, a columnist for the Concord paper, gave voice to these suspicions: "It's remarkable how old Struttin' Bud Shaney has managed to chalk up nine straight victories this season. And just last season he was washed up.... But he was off to Florida last season, and from the looks of the Strutter this season he found the Fountain of Youth.... Of course, there have been assertions that Shaney isn't pitching on the up and up."

The Charlotte media reported a different story. After his 12th consecutive victory on June 30, Wade Ison of the *Charlotte News* wrote: "Bud Shaney ... has become one of the Charlotte Hornets immortals. Believed by professional baseball moguls to have been through a year ago, Struttin' Bud has just pitched his 12th consecutive victory in one of the toughest leagues in the nation." After his next victory, *Observer* sports editor Jake Wade wrote, "Bud Shaney's amazing control this season has been one of the prime reasons he has won 13 consecutive games. He has walked only fifteen men in all those contests and pitched seven complete games without issuing a single free ticket."

The streak finally ended against the Kannapolis Towelers on July 21. Shaney lost the 12 inning contest 13–11. Jake Wade's description of him that day is memorable: "The Strutter never did have much, but he was able to cut loose with those occasional 'sailers' that had his foes' back breaking.... And the Strutter jabbered out of the corner of his mouth and strutted. Jabbered and strutted, indeed, even when he wavered in the late innings ... even when they got to him for keeps, in the 12th inning as the midnight hour bore down."

The team management claimed that he pitched only in Charlotte because he could draw 2000 fans from the visiting team's county. Other teams asserted that he played only at home because he was doctoring the ball. In the Carolina League, home teams provided the balls and could use "dead," "lively," or whatever type they could find or choose. Shaney was accused of cutting, roughing, or shining the balls in order to make them do tricks. The ultimate accusation claimed that his pre-game preparation included a process by which he carefully laced the baseball seams with old time gramophone needles. These needles, which resembled small nails, when embedded in the seams of the baseball, would throw it out of balance. The pitcher then could throw a ball that would move in its trajectory in such a way that it was nearly impossible to hit. As one might imagine, Shaney's games often lasted longer than normal because opposing players constantly asked the umpire to look at the ball. Bud's antics were most likely more a matter of psychological gamesmanship than anything. He, in fact, told his wife that he never laced a ball with needles.

Bob Terrell, a long-time sports editor for the *Asheville Citizen-Times*, had this to say about "Struttin' Bud" in a March 1970 article:

> He was of the old school, a man who spat on the ball and threw the juicer, who rubbed the ball on his wool trousers until he slicked one side and threw the shiner. He was accused of doctoring the ball with every imaginable device because his pitches were so effective, but he denies that.
>
> "Bobby Hipps used to take baseballs that I'd pitched and saw them in two and shake 'em over paper to see if any phonograph needles or anything else came out," Bud laughed. "But I never used anything like that. I didn't need to. I could make the ball do things and that was enough. If I'd used emory paper, they could've seen the scars on the ball, but I was never thrown out of a game in my life for doctoring a baseball.
>
> "Eddie Cicotte, who was banned from organized professional baseball for life for taking part in the Black Sox scandal in 1919, showed me how to shine a ball. Jeff Tesreau, the old New York Giant pitcher, taught me the spitter. With my speed and strength, those were all the pitches I needed besides the curve, and I could always throw the curve."

Tracey Hitchner, the pitching ace for the Carolina League Hickory Rebels (who had jumped his contract with Albany, NY, one step from the big leagues to play outlaw ball), when told of the Strutter's remark about never being thrown out of a game, replied, "Yeah, but a lot of the baseballs he was throwing were thrown out of the game." Other of Shaney's competitors would seem to concur. In a 1951 interview, Jim Hemphill of the Forest City club told how he and a Forest City pitcher brought back two balls from a game that Shaney pitched in Charlotte, took them apart and found gramophone needles.

In 1936, Bud Shaney playfully demonstrated his method for doctoring a ball (courtesy *Charlotte Observer*).

5. The Showman

John Church, scorekeeper for the Valdese Textiles and son of Mitch Church, a member of the Textiles board of directors, related the story that follows in a 1991 interview. The Valdese team was going to Charlotte to play the deciding game of the first round of the 1936 playoffs. Red Evans, the ace Valdese pitcher, was scheduled to face Bud Shaney in a monumental showdown.

> As I remember, we went down to Charlotte for the game and there had been some discussion about whether Bud Shaney was using phonograph needles in the baseballs and most of our players agreed that he did and decided to do something about it. We supplied two dozen baseballs for the ball game and took them down and discussion came about with the umpire Skidmore that Charlotte's baseballs were not to be used in this game because we were pretty sure they had been loaded with phonograph needles. Rod Evans, our starting pitcher that day handed the umpire two dozen baseballs and used some profanity handing them to him and telling him "don't miss a ball or strike on me at any time and use these baseballs. We will use good baseballs." When Red got through talking to the umpire, we see that Shaney is not pitching for Charlotte, possibly because he could not use his phonograph needles. That's what some of our players said. But as the game progressed, Red Murray, our catcher, got five hits; the last was a triple that hit the right field fence. If I remember, I think the score was 10 to 5. I remember it being a low score for Charlotte. The rest of what Red Evans had told Mr. Skidmore, the umpire, was "I've been paid already and you can't fine me because I have already received my final pay check and when I get through with this ball game, if you miss one decision on calling balls and strikes on me, I'm going to break your neck." And then he reinforced that with some choice words.

News reports in the *Concord Tribune* confirm John Church's memory. The score was 10 to 5, and Red Murray did get five hits. The subheadline above the game report stated: "Shaney did not take part in closing game."

After his spectacular 1936 season, Shaney remained a legendary sports figure not just in the region, but a rather far-reaching sort as related by his wife. One of her sons while working in Saudi Arabia in the 1980s was asked by a friend from North Carolina if he by any chance was kin to that Bud Shaney that used to pitch for the Charlotte Hornets. When he replied that Bud Shaney was indeed his father, the man smiled and said, "Bud was a helluva pitcher. Nobody could hit him. The players said that he was a cheater, but the fans loved him." Nearly fifty years after he won 17 games before he was defeated, the story of "Struttin' Bud" Shaney was being told on the other side of the world.

Charles R. Shaney, who lives in Charlotte, also notes how people still recognize his name when he writes a check and are quick to talk about his father. In speaking about his father's hands and sheer physical strength, Charles perhaps reveals the secret to "Struttin' Bud's" process on the mound.

He said that up to the last year of his life, Bud had fingers strong as steel springs. He could take a baseball and move it around in his hand less than a minute and find the end of the seams tucked inside the leather cover. Once this constant rubbing loosened the seams only slightly, Bud knew he had found the end of the seams and proceeded to rub until the seams were raised slightly, creating additional wind resistance at that point on the ball. These raised seams were enough to cause a baseball to do strange things. Even now, a major league pitcher will return a ball to the umpire if he thinks the seams are too tight (flat) on the ball.

After his phenomenal year in the outlaw league, Shaney continued to play. His last two full seasons were in 1940 and 1942 as player and manager with the Class D Hickory Rebels. During 1942, his last year, he posted a remarkable 8–9 record with an ERA of 2.92. This was mainly significant because this version of the Rebels was one of the worst teams in minor league history, finishing with a record of 18–80.

Shaney did not, however, play his final game in 1942. Given his nature, he could not stray too far from the game. Eventually, he became the groundskeeper for the Asheville Tourists. Starting in 1953, for three years, the team brought him to the mound for a start at the end of the season. The 1954 game marked another milestone for "Struttin' Bud." At the age of 54, he recorded six innings of

Bud Shaney with his wife, Alice, and two sons, Charles and Richard (in mother's arms) in 1931. While pitching for the Charlotte Hornets, Shaney led the Piedmont League with 24 wins while losing 10 games. His 280 innings pitched also led the league (courtesy Charles R. Shaney).

shutout ball and recorded the 235th and final win of his storied minor league career. It should be noted that the game was played by special arrangement with the Knoxville team. In an *Asheville Citizen* article, Bob Terrell suggests that the two teams seemed to be playing purely for the fun of it. Regarding Shaney, he noted that he "didn't show a fast ball at all — just stuff." However, he also says that "some of the Smokies played along with him; others tried to beat his brains out. None of them were very successful." He further describes Shaney's fifth inning trip to the plate as "worth the price of admission.... Swinging mightily at a 1–2 pitch, Bud popped the ball weakly in the air in front of the plate. Catcher McConnell scrambled to field it while Shaney chugged off down to first base. McConnell took his time about fielding the ball, letting Bud have a good start down the baseline. Then the catcher picked up the ball and fired to first — lo and behold, Shaney was already there, safe on a close play." Shaney lasted five innings and combined with Tourists manager Ray Hathaway for a four-hit shutout, capping what could have been a storybook ending to his career. The next year, however, he was knocked out in the second inning of his final game.

The reader can believe what he wants about "Struttin' Bud" Shaney. What cannot be denied is that he was a fan favorite everywhere he went. An interview with Mrs. Shaney verifies Shaney's popularity and his enthusiasm for the game. "Baseball was his life, and everywhere he went, from Milwaukee to Charlotte, the fans loved him. He never had a sore arm. And he was a ball player until the day he died. It was kind of sad. He was in the hospital, and his mind was wandering just before he died. He was still talking baseball. He asked me, 'Did I get in the Hall of Fame?' He was sure he did. He wanted to know if it was in the paper. I said, yes, you did and it was in the paper.

He asked, 'Did you save the clipping?' and I said, yes."

6

The Manager: Bobby Hipps

Born: 1905 Canton, North Carolina; died: March 31, 1980, Asheville, North Carolina

Robert Elwood Hipps was born in 1905 in the western North Carolina mountain town of Canton. Known mostly for its huge paper mill, Canton is located in a river valley southwest of Asheville. Canton was a hotbed for sports, and Hipps excelled in many of them. But it became apparent during his years in the Canton school system and later at Oak Ridge Military Academy near Greensboro that baseball would be his sport. He displayed a talent and enthusiasm that would keep him involved in that game for nearly half a century.

After high school, Hipps enrolled at nearby Weaver College but only stayed for a year before transferring to Furman University. At the Greenville, SC, school, Hipps had a stellar athletic career. He was named to the All-State baseball team in both 1925 and 1926, but his success was not limited to the diamond. He also received honorable mention on the All-State football team and even played a season of varsity basketball. As a senior in 1926, Hipps was elected captain of the baseball squad and was named Furman's most valuable player in a year that he finished with a .435 batting average. For this honor, he was awarded a full-size silver bat. His accomplishments did not go unnoticed, and when he graduated, he signed a contract with Connie Mack's Philadelphia Athletics.

Furman University's yearbook, the *Bonhomie* sang the praises of its star athlete:

> Bob is a native of North Carolina who has brought fame to Furman. Because he brought credits from another college when he entered Furman, he is able to finish in three years. He is a star athlete: one of the best football and basketball stars Furman has turned out in some years. In baseball, however, he has gained most of his glory. He has been for the past two years the best first baseman in South Carolina, and has already signed a contract with the Philadelphia Athletics to whom he will go as soon as he has the diploma

6. The Manager

tucked away. Last year he was voted the best looking man at the University; this fact, coupled with that neat little coupe that is at his disposal at all times, has served to make him the University Beau Brummel. If it is his will, and he has a strong one, we shall see him become one of the best first sackers in the major leagues.

Unfortunately, like many promising prospects of his era, Hipps would never achieve the major league stardom as predicted in his college annual. He did, however, have a successful minor league career. He was shipped, fresh from the pomp and circumstance of graduation, to Philadelphia's Class A Hartford Senators. Hipps did fairly well, batting a respectable .270 in 39 games, but the big league club decided to see how he would fare in the Class A Southern Association. Hipps joined the Chattanooga Lookouts at midseason and was immediately given the opportunity for additional playing time. His response was exceptional: a .339 batting average.

The 1927 season would also be split between two teams; for the first half, Hipps was with Chattanooga again before being sent down to Asheville in the Class B South Atlantic League. Hipps got to play regularly in both cities, but his batting average fell to the mid–200s. In 1928 he was assigned to the Durham Bulls of the Class C Piedmont League where he suffered an injury which limited him to 46 games. Again, he managed to hit just .257.

During the off-season, beginning in the fall of 1927, Hipps worked in the Asheville area as a teacher and a coach at Weaverville and Grace High Schools. In 1934 he was hired as assistant baseball coach at Asheville's Edwards High School.

In 1929, at the age of 24, Hipps returned to play for the Asheville Tourists. For three consecutive seasons, he was the team's star first baseman, increasing his outstanding numbers each season. In 1931, as a result of the financial difficulties created by the Great Depression, the South Atlantic League folded. The Asheville Tourists, who wanted to continue to field a team, managed to switch to the Class C Piedmont League. That year Hipps put up the best numbers of his career. Not only did he bat .360 while driving in 106 runs, but he also rang up 63 total extra base hits, easily a career best. For those three fantastic seasons, it appeared that Bobby Hipps had matured into a major league caliber player who would soon make true those college annual predictions. But the call from the big leagues never came.

For the 1932 season, Hipps made a dramatic geographical move, signing with the Tulsa Oilers of the Class A Western League. There he played well, hitting .289 with 75 RBIs and 171 hits. His play helped the Oilers win the league championship, after which they swept the Oklahoma City Indians in the playoffs. The trip to the other side of the Mississippi only lasted a year, though, as Hipps opted to come back east and sign with the Knoxville Smokies of the Class A Southern League for the '33 season. Hipps duplicated his

.289 average of the year before and upped his RBI total to 81 in 122 fewer at-bats.

Despite his excellent play, he was back near home in Asheville for the start of the 1934 season. A month into the season, he headed north to play for the Williamsport, PA, Grays in the Class A New York–Penn League. Williamsport would be the last organized professional baseball club for which he would play. His totals there fell some. He finished the short season with a .260 average and 59 RBIs, but his play helped the club win the league championship.

In 1935, at the age of 30, Bobby Hipps made a career-changing decision that kept him in the game for an additional four years and laid a foundation on which he built a business career. He dropped out of organized professional baseball and began to play for the Cooleemee Cools in the Carolina Textile League. Cooleemee was one of many North Carolina villages built around a single textile mill. It joined Landis and Mooresville, also single-mill towns, and together with the slightly larger multiple mill towns of Concord, Kannapolis and Salisbury formed the Carolina Textile League. The league was highly competitive, and Hipps soon found that he was only one of many league players with professional experience. In midseason 1935, he switched teams and took over as a player-manager for the Kannapolis club. Hipps had an outstanding year, hitting .342, and was named to the league All-Star team at first base.

During the winter of 1935–36, the Carolina Textile League reorganized and transformed itself into a fully professional league. Called the Carolina League, it operated outside the auspices of the governing body of the National Association of Professional Baseball, minor league's governing body, thus earning itself the title of an "outlaw" league. Players didn't complain about the stigma though since the league offered more money and the year-round security of a job in the mills. The professional baseball establishment, on the other hand, attempted to shut the league down and threatened to ban all players who participated in its games.

As the Carolina League members mounted one of the early challenges to baseball's reserve clause, Hipps and fellow player-managers Art Hord and Jim Poole could be found in the background offering advice to the textile mill owners and civic leaders. In reality, they didn't challenge the reserve clause (which, in essence, stated that players were the sole possession of the team they signed with until that team said otherwise) as much as they ignored it. It would be years later, in the 1970s, before professional players would finally successfully challenge the reserve clause in the courts of the United States.

Hipps had three outstanding years in the outlaw league, the first two with Concord and the final year with the hard hitting Lenoir Finishers. In

6. The Manager

After a minor league career that began in Hartford and Chattanooga, Bobby Hipps finished his playing days with three solid seasons in the Carolina League where he played for and managed first the Concord Weavers and then the Lenoir Finishers. Hipps later served as the president of the Class B Tri-State League for five years from 1951 to 1955 (Hank Utley).

that last season he batted .361 and knocked in 50 runs in 338 at-bats. In the three seasons, he hit 28 home runs and drove in a combined 148 runs. The Carolina League proved to be a great place to finish his playing career.

After the collapse of the Carolina League at the end of the 1938 season, Bobby Hipps made his first move into business management. He was selected to be general manager of the Central Motor Lines in Lenoir, NC. The president of Central Motor Lines, Robert Hayes, was closely associated with Cannon Mills in Kannapolis. How a man who had managed only baseball players could be named manager of a trucking company can be explained by a conversation businessman Cork Caldwell recalled that had taken place between Dick Rankin, a prominent doctor in the Kannapolis area, and Cannon Mills executive Alex Howard. He remembered Dr. Rankin saying, "Alex, I see where Bobby Hipps has been named general manager of Central Motor Lines in Lenoir. What does that man know about managing a motor line? He's done nothing but play baseball all his life."

Alex Howard replied, "For four years in the Carolina League, Bobby

Hipps has shown leadership abilities and has proven he knows how to manage men. That type of man is hard to find. We can teach him the technical end of the trucking business, but you cannot teach a man management skills on the job. Hipps knows how to manage men."

Though Hipps' playing career was over, his love for the game was too great to allow him to stay away for long. From 1941 to 1947 he was a baseball scout, first for the Atlanta Crackers and then for the Pittsburgh Pirates. In 1947 he resigned from the Pirates and went into the used car business in Asheville. Soon, he became part of Sam's Motor Sales, the city's Lincoln and Mercury dealer. (He would retire as the company's vice-president and treasurer in 1971.) Hipps was also a prominent civic leader, serving as commissioner of the Asheville Housing Authority.

Even while becoming a business leader in Asheville, Hipps couldn't stay away from his beloved game. In 1951, professional baseball called again. The presidency of the Tri-State League, a Class B circuit in North Carolina, South Carolina and Tennessee was offered to him. Hipps eagerly accepted the job.

Hipps applied his skills as a baseball manager to the business arena where he succeeded in the trucking business (Hank Utley).

It is ironic that Bobby Hipps, a man who loved and gave so much to the game of baseball, would have to shoulder the pains of the demise that minor league baseball was going through during the early part of that decade. The entertainment world was changing, led by the burgeoning television industry, and fans were no longer coming out to the ballparks in record numbers like they had just a few seasons before. For five years, from 1951 to 1955, Bobby Hipps was a man possessed by optimism and drive, trying to save professional baseball in the region. In the end, however, it proved to be a fight that couldn't be won.

After Hipps died in 1980, Bob Terrell, sportswriter for the *Asheville Citizen Times* wrote the following eulogy:

Hipps was league president for five years, until the league folded after the 1955 season. Had it not been for his efforts, his tireless work, and his many contacts in baseball, the league would have gone under a year or two before it did. I came to know Hipps as perhaps the most honest man I ever had to approach for a story. When you asked him a question, he gave a straight answer. He didn't beat around the bush, and he didn't try to hide anything. He was an optimist. He believed that through honest effort, he could hold the Tri-State League together. In 1954 and '55, when the league threatened every month to cave in, Hipps played every possible angle and held it together. I remember two headlines in the Times. One read "Hipps Smiles While Tri-State Totters," and the other, in February of 1955: "Will it Take Miracle Work to Save Tri-State League Now?" Hipps saved it. Most of the cities had folded up, but Hipps promoted a four-team league in 1955 consisting of Asheville, Spartanburg, Greenville, and Rock Hill, and played the entire season. At the end of the 1955 season, the league folded. Nothing, not even Bobby Hipps, could have saved it.

Baseball did eventually return to Asheville in the 1960s, but by that time, Bobby Hipps' only official involvement with the game was as an avid fan. Unofficially, however, he still helped guide the careers of players and league presidents alike by sharing his years of experience. Even today, more than twenty years after his death, his contributions to the game he loved are not forgotten.

7

A Gang of Two

The Forgotten: Richard Grey Clarke
The Scout: Edwin "Cy" Williams

Richard Grey Clarke and Edwin "Cy" Williams were two of the many minor league players who were caught up in Branch Rickey's vast and complex St. Louis Cardinals minor league system. Clarke, who hailed from Alabama, had spent several seasons as a professional ballplayer before he arrived in Kannapolis to play for the Carolina League Towelers. Williams, who came from the opposite side of the country in Buffalo, New York, had begun his career earlier as well. Both men loved the game, but while Clarke remained in the area spending his work career at Cannon Mills, Williams returned to the Northeast where he became a near-legendary baseball scout.

The Forgotten: Richard Grey Clarke

Born: September 26, 1912, Fulton, Alabama; died: November 23, 1993, Kannapolis, North Carolina

Grey Clarke was the third baseman for the Kannapolis Towelers in 1936, the first year of the Carolina League. Clarke, born in 1912 in Fulton, AL, was 24 years of age at the time and had already played several years of professional baseball. This interview with Grey Clarke was conducted July 12, 1991, as Mr. Clarke was approaching his 79th birthday.

His baseball career began in 1934 with a season spent in the Mid-Atlantic League with Huntington. Clarke spent 1935 with Houston in the Texas League, a farm club for the Cardinals organization. That year he established himself as a productive hitter, batting .279 and driving in 53 runs. Clarke began the following year in the Piedmont League with the Asheville Tourists. He was hitting well at the beginning of the season with 11 RBIs and a .352 average. When he developed a sore arm which forced him to throw with an underhanded motion from third, he was released by the club. Regarding his release, Clarke noted that during the Great Depression there were so many good ballplayers looking for work that the professional teams in organized ball would release you if you could not perform at your peak level.

Bobby Hipps, the manager of the Concord Weavers in 1936 and former Kannapolis Towelers manager, told Kannapolis management about Clarke after the Kannapolis third baseman, Bob White, broke his leg early in the 1936 season. Such was the spirit of the outlaw Carolina League; teams would often help other teams secure players that they did not need themselves.

Clarke signed with Kannapolis for $25 a week. He had been earning $150 a month at Asheville. His Kannapolis contract did, how-

After a ten-year minor league career, which included a stint in the Carolina League with the Kannapolis Towelers, Grey Clarke realized his baseball dream. In 1944, at age thirty-one, he played his final season with the Chicago White Sox (Hank Utley).

ever, offer a $100 bonus at the end of the season if he was still with the team. Clarke said that the bonus helped him average about $35 per week for the season and his arm did eventually recuperate so that he could perform satisfactorily in the field.

Unfortunately only midseason statistics are available for that season, but they show that Clarke was having no trouble with the Carolina League pitching. In 198 at-bats he managed to get 64 hits including 11 home runs and drove in 56 runs.

After the 1936 season, Clarke signed with Macon in the South Atlantic League. During the winter of 1936–37, there was a great deal of discussion about the National Association taking over the Carolina League and making it a Class D league. Clarke had played at higher classifications in Houston and Asheville and didn't want to get stuck in Class D ball. For this reason he signed with the Class B franchise in Macon for the 1937 season.

Like many of the Kannapolis Toweler players, Clarke was given a winter job at the Cannon Mills plant. During the '36–'37 winter, he met his future wife while working there. She was Miss Nell Mauldin, sister of Dr. Mauldin, and he met her at Christmas of 1936.

Except for the winter of 1937–38, Clarke returned to Cannon Mills and worked for Ray Propst each off-season. Clarke noted that a Mr. Payne of Cannon Mills was upset with him for signing to play with Macon earlier in the year. But Mr. Propst knew he had only gone there to avoid dropping down to Class D play. After all, he had the opportunity to sign with Martinsville in the Bi-State League when his arm recuperated in 1936 but chose to stick with the Kannapolis club.

While Clarke was with the Cardinals organization in Houston in the Texas League, he recalled that the Cardinals had signed so many minor league players in Branch Rickey's infamous St. Louis Cardinals "chain gang," that the Cardinals had four or five of their farm hands on several other clubs in the Texas League. He said it was like the entire Texas League was a St. Louis Cardinals League. Of course, this was against the rules of organized baseball and eventually in March of 1938 Judge K. M. Landis, the Major league commissioner, freed 80 to 90 St. Louis minor league players who were then eligible to sign with any organized baseball team in the country.

At this time, St. Louis controlled over 500 minor league players, enough to field 25 or thirty teams. Obviously, they could not afford to maintain that many teams, so Branch Rickey made gentlemen's agreements with various independent ball clubs, including some textile league teams. The agreements allowed the Cardinals to "lend" players out and have them returned when they decided that they needed them back. When Landis voided all those minor league contracts, he freed up several future major league players including Pete Reiser who signed with the Brooklyn Dodgers and led the National League in hitting three years later, in 1941, with a .343 average.

Clarke had an excellent year in 1937 in Macon where he batted .335 and knocked in 79 runs. He spent the next four seasons back in the Texas League, this time playing for Dallas. His final year there, he batted a career high .361 and led the league with 96 RBIs. He spent the following two seasons with the triple A Milwaukee club of the American Association. In 1943 he batted an exceptional .346 and again led his league with 96 RBIs. Finally, in 1944, at the age of 31, Clarke realized his dream and made it to the Big Show. He played that season in Chicago with the White Sox where he batted .260 and drove in 27 runs. This is where his professional baseball career ended.

When Richard Grey Clarke, Sr. died on November 23, 1993, his brief obituary made no mention of his baseball career. The man who had it made it all the way from Kannapolis and the outlaw league to Chicago and the major league was only listed as "retired from Cannon Mills."

The Scout: Edwin "Cy" Williams

If ever the old cliché, "They played the game because they loved it" was true, it described many of the players that played in the outlaw Carolina League of 1936–38.

One of the best examples of such a man is Edwin "Cy" Williams, who was living in the Buffalo, NY, area at the time of the interview (1992). Cy has spent 51 years in baseball, doing one thing or another. He was inducted into the Greater Buffalo Sports Hall of Fame in 2000.

He was signed as a twenty-year-old shortstop by the St. Louis Cardinals in 1935. This was the heyday of Branch Rickey and his infamous chain of farm teams called appropriately "The Chain Gang." Williams' first contract was $75 a month, a considerable sum of money in 1935, even though it was for the length of the season only.

He reported to the Cardinals' minor league camp in Asheville, NC, along with several hundred other ballplayers. Branch Rickey had more ballplayers than he had minor league teams on which to place them. However, Rickey, ever mindful that any of these young prospects could develop into a future star, helped place most of the players with some team — sometimes outside of organized baseball. Of course, Rickey still maintained control of the player's future by holding him under the now infamous "reserve clause" of organized baseball's standard contract.

Cy Williams was one of many players in Asheville in 1935 that Rickey helped find a position in the newly formulated Carolina Textile League, forerunner of the outlaw Carolina League. In fact, "Tiny" Stewart, manager of the Salisbury Greyhounds, found several of his players at this Cardinal camp.

Whereas the Cardinals had Cy signed to a $75 a month contract, the Greyhounds "paid me a little

Edwin "Cy" Williams is seen here while playing with the 1935 Salisbury Greyhounds in the Carolina Textile League, a forerunner of the Carolina League. After his playing career, Williams was a highly successful professional scout (courtesy Cy Williams).

more, even though we played only three to four games a week." Cy Williams' career in the Carolina Textile League was, however, cut short by injury.

Cy, being young and naïve, didn't realize he was still the property of the St. Louis Cardinals until the next year when he hit .308 for Oswego of the Canadian-American League. In 1937 he hit .321 for Zanesville, OH, of the Middle Atlantic League before being transferred to Perth-Cornwall of the Canadian-American League where he hit .377 in eighteen games.

That was the end of Cy's playing career except for a few wartime games with Albany of the Eastern League in 1943. Cy, like many other youngsters, could not live on the meager minor league salaries and the costly relocation twice each year. There was also practically no off-season work available because of the Great Depression.

Williams continued to play amateur and semi-pro ball while raising his family, working at one time or another as a steel worker, construction worker, plant security guard, car salesman, private detective, and grave digger.

In 1945, playing shortstop on a Buffalo All-Star team against the Kansas City Monarchs at Brian Stadium, he impressed Detroit Tigers scout Aloysius Egan and was offered a contract to join the Tigers' top farm team, Toledo, of the American Association. Although flattered by the offer, he was too old for such a venture by that time. Cy refused the offer. He couldn't afford to take the chance with a wife and three children. Plus he had a good year-round job with General Motors.

The meeting with Egan did produce some unexpected benefits for the former player. Williams later became a part-time and then a full-time baseball scout for the Detroit Tigers organization. It was this second baseball career that earned Williams many accolades. His forty-two plus years as a scout made him a legend in that demanding world and earned him a place in the Greater Buffalo Sports Hall of Fame.

Cy began his work for Detroit in 1945, traveling to the isolated areas of Pennsylvania, New York, and West Virginia. His hard work paid off in 1955 when he was appointed to be the director of scouting for the Tigers in the Eastern United States and Canada. During his twenty-nine years with the Tigers, he earned two World Series rings: 1945 and 1968. Williams was responsible for signing key players for the powerhouse 1968 team including Dick McAuliffe and John Hiller. He also signed fellow Buffalo Hall of Famer, Pat Dobson. His final job was with the Major League Scouting Bureau, a time in which he signed Mel Hall and Dave LaPointe among others. By the time Williams retired in 1987, he was credited with signing forty-three players who eventually made it to the major leagues. Before he retired, he completed 51 years of association with his lifelong love—baseball.

8

The Brain: Richard Broadus Culler

Born: January 15, 1915, High Point, North Carolina; died: June 16, 1964, Chapel Hill, North Carolina

Looking back and analyzing the rise and fall of the outlaw Carolina League, it is easy to come to the conclusion that Broadus Culler's up and leaving Concord was the first crack in the breakup of the outlaw league after the 1938 season.

Culler, granted, was only one player, but from the day he left Concord one rupture after another shattered the league. Whether this was merely a coincidence or a sign of the legitimacy the once and future major leaguer gave to the league is hard to determine. Several other factors indicate that Broadus Culler, a rising young star with a college degree, began to see the handwriting on the wall and sensed that his future was not in the outlaw Carolina League. Professional baseball, even the Class D NC State League, was beginning to show the area fans the stability that only professional baseball could offer. The NC State League was in only its second year of operation, but fans were already starting to notice the absence of all the disputes and altercations among the executives of the teams and the league and most of all the absence of continuing to lay and raise money to pay the ballplayers. To put it simply, professional ball kept a lid on its budget that maintained the competitiveness among the league's teams. Granted, the level of Class D baseball was well below the outlaw league, but it was the teams' management that controlled the finances and not the overdemanding players in the outlaw league.

Another factor was the outlaw league's fans. Being asked for more and more money in addition to the cost of the tickets, they took their bitterness out on the players—even the home team's players.

In an interview with Broadus Culler's widow, now Mrs. Evelyn Foster of Thomasville, North Carolina, she quickly pointed out that she did not believe it was money that made Culler leave for the Bi-State League. The fans were really getting on Broadus and he just got fed up with it. Culler had gotten off to his worst start in three years in Concord. Hindsight indicates that he may not have been as well prepared for the season as in past years. In 1936 he completed a full college baseball season at High Point College and was in excellent midseason shape when he reported to Concord. In 1937 he had the benefit of spring training with the Philadelphia Athletics in Mexico City. Although he had lost considerable weight, along with other members of the Athletics, as a result of "Montezuma's Revenge," his baseball skills were highly tuned. In 1938, however, Culler started playing without the extensive preparation of the previous two years. He had just completed his first year teaching math in the Concord school system. There is no question that his preparation in 1938 was far less than the previous two years. Mrs. Foster pointed out that the fans in the outlaw Carolina League, as a whole, were the most demanding and least forgiving fans in all of baseball — having experienced most organized baseball in the Bi-State League, Southern Association, American Association, and the American and National major leagues. They were rough. Ulmont Baker, who played third base for Concord in 1938, would even venture to say, "They were brutal."

Culler was his own man, and being young with professional scouts after him, he just said "to heck with it" and joined Reidsville, North Carolina (home of Lucky cigarettes which owned

Richard Broadus Culler was one of the players who helped lend credibility to the Carolina League. He split the 1936 season between the Concord Weavers and the Philadelphia Athletics (courtesy Evelyn Culler Foster).

8. The Brain

the Reidsville franchise), in the Class D Bi-State League. He was also given a job teaching in Reidsville.

Earlier, it was mentioned that Broadus signed with the Philadelphia Athletics at the end of the 1936 Carolina League season and played nine games in the majors that year.

Culler's keenness of insight was evident when the contract he signed with Connie Mack specified that he would be given his "unconditional release" if he was not assigned to Triple A baseball or the majors. That is why he ended up back in Concord after major league spring training in 1937. He could simply come out better economically by coming back to the Carolina League and a teaching position.

And in June 1938 Culler's own maturity probably made him realize that he did have major league potential and that the way to get there was through the age old process of professional baseball—making one's way through the minor league system—one step at a time. Broadus, at the age of 23, was still young enough to do it.

As he progressed to the majors, he showed "baseball savvy" far beyond his years because he had cut his teeth in the Outlaw Carolina League. His physical skills needed to be honed by experience, but having played nearly three years with professionals of ten to fifteen years experience, his mental preparation was already Major League.

Richard Broadus Culler was born January 15, 1915, in High Point, North Carolina. He died at the early age of 49 on June 16, 1964—stricken with regional enteritis, a form of Crohn's Disease. He stood 5' 9½" tall and played at 155 lbs. Broadus, as he was called until he entered professional baseball (it was "Dick" after that, a nickname for Richard), married his college sweetheart, Evelyn Williams of Graham, North Carolina, on October 30, 1936, the fall after his graduation from High Point College.

Culler's chief interest throughout his life was athletics. He not only starred in baseball and basketball at High Point College, but he also played soccer for four years and was coach of the team the last three years. He was captain of the basketball team and after his last basketball game, his jersey, No. 9, was retired, the first time this honor had been made in the school's history—an honor that was not to be repeated for 28 years, when, in 1964, Donny Seville's No. 32 was retired. At graduation ceremonies, he was named the most outstanding athlete in the school's history.

Outside of his college and professional playing careers, Culler remained deeply involved in sports as well. After his retirement from baseball, he devoted much of his time to officiating basketball games. He officiated games from high school all the way up to the ACC. His career as an official ended in an unfortunately early manner when a disagreement with a fan at a State College home game in Raleigh nearly came to blows.

At the time he announced his retirement as an official in February 1948, Frank Spencer of the *Winston-Salem Journal* described him as a man "who ranked as one of the top basketball officials of North Carolina."

After leaving Concord in June 1938, Culler played with Reidsville the remainder of '38 and 1939. In 1938 he had hit .330.

The winter before leading the 1939 Bi-State League in hitting, Culler and his wife thought his baseball career was at an end. His widow, Mrs. Foster, said even when it looked like her husband would not play baseball again that she had no doubts about their future. She knew Broadus had his college education, was already a successful school teacher, and so she had no doubt, economically, about their future. Her faith was strong.

Here are Broadus Culler's own words taken from a newspaper clipping in his wife's scrapbook:

> I was instructing in a high school physical education class. I was doing one of those movements where you use your neck for power and then flip yourself to a standing position. Well, I tried it and when I did the cartilage between the two vertebrae was crushed.
>
> I was in a cast for eight weeks. There was no way to keep the vertebrae separated with the cartilage crushed, so they grew together. In 1938, that was before I went to Nashville, something snapped and kept pulling my chin down to my chest. I couldn't even move my head. Strangely, one night I was lying on the couch at home, with one of those small sun lamps on my back. My wife said it was time to go to bed. I told her I'd go soon and just then I broke out with a big sneeze. The next morning my back was as good as ever and I guess when I sneezed it snapped something into place.

The back never bothered him again except for periodic stiffness that would quickly clear up. Of course the two vertebrae that had grown together kept him out of military service in World War II.

The Nashville Vols manager, Larry Gilbert, in March 1940 at spring training, quickly named "Dick" Culler, despite his size, his shortstop. As reported in the *Nashville Tennessean*, Culler, confident to the point of cockiness, was quoted as saying, "I think I'm gonna make this club, but if I don't, it won't be because of my size. I hit .347 at Reidsville last year."

By July 16, 1940, the *Nashville Banner*

Culler played for the Nashville Vols of the Class A Southern Association during the 1940–41 seasons (Hank Utley).

quoted manager Larry Gilbert, "I've seen Culler make plays this year that no shortstop in the game, big league or otherwise, could beat. He's hitting .250. If he could hit big league pitching, he'd be a sensation in the Majors. He's the best shortstop I've ever seen in the Southern Association League in 25 years."

"Dick" Culler was not only showing his fielding and hitting ability, he was also establishing his reputation as a "brainy ballplayer."

Fred Russell, long time sportswriter in Atlanta, wrote the following report about a game on August 19, 1940. In his column "Sideline Sidelights" on August 20, he wrote:

> One of the oldest gags in baseball decided one of the season's most important games for Nashville last night. The villain was Dickie Culler, the victim Emil Lochbaum.
> With the score tied 2–2 in the tenth, Culler was on third base, two outs, John Miholic at bat and the count one ball and one strike. Lochbaum got the sign from catcher Williams, glanced at third, then started his windup.
> Suddenly, a voice screamed: "Time! Time!"
> Lochbaum stopped right in the middle of the windup. It was a balk. Too late it dawned on him that he had been foxed by the crafty Culler.
> Culler is a sharpie. He's trying stuff like this all the time. It is fortunate that the one time in fifty that it worked be so profitable.

Culler walked home with the winning run. Mrs. Evelyn Culler Foster, Culler's wife, recalled that he was so excited he called her up after the game from Atlanta to tell her about winning the game.

Culler's quick thinking was evident the night before when the Atlanta Crackers won that game in the ninth inning. Ed Danforth, sports editor of the *Atlanta Journal* wrote in his column August 19, 1940:

> Charley Glock, Cracker second baseman, hit a long drive to left center with one down, bases loaded and score tied. Hockett, Nashville centerfielder, ran for it, saw he could not reach it, let it fall and swung on toward the clubhouse. That was boner #1.
> The Crackers Willard Marshall on first cut short his run towards second and left the field; so did Burge going to third. Boners 2 and 3. Anderson scored the winning run from third due to form.
> Culler, Nashville shortstop, alone had his wits. He rushed to the outfield for the ball, but a Negro boy jumped out of the stands and beat him to the ball. Then Culler, joined by Nashville manager Gilbert, protested the irregular disappearance of the baseball. They demanded a ball be put in play so they could touch second and third, getting force outs on Marshall and Burge, and end the inning in a tie instead of defeat.
> The umpires hit on the only solution—a brilliant one after 3 boners by the players. The ball had been hit into the crowd—at least a member of the crowd—and he by that time was running for dear life, rounding the corner of

the neighborhood Wheat Street Baptist Church with the ball in his pocket. Therefore, that was a ground-rule two base hit; the ball went into the crowd which eliminated the possibility of any force play. If Culler could have found the ball, he could have wiped out the winning run and they could still be playing ball.

And Dick Culler, except for a creative decision by the umpire, might have gone down as one of the smartest players in the history of the game.

The Nashville Vols, after winning the Southern Association playoffs, defeated Houston, winner of the Texas League, four games to one in the Dixie Series.

The Houston team, managed by Eddie Dyer, later a St. Louis Cardinals manager, was called one of the best teams in minor league history. The team included pitchers Ted Wilks and Howard Krist who later played with the St. Louis Cardinals.

Culler's toughness showed when he remained in the final game after being spiked by Danny Murtaugh, a future major leaguer and manager of

The 1940 Nashville Vols infield set a Southern Association record with 208 double plays. Left to right: Bob Boken, 3B; Dick Culler, SS; John Mihalic, 2B; Mickey Rocco, 1B (Hank Utley).

the Pittsburgh Pirates. One inning later he was hit in the jaw with a pitch from Howard Krist when Culler tried to squeeze bunt a run from third.

The Houston team had won 105 games in the Texas League that year and finished 16 games in front of their nearest rival.

The players' cut of the Dixie series was $338.29 each for the winning Vols. The Houston players received $225.53 according to news clippings in Culler's scrapbook.

In 1941, the Nashville Vols again won the Southern Association Championship and became the first Southern Association team to win the Dixie Series against the Texas League (Dallas) two years in a row. Grey Clarke, who played third base for Kannapolis in the 1936 Outlaw League was the Dallas third baseman and led the Texas League in hitting — .361. However, he was not able to play against his old outlaw rival from Concord because of an operation. Culler hit .280 for Nashville that year. The Vols swept the Dixie Series with four straight wins. Vols players received approximately $400 each as their cut of the gate.

Jimmy Hamilton, Vols business manager, was quoted by a Nashville newspaper, in reference to Culler, as "another Pee Wee Reese — he's the best shortstop in the Minors and will be in the Majors in a year or less."

In 1942, Tuck Hannah, manager of Memphis in the 1941 Southern Association League, was named manager of the St. Paul, Minnesota, team in the American Association; Triple A baseball — one step below the majors. His first acquisition was Culler's contract from Nashville.

Culler's prowess was quickly noted when, by midseason, St. Paul newspapers were calling Dick Culler and second baseman Frank Drews the best double play combination since Phil Rizzuto and Gerry Priddy were at Kansas City in 1940.

George Edmond reported in his column, "The Sporting Thing" that Oliver Morton, Sr., a fan back in 1915, said, "Culler's the best shortstop since Everett Scott in 1915 and that includes Leo Durocher of later years."

Dick Culler hit .260 for St. Paul in 1942 and was drafted by the Chicago White Sox.

During the 1942 season, Dick Culler's baseball savvy showed up once again.

From an article in Culler's scrapbook, Ted Wilks, then a St. Louis Cardinals relief pitcher told the following story about his biggest "boner" in baseball.

> My biggest boner happened with Columbus in the American Association in 1942 and it gave Manager Eddie Dyer, later with St. Louis a big knot on the head.
> It was in St. Paul June 14, 1942. We weren't going so well, and Manager Dyer wasn't happy.

We had the game tied up going into the last inning of the second game of a doubleheader. Dick Culler opened the inning with a triple.

Naturally, with Culler on third, I was taking a full windup. He started off third base, taking a normal lead, as I started to windup.

I was already into my windup when he suddenly yelled: "Time, I want to tie my shoe!" I stopped my windup. Culler and the rest of the St. Paul players hollered, "Balk," and the umpires sent Culler home with the winning run.

Dyer jumped up out of our dugout, started after me. When he jumped up, his head hit the top of the dugout. I started for the clubhouse.

The blow on the head didn't knock Dyer out, but they tell me it dazed him to where he was just running around in front of the dugout.

I was running for the clubhouse. We had lost the first game — that cost us the second game — so I knew what was coming.

I thought Skip was going to pop me when he finally got to the clubhouse. He raved and he ranted, he walked up and down.

You so-and-so Polack, he raged, I ought to fine you every penny you've got, falling for a busher trick like that. If I had a gun I'd shoot you! He was mad.

And all the time he was rubbing his head. That was my biggest boner, and I'll never forget it.

In 1943, spring training was held in the Northern climate of the United States because of wartime restrictions on travel.

Culler reported to White Sox manager Jimmie Dykes at French Lick, Indiana.

Because future Hall of Famer Luke Appling was playing shortstop, Culler was moved to second base. In one spring training game he stole home with the winning run. Dick, after riding the bench for a while, demanded that he either get into some ballgames or be traded. He was shipped to the minors — the Milwaukee Brewers of the American Association.

He was still with Milwaukee in 1944. That team, managed by Casey Stengel, and independently owned, sold seven players to the major leagues at the end of the season. The Brewers were the American Association pennant winner but lost the playoff to Louisville four games to two.

Culler hit .308, stole 19 bases and had enough power at the plate to include 30 doubles, 4 triples and 5 home runs among his 194 hits. He tied for fourth in the poll for the American Association Most Valuable Player, missing third by one vote. As a result, Bob Quinn, president of the Boston Braves, purchased Culler's contract.

Other players off the '44 Brewers sold to the majors were outfielder Frank Secory to the Cubs, outfielder Hersh Martin to the Yankees, outfielder George Binks to Washington, outfielder Hal Peck to the Philadelphia Athletics and third baseman Bill Nagel to the White Sox; first baseman Heinz Becker was already the property of the Cubs.

8. *The Brain*

As the Boston Braves regular shortstop in 1945 and '46, Culler hit .262 and .255 respectively. Playing in only 77 games in 1947 he hit .248. His fielding was superb.

On opening day in 1947 he played against Jackie Robinson in Robinson's first major league game.

Always competitive and outspoken, Culler was quoted in August 1947, "I'm far from being a great all-around shortstop, but I know I'm better than either Sibby Sisti or Nanny Fernandez." And he showed the Braves' manager, Billy Southworth, percentages showing how much better the Braves played when he was in the game.

Culler's opponents also felt the sting of his fiery brand of baseball. A news item in his scrapbook from 1945 said, "A fist fight between Ed Stanky, second baseman of the Brooklyn Dodgers, and Dick Culler of the Braves intervened the proceedings at Ebbetts Field where the Dodgers took two from Boston, 4–0 and 4–3."

Apparently Eddie Stanky, also a fire brand, tagged Culler out at second by jamming his glove in Culler's face. After a few heated words fists began to fly.

Broadus with his family circa 1950: Standing, son Richard Broadus, Jr., and daughter Nancy; sitting, Broadus, Larry and wife Evelyn (Hank Utley).

In 1947, another news item reported: "The Cubs Phil Cavarretta was kayoed sliding into second base in the eighth, trying to breakup a twin killing. He ran into Dick Culler's knees, which might have been deliberately placed in the way of Cavarretta's head in self-defense of Cav's head slide."

On February 29, 1948, the *Boston Sunday Globe* reported that Dick Culler and Braves pitcher Walter Lanfranconi were traded to the Cubs for 27-year-old infielder Bob Sturgeon. The news item continued:

> Culler was personally unpopular with Manager Billy Southworth. Culler was too independent to satisfy Southworth's old school demands. He was outspoken, especially when it came to grievances held by ballplayers against management, and was known as a clubhouse lawyer.
>
> One Brewers pitcher said, "A little fresh, Dick was, but I'll say he was a pretty good player for a fellow his size."
>
> Culler fell into disfavor with Southworth for leaving training camp at Fort Lauderdale in the spring of '47 to referee a basketball game at North Carolina State.
>
> Culler, upon hearing of his trade to the Cubs said, "I know the Cubs have been after me. If I don't make it next season I think I'll quit and stick to my sporting goods business in High Point."

Dick's contract for 1948 with the Chicago Cubs was for $10,000.00. He played in 48 games and hit only .169.

Until midseason in 1949 he was with the New York Giants. They sent him down to the Jersey City Giants where he played backup at three infield and one outfield positions.

In 1950 the Baltimore Orioles claimed Culler on waivers from the Giants, but Culler retired from professional baseball at the age of 34.

Richard Broadus Culler returned to his sporting goods store in High Point. In addition to his sporting goods business, Culler started another business—the Autographed Ball Company. Seeing the great demand for baseball players' autographs while playing with the Chicago White Sox in 1943, Culler over the years developed a technique to transfer a major league player's autograph to a baseball. His son, "Dickie" Jr., continues to operate the business and sells thousands of baseballs each year at Major League park concession stands with entire teams' facsimile autographs printed on them.

There was more to this baseball player than meets the naked eye—and it was gray matter, an intelligence that was uncommon to the professional baseball players of the pre–World War II vintage.

9

The Wives

Winnie Taylor and Edna Carrier

Winnie Taylor

Born: July 2, 1910, Coddle Creek, North Carolina; died: September 15, 1970, Concord, NC

Interview with "Coddle Creek" Taylor's widow, Ms. Winnie Taylor (born May 7, 1918, now Mrs. G.C. Watkins of Kannapolis), by R.G. (Hank) Utley on January 31, 1992.

Additional information from scrapbook.

"Creek" as she called him was born in 1910 near Coddle Creek in northwestern Cabarrus County (between Concord and Kannapolis). He died of cancer in 1970. In 1959, he coached the Kannapolis American Legion baseball team to the state finals, losing the championship game to Wilmington. "Creek" was a World War II veteran who saw service at the invasion of Normandy Beach and the Battle of the Bulge.

In his early years, "Creek" practiced pitching year-round in the barn on his family farm, throwing at a knothole in the wall until he had battered the wall to such an extent that the knothole became big enough for the ball to go through, and then he moved on to another knothole.

Winnie said "Creek" had good control and developed a good knuckleball, "whatever that is."

Taylor's reputation as a crafty pitcher reached far beyond the local area. He had two, three, or four teams after him every year, but he just didn't want to leave home, plus there was a financial advantage in avoiding the relocation costs each spring and fall. He also knew that he could always find winter employment with one of the local companies that supported the baseball teams.

Winnie related a story about a trip to Kinston, NC, in 1939 after the outlaw league had folded. Creek was set to try out for a position on a Class

D team in the Coastal Plains League. It was an all-day trip across the state in their Willis automobile. She said she prayed the whole time he was pitching his three innings that he would do poorly so that they could return to Kannapolis. As luck would have it, Creek impressed the owners, and he signed a contract with Snow Hill, NC, receiving over $500 at the signing. With more money than they had ever seen at one time, Winnie said they drove all night back to Kannapolis, fearing they would somehow lose the money if they dared to stop.

Winnie had fond memories of their days in the Coastal Plains League. They lived for a while with a Mr. Exum, whose son became a state supreme court justice, and she still has many friends in that area.

Creek often said the baseball in the outlaw Carolina League was much better than the quality of the ballparks. In Kannapolis, the players had to dress at the high school, over one mile from the ballpark. Creek said the parks that did have dressing rooms under the grandstands were usually so dirty that he would stand on a bench while dressing to keep the bugs off his feet and legs.

Winnie recalled having to massage his sore arms with alcohol and put a hot light on them. But she noted that "Creek never had arm trouble bad enough to keep him from pitching." Ironically, he did have arm trouble with his left arm once during the 1936 season, when he pushed it through a window on the team bus during horseplay. Winnie said that he came home that night with blood running out through his bandages and scared her to death. "I was so scared that I thought at first that it was his pitching arm. The arm kept on bleeding, and my daddy ended up taking Creek back to the hospital that night."

Virgil "Coddle Creek" and wife Winnie Taylor circa 1938. Taylor was an outstanding pitcher from the Coddle Creek area of Cabarrus County (courtesy Cy Williams).

9. The Wives

I met Creek at my aunt's house in Concord. I am originally from Gastonia. Creek had been dating my aunt's daughter. I don't know if they were really dates because it would be a group of girls and players go out dancing. Anyway, after I married Creek, my aunt told me, "You would marry the one I warned you about." Creek had a reputation for loving them and leaving 'em. All the ballplayers had that reputation.

After we were married in October 1935, one day the manager came by our place to eat lunch. It was 1936, and they were talking about one of the pitchers not doing so good. He was in a slump and not pitching too well. This guy was dating one of those cute local girls. Everybody knew, and I had heard Creek say it earlier. So I was trying to be a part of the conversation, and I said, "Well, I heard Ruth got his fast ball."

You could have heard a pin drop. Creek was really embarrassed and turned real red. I really didn't know what it meant, but I had heard Creek say it. Later, after Creek told me what it meant, I was embarrassed to look at the manager. Ballplayers sometimes have their own language, and I learned some of it the hard way.

We had a good time. Everything was exciting. It was fun. Creek made good money playing ball, especially when you think what other people were making, and some of them didn't have any job. I knew that when we came back to Landis, he worked in the mill for $14 a week, and he had been making $60 or $75 a week playing ball. We had to change the way we lived every winter. It was a big difference.

We had an old Willis coupe that we traveled in. Many times we would have Creek and I and some other friend packed in the front seat.

When we played out of town games, the fans would say some awful things to the players. I remember a man in Concord. His name was Tony Means, and he always sat in the grandstand behind the visitor's bench. He would make me so mad I could have stomped him. I never showed myself by losing my temper. I held it in. I got so mad at one game that I broke my watch by beating my hand against the chairs in my box seat.

That Tony Means always hollered and wanted to know if Creek had ever had any shoes before he put on baseball shoes. They never let him forget he was a country boy. It's a wonder that there were not more fights than there were. The fights would usually start between the players or between the players and the umpires, and before you knew it, the fans were all over the field. The players would gather together with their bats to protect each other and even the umpires, and then the fans would fight among themselves.

I remember at Snow Hill we had this big catcher, and he had a woman that looked old enough to be his mother — and he said she was his mother. But the way they acted when they were out with the other players started rumors that she wasn't his mother, but his girlfriend. I guess that's how they kept living together — saying she was his mother. You knew you didn't do things like that in those days.

Edna Carrier

Summary of interview with Mrs. Edna Carrier, wife of William Houston "Bill" Carrier.

Mrs. Edna Carrier remembers well her May 1936 introduction to being a ballplayer's wife. During the height of the Great Depression, her husband, Bill, had quit playing ball. Baseball jobs, like other jobs all over the country, were becoming non-existent or paid so little you could not afford the two moves a year that it took to play professional ball.

Bill received a call from Baron Hinson, legendary owner of the Charlotte, NC, Hornets. Charlotte had lost its franchise in the Class C Piedmont League because they refused to schedule games on Sundays, a big no-no in the Bible Belt of the 1936 South. Hinson was in the process of assembling a team to compete in the newly-established independent Carolina League, a league made up of dissatisfied players from the minor leagues of the National Association of Professional Baseball Leagues and top-flight regional college players. Bill had played for the 1931 Charlotte Hornets when they won the league championship by 13½ games and then defeated the second place Raleigh Capitols 4 games to 2 in the playoff championship. Carrier, who threw and hit from the left side and played in the outfield, had hit .313 with 210 total bases on 150 hits with 96 RBIs in 123 games. The 1931 Hornets were one of the strongest teams to ever play in North Carolina. The club included "Struttin' Bud" Shaney who won 24 games, Jim Lyle who accomplished a 1.92 earned run average, and Frank "What-A-Man" Packard who led the league with a .336 average, scored 145 runs, got 185 hits, and knocked in 123 runs while belting 21 home runs. It was a sensational season filled with sensational performances.

Now, five years later, Bill Carrier was returning to Charlotte as a disgruntled professional and joining what the NAPBL would soon brand an outlaw league.

Carrier had been working as a carpenter in Lynch, VA, in 1934–35 when Edna fell in love with and married him. After the phone call from Baron Hinson about playing ball again, he was raring to go. He left to join the team, and nineteen-year-old Edna, nearly nine months pregnant, would join him in Charlotte once he found an apartment.

It was on the morning of May 6, 1936, that the young expectant mother missed the first bus in Bristol, Tennessee. She caught a later one that took her to Charlotte later in the afternoon. She was excited. She would soon be joining her husband. Bus travel 1936 style was no picnic. The two-lane mountain roads were filled with pot holes and hairpin curves. The bus driver felt a great deal of anxiety. At every small town stop, he would ask Edna if she was comfortable. Edna noted that she was not nearly as concerned as the driver, but the bumpy roads did reinforce the fact that she was very close to having her first child.

The very next day, May 6, 1936, Edna Carrier gave birth to her first child, a beautiful baby girl. When asked about how they chose the baby's name, Edna told a familiar story about the thought process of a professional baseball player when choosing a name for his first child. No names except boys' names were even discussed before the child's birth. The child was going to be a boy.

And like most ballplayers, a proud new father, jubilant not only about the birth of his first child, but also a return to baseball, just couldn't come up with a girl's name. The doctor, knowing about Edna's ride to Charlotte, suggested the name Charlotte.

10

The Star: Lawrence Columbus "Crash" Davis

Born: July 14, 1919, Canon, Georgia (moved to Gastonia, North Carolina, age four); died: August 31, 2001, Greensboro, North Carolina

Long before screenwriter Ron Shelton picked his colorful name out of the 1948 Carolina League record book, Lawrence "Crash" Davis was a star in his own right. After moving to Gastonia, NC, at a young age, he began play on one of the city's auxiliary American Legion teams at the age of 11. By 1935, at the age of sixteen, he was a star on a national championship team and a local hero. Davis then spent three seasons, from 1938 to 1940, on the team at Duke University, where he finished with a career .330 average and served as captain for coach and former big-league pitcher Jack Coombs. Summering as a young collegiate star, he lent credibility to the outlaw Carolina League during its first season. It was however not a memorable season for the last place Gastonia Spinners, nor for their second baseman.

Davis's experience would help prepare him for the three major league seasons he spent with Connie Mack's Philadelphia Athletics in the early 1940s. His career was interrupted, in 1942, by service in the U.S. Navy. When World War II ended, Davis found himself back in the minor leagues. There he continued to play at a high level for several seasons, setting defensive records during his stops with the Durham Bulls, Raleigh Capitols and Reidsville Luckies.

After retiring from pro ball at the end of the 1952 season at the age of 33, he coached at Gastonia High School 1953–55. He won two state championships (1953–54). He coached the Gastonia American Legion baseball team to the little World Series in 1954 at Yakima, Washington, where they were defeated by San Diego, California.

From 1956 to 1985, Davis worked for Burlington Industries spending much of that time as a personnel executive. In 2001 during the final months of his life, he helped found the Minor League Baseball Alumni Association. Davis had this to say about his career during an interview.

> Growing up in Gastonia, the ultimate in life was to be on the American Legion baseball team. At the age of 11 I made one of the teams. Gastonia was set up with about six auxiliary teams. An All-Star team was picked every year to represent Gastonia. I probably played American Legion ball longer than anyone ever played in Gastonia because they had these auxiliary teams and no Little League back then. I started off and they called me "Little" Davis cause I was just a tiny thing. I played shortstop and then at the age of 15, I made the All-Star team in Gastonia and that team was coached by "Doc" Newton, who at that time was a college coach. So I made that team. I started off being called "Little" Davis, and then I was called Squeaky because I had a lot of chatter, all my life. Kids don't do it today. I made the 1935 team. We moved forward. We won the National American Legion Championship that year. We beat Sacramento, CA, in Gastonia, a town of about 20,000 people. One of the games of the Little World Series in Gastonia had 11,000 people there, incredible for a town of 20,000 people.
>
> All three games were played in the Gastonia High School stadium. And that was where I picked up the name "Crash." This is a true story, embellished somewhat. I was playing shortstop in a game, and we had a guy by the name of Bob Russell that played left field. Somebody hit a short pop fly to left field, so I went back, and he and I collided. At that time I was called "Dynamite," "Dynamite" exploded to "Crash," so I've been "Crash" all my life. It followed me through my school days, my professional career, right up to the movie *Bull Durham*.
>
> But that American Legion

Davis first earned his reputation on the state champion Gastonia American Legion team (courtesy Lawrence Davis).

ball probably influenced my life more than anything. One reason I remember, too, we had a parade there after we won that championship and little things like that, a parade going down Main Street, and they let me ride on the fire truck. I thought that was something.

And then Warren Gardner had a clothing store, and he gave each of us a suit. I had never worn a suit. That was such a thrill. That was probably the most thrilling thing that ever happened to me. Things like that just put you a notch ahead, and you have to take advantage of those things as they occur in life; otherwise, you just don't go anywhere.

I remember before I made the big team, the All-Star team in Gastonia, I was playing second, and the other team had a man on third base. I went up to the pitcher and I said, "Give me the ball," and I went back to second base. When the runner was not looking, I was going to flip the ball to third, and we would get him out. But as I was walking back to second, the man scored. So they called me "Bonehead" for a while. I had lots of names.

The next year (1936) in Legion ball we got beat in the North Carolina State finals. But that American Legion ball contributed as much to my well-being or to my success as anything that ever happened to me in my life.

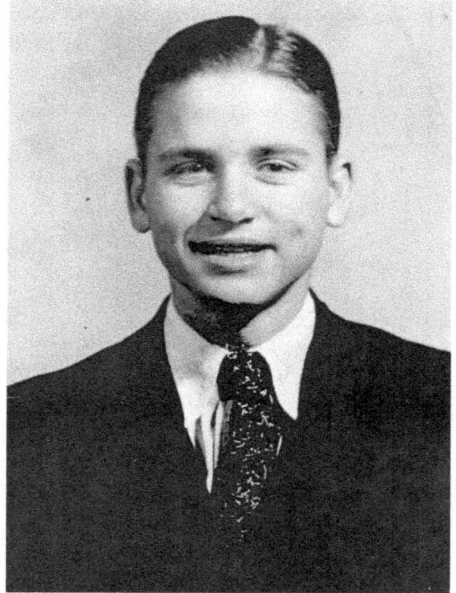

Crash Davis is seen here during high school days (courtesy Lawrence Davis).

10. The Star

One of the players on the '35 team was Howard Moss. Howard played with me two years later on the 1937 Gastonia Spinners team in the old outlaw league which was probably the best baseball [league] I ever played. I got more experience from the outlaw Carolina League in 1937 than any other outside the big leagues.

Howard Moss, what a hitter. He could hit. He hit 30–40 [actually 22 HRs, second in the league with a league leading 93 runs batted in and .362 batting average, fifth in the league] in the Carolina League that year.

A lot of kids back in those days wouldn't leave home. That '35 Legion team had a lot of talent, but they just wouldn't leave home [influence of the Great Depression, as there was security at home]. And some of them were a lot better ballplayers than I was. There's always that one opportunity you get in life, and if you don't take advantage of it, you're left.

I always studied hard. I was a pretty good student because I did well in my books, and I studied and worked hard. I loved baseball, and I would be so tired when I got home. I would get up at 5 o'clock in the morning and study my lessons.

There was a man that took a special interest in me in Gastonia. "Boo" Boshamer was the postmaster in Gastonia, and he was quite a politician. He was a Duke graduate, and he took an interest in me when I was playing American Legion ball. He was the one that carried me to Duke and introduced me to Coach Coombs. He was the one responsible for me going to Duke University.

And Jack Coombs, he was like a father to me. When I had a problem, I would go see Coach Jack. He was a listener. I really don't think he ever gave me an answer. He just let me talk it out. He was a smart man.

I remember that '39 team at Duke [sophomore year] lost only one ball game—to Maryland, up in Maryland. I remember a story about that year. Back in those days we didn't have all the trainers they have now. One of our players slid into second base and hurt his ankle. So one of the guys picked up the medicine kit and rushed out to second base and opened the bag, and all that was in there was a pint of whiskey. We had just gone to a baseball class. Coach Coombs really knew the ins and outs of baseball.

Some of those ballplayers in the outlaw [Carolina League] league were tough. They were just great ballplayers. I was only seventeen years old [at the beginning of the season and a freshman at Duke], and I really grew up. We had a manager named Frank Packard [called "What-a-Man"]. He was one of the toughest managers I ever played

Larry "Crash" Davis is pictured at the time of his interview, and posed with a cutout of himself in his days at Duke University (courtesy Lawrence Davis).

for—I mean in my whole baseball career. He was tough—particularly on pitchers. He would call time-out, and he would give those pitchers holy hell. We had a team coming, one there and one going. They were so anxious to win, but I made the ball club. I had been there a week or so—I'll never forget this—there's always certain little things you remember in your career. I was struggling a little bit, but in the 8th inning of a game—I forget who it was against—I hit a high fastball over the left field fence and won the ball game. That sort of set me on fire and moved me forward, and from then on, I had a pretty good year. I was always a little better fielder than I was a hitter, but back in those days I could hold my own pretty good and playing with those fellows gave me confidence. I could make the doubleplay as good as anyone.

In 1937, in the old Carolina League, I had my only fight in any league. I had a fight with a guy named George Andrews. He was a left-handed hitter, had his head shaved, probably in his thirties. He just didn't like college players. I don't know why. But we had a fight in the club house in Concord. We had a real fight. I didn't know I could fight that well. Frank Packard got rid of him the next day [*Note:*

10. The Star

George "Tar Bucket" Andrews was signed up by Concord. He rejoined Bill Selph (Steineke) whom he had played with in the 1936 semi-pro Florida State League.]

It was either the first or second day I reported to Gastonia. The team had its office in the old National Bank building. They had a club meeting, and "Alabama" Pitts and manager Frank Packard had a fight. So they traded Pitts to Valdese.

I grew up! I got more experience in that league than I got in the big leagues. It was incredible. The next time we played in Valdese, "Alabama" Pitts got on first base, and Frank covered second on a steal. "Alabama" slid head first and hit Frank right in the belly and nearly knocked Frank out. Frank couldn't get his breath. I was playing second, and I thought he was going to die. And "Bama" was hollering, "Frank, don't die, don't die; they will put me back in jail."

Hickory had a pitcher, Kermode, and I had hit a ball up against the fence the first time I was at bat. Kermode was a big guy. When I went up the second time, I sort of pointed like I was going to do it again, and he hit me in the head with the first pitch. We didn't have helmets in those days, and I was really hit.

For me, it [1937] was an amazing year, playing against players like Bobby Hipps and with Stuffy McCrone. They were really experienced ballplayers.

During the summer of '38, after my sophomore year at Duke, I played in the New England League for Rutland, Vermont.

They were all college players. Jack Berry, a college coach, was our manager. I slid into second base on July 4th in Montpelier and broke my ankle, and that slowed me down a little bit. That ankle still bothers me.

In '39 I played in the North State League, another college league. I played for Sanford, NC — made $140 a month. Eddie Shokes, a Duke teammate that later played for the Cincinnati Reds, was also at Sanford. We didn't lose many games that year and had more fun.

In the spring of 1940, after his senior year at Duke, "Crash" Davis entered the big leagues. Davis continues:

Being a southern boy, I hadn't traveled too much, but when I got to Shibe Park in Philadelphia, Mr. [Connie] Mack said he was going to give me $3,000. I said, "Mr. Mack, I won't play for that. I'm making about that much now." He said, "Well, young man, if you don't want it, just go home." I didn't have any money, so I signed.

But Mr. Mack was really a gentleman. I was in awe. Big leagues back then meant more than they do today — only eight teams in a league, two leagues, no television. You would read about all these guys. I was simply in awe when I saw Ted Williams, Joe DiMaggio, guys you had read about, like God.

I didn't get in a game for about two weeks. I was sitting at the end of the bench. Mr. Mack called, "Davis." He couldn't remember names very well. He said, "Davis." I said, "Yes, sir." He said, "I want you to pinch hit."

I grabbed a couple of bats, rushed up to home plate and the umpire said, "Wait a minute, son; you have to let this man hit first."

The first man I hit against was Bob Feller. I could make a long story short, but he was fast. But I did hit a pop fly to the catcher.

In 1941 I did really well in spring training, but I just didn't do it after the season started. We had spring training in Anaheim, California. Back in those days, Mr. Mack sat on the bench and moved players with his scorecard. He loved to sit in the lobbies of the hotels, too hot to stay in the rooms. He liked to meet people. Shibe Park was built before 1910 and was the first concrete cement stadium ever built in America. Before that, it was wood.

I played with good ball players—Al Simmons, Wally Moses, Bob Johnson. In 1941 when Ted Williams came into Philadelphia hitting just over the .400 mark, on Saturday he went none for four and went down right on the .400 mark. He could have sat out the double-header the next day and still hit .400, but he elected to play. I played in both of those games. I played second base in the first game and first base in the second. That's a good story. We were in Chicago earlier and riding down the elevator, and Mr. Mack said, "Davis, can you play first base?" I replied, "I can play it," so that day I played first base against the White Sox in Comiskey Park. And this is true too—when you play second base and a ball goes through you, you don't chase it. Anyway a ball went over my head that day at first. I didn't really hustle. My cap came off, and I went over to pick up my cap before I picked up the ball. The next day's paper said, "Davis retrieves cap before ball."

That was the year DiMaggio had his 56-game hitting streak. I had a lot of good experiences. I wasn't a real good ballplayer in the big leagues. I made the team and got a lot of recognition. I remember going from Cleveland to Detroit on the boat at night. We didn't fly. We had trains. In spring training, we worked our way back from the West Coast with the Cubs and Pirates. So, I did get to hit against the Big Diz [Dean]. He didn't have nothing then. That was in spring training. It was a wonderful experience for a young unmarried guy. I took it all in.

10. The Star

Connie Mack's 1941 Philadelphia Athletics infield included two Carolina League products: Larry "Crash" Davis and Fred Chapman(second and third from left, respectively). Also pictured are first baseman Dick Siebert and at right third baseman Joe Gantenbein (courtesy Lawrence Davis).

My first roommate was Chubby Dean. Chubby was a Duke guy. Chubby was a good looking man — a nice looking guy. On my first road trip, Chubby had too many women. He wasn't married, so the women were after him. I grew up as far as baseball in the ballpark in the outlaw Carolina League, but I grew up in other ways in the big leagues. For a young man out of the South, it was just an education. Didn't think much about it at the time, but I wouldn't take anything for it.

You have to be ready for changes in life. The opportunities only come once, twice or three times, and you have to be ready. I never thought I would be a movie star in later life.

I was drafted. I went into the Navy. My first station was in Norfolk, November 1942. I got in the physical education program. In 1943, at the Norfolk Air Station, all I did was play baseball — Dom DiMaggio in center field, Pee Wee Reese at short, Eddie Robinson played first. Hugh Casey was a pitcher. At Norfolk Naval Base, just across the fence, was Bob Feller and other big leaguers. All I did was play ball.

In the fall of 1943, I was transferred to Harvard University. I was officer of the day up there. I became a squash coach, and I didn't even know what squash was. Then I was moved to the Harvard baseball team. So, in '44, I helped Floyd Stahl with the Harvard baseball team. Then I became coach of the JV team at Harvard. We played the prep schools around New England.

Was married in Norfolk in 1943, and my wife was with me, and we lived at Harvard Square. My wife, Harriet, taught at Gastonia High School. We had two daughters. Diana is in Denver, an excellent salesperson doing really well. Sharon is at Gardner-Webb College. She is director of the deaf and blind program. We are divorced now [August 1997], but we had many fruitful years together. Harriet now lives in Denver, Colorado.

At Harvard, I had Bob Kennedy under me. He wasn't a real standout. He was just an ordinary guy. He certainly didn't lead the class. He was not a battalion leader, nothing like the way he developed. Some guys get opportunities; others don't.

I had a lot of names—Little Davis, Squeaky, Dynamite and then Crash. At Harvard I started playing as Chuck Leary because the Irish were big in that area. I played in the New England Semi-Pro League three to four games per week. We made good money, and it was extra and above my Navy money. Later, I played as Bob Palliteria—a French name. There were a lot of French people there. My wife was at one of the games, and one of the French background fans said, "Bob Palliteria is a good ball player. Does he speak English?" I also managed at Lawrence that same year.

We were playing in Providence, Rhode Island, and all those players were using assumed names. Jimmy Gleason was playing in that league, and first base was open, so I elected to walk Gleason because I didn't know that little guy that was hitting next, but I knew Gleason. That little short guy looked about 18 or 19 years old, and it turned out he hit a home run with the bases loaded, and his real name was Yogi Berra. Yogi was at New London in the Merchant Marines.

After the war (I was discharged in November 1945), when Philadelphia cut me, I went back up there and played for Lawrence in 1946–47 in the (Class B) New England League [Davis completed the '47 season playing in Lowell and Pawtucket and made the all-star team at second base both years]. Don Newcombe and Roy Campanella were at Nashua, and Roy tried to get me to go barnstorming, after the '47 season, to the Caribbean. Both were great guys. Branch Rickey knew how to pick them.

When I was cut by Philadelphia in spring training in '46, to show how cold baseball is, they didn't call you in and say we're sorry you didn't make it. They just left a pink note in your box. I needed to be a step faster. I lost that during the war.

After I left Philadelphia, I always had in my contract that I got my release at the end of the year.

In 1948 Crash Davis came back to North Carolina. He signed with the Durham Bulls of organized ball's Class C Carolina League. That year, 1948, "was the greatest year of playing baseball in my life." Davis hit .317 and led the league in doubles with 50. He also made the league all-star team.

Legendary minor leaguer "Willie" Duke was manager of the '48 Durham Bulls. Davis said, "Willie Duke (before there was Willie, Mickey, and the Duke, there was Willie Duke) was one of the greatest left handed hitters I ever played with. I mean he could hit. Not like Ted Williams 'cause Ted was the greatest hitter that ever lived."

"I remember the ump made a bad decision in Durham on a Sunday afternoon, and Willie took a bucket of ice water and threw it across home plate. The ump kicked him out. Willie became one of the greatest promoters of baseball I ever knew. He started the Hot Stove League in Raleigh. Willie Duke is responsible for me being in the North Carolina American Legion Hall of Fame. He sponsored me. Baseball was all he lived for till his dying day.

In the 1948 Carolina

Davis is pictured here with Durham Bulls manager Willie Duke. Davis, playing second base, helped an otherwise mediocre team lead the league in double plays (courtesy Lawrence Davis).

League All-Star game in Greensboro, Davis hit two home runs and drove in five runs.

"All my brothers played baseball. Hutt and I played together one year in the New England League. 'Toad' was a catcher. He died a few years back. Bobby also played organized baseball. My dad was a Sunday school teacher and choir director. We had good training. Dad wouldn't let the family cheer at ballgames even though they were at all the games."

11

The Pro: Lee Ravon "Buck" Ross

Born: February 2, 1915, Norwood, North Carolina; died: November 23, 1978, Charlotte, North Carolina

Buck Ross was one of those rare individuals who was able to hurdle the minor league baseball system, and at the age of twenty-one, go directly to the major league. The Philadelphia organization had discovered him while he was pitching in the 1935 Carolina Textile League, the highly competitive precursor to the outlaw Carolina League. Despite his lack of physical prowess with a scant 160 lbs. spread over a 6' 2" frame, he impressed Connie Mack in spring training and made his major league debut on May 7, 1936.

Unfortunately for Ross, he arrived in Philadelphia just after the fire sale of players such as Jimmie Foxx. Desperate for cash flow, Mack had been forced to sell off his best hitters. The lackluster team that was left simply could not score runs. The *Sporting News* once said of Ross's situation with the A's: "Buck Ross should be given a plaque for carrying his non-hitting infielders on his back for several innings, then seeing them convert easy plays into game-losing bobbles." During his five full seasons with Philadelphia, Ross allowed 115 unearned runs, a remarkable total. He did manage to win 34 games, but lost 65 before he was traded to the Chicago White Sox.

While he was not used as extensively in his five years at Chicago, Ross did have a few successful seasons, most notably 1943 when he posted an 11–7 record and a 3.19 ERA.

This was also the year that Ross flirted with baseball immortality. On May 14, 1943, in Chicago, Ross pitched a controversial one-hitter against the New York Yankees— winning the game 3–0. Fans and sportswriters alike thought Ross had pitched a no-hitter when the game ended. When the public address system announced at the end of the game, "For New York, no

On May 14, 1943, Buck Ross pitched a controversial one-hitter against the New York Yankees. At the conclusion of the game, everyone in the stadium thought he had thrown a no-hitter until the public address announcer informed the crowd that the Yankees had one hit (courtesy Mrs. Buck Ross).

runs, one hit," you could have heard the White Sox fans booing from the south side of Chicago all the way to the Cubs' Wrigley Field on the north side. The White Sox players raved, but the decision stood.

Buck explained it this way, "I'll never forget that one. It was one of the few games I set down New York. I shut 'em out, and when the final out was made, everybody in Comiskey Park thought I had a no-hitter but the official scorer. In the early part of the game, Nick Etten hit a bounder to me that I fumbled. It was one of those debatable plays; it could have been called a hit or an error. Etten received credit for a bingle. In spite of the lone hit, that game — that was my biggest diamond thrill."

The Associated Press news account of the game showed why the fans and White Sox players were upset. There were possibly two errors on the play that was called a hit. A passage from the AP report follows:

> The 28 year-old right hander from Norwood, NC, pitched to only 28 batters. Only Nick Etten, the reformed Phillie, now handling first base chores for the American League champs, could not do a thing with Buck's Sunday shoots. Nick clicked for the only hit off Ross in the second frame, and then became the only other man to reach base by drawing a walk in the eighth. His second

inning hit, however was strictly from luck, for it was a bounder that bounced off Ross' pitching hand. At that, Ross recovered the ball and would have had Etten at first if his throw had not pulled Kuhel off the bag. Nick was wiped out immediately after by a double play.

So goes the fickle Dame Fortune.

When World War II ended in 1945, the market for ballplayers was glutted, greatly devaluing their services and forcing many veteran players to accept minor league contracts. Ross finished his career in Milwaukee and then Toledo. His final season in Toledo in 1948 featured two highlights. On August 1, he pitched a no-hitter against the Minneapolis Millers. In the weeks following, the club had a Buck Ross Day where he was honored by the fans with gifts of hunting and fishing equipment. It was a great way to end his career. In the off-season that year, arm surgery and common sense forced his retirement. Ross was employed at a textile mill near Albemarle where he had worked during the winters of his baseball career.

Ross finished his big league career with a 56 and 95 record. His ERA of 4.94 is not outstanding, but he proved to be more durable than his size suggested. Ross completed 65 games, over a third of the 182 that he started. He was also an outstanding fielder who only committed thirteen errors in his ten year career. For his last four seasons, he had a perfect fielding percentage.

Mrs. Buck Ross was interviewed by R.G. (Hank) Utley — June 30, 1992, in Albemarle, NC.

> We knew each other growing up, married in 1938. Buck didn't make enough money until then so that we could get married. He had been in Philadelphia since 1936. Buck signed at the end of the 1935 Carolina Textile League season. He didn't get anything for signing, but Connie Mack sent him $100 per month the winter of '36-'37.
>
> He made very little. There were a few high salaries such as Bob Johnson and Frankie Hayes. Then in Chicago it was Luke Appling — just a few others that made any money.
>
> The wives of the other players helped me when I first moved to Philadelphia after we got married in '38. Our first apartment cost us $45 a month — that included everything, completely furnished. I think Buck was making about $1800 that year. That was about $250 per month covering the season from spring training through September. He didn't make that much in '36 or '37 'cause it wasn't enough to get married on and move back and forth and, with the Depression, try and send some to the folks at home. The depression was pretty rough.
>
> Some of our best friends were Bob Johnson, George Cooper, and Helen Brucker. A lot of the players were not married.

When the players were on the road for two or three weeks at a time, all we could afford to do was visit each other and go to a movie. Later in Chicago, after '41, a couple of us would play golf. We managed. Really, the only thing we had was the movies—we had no TV back then, and we would listen to the ballgames on the radio in the afternoon. On Sunday at 7 PM, all baseball stopped—no playing after seven o'clock.

Buck's best years were the last couple of years in Chicago. He was sold to the Phillies in '45 by the Chicago White Sox. That was the year the war ended. He went to spring training with the Phillies in '46. With all the young players back from the war, Buck was thirty-one that year—they told him they could get all the young players they wanted at half of what the regulars were making, and Buck wasn't making much money at all. He was up to about $8000, and that was after ten years in the majors. The young players were getting a whole lot less. So Buck signed with Milwaukee, and he played there two years ['46 and '47]. Then he was sold to Toledo. After Toledo he retired. He was supposed to report to Little Rock. All the players said that was the jumping off place—it was so hot and muggy. By that time Buck was about thirty-three years old; he had bone chips removed from his elbow by Dr. Hyland in St. Louis. Dr. Hyland was about the only doctor in the country that the players would let operate on their arms. So Buck said it was time to quit, and we moved back home. You know if Buck had gotten just eight more days in

Lee "Buck" Ross and his wife to be, Mary Boyd Hawkins, in 1936, Ross's first year with the Philadelphia Athletics. Boyd, as Buck called his wife, said Buck did not make enough money, even in the major leagues, to get married until 1938. It was because of the Great Depression and his need to send money home to his parents (courtesy Mrs. Buck Ross).

the big leagues before he went to the minors he would have gotten a pension. That pension pay was real new after the war.

Our son was born in Chicago. You just learned to pack up and go when you had to — every spring and every fall. You lived with two bags packed. I remember he came home from the ballgame one afternoon in Milwaukee, and he had been traded to Toledo. The wives would just have to pack and follow them, and away we went. It was tough, and that was the days before disposable diapers. But it was exciting. I wouldn't take anything for our experiences.

All the players traveled by train. The wives would follow by car, or bus or train. When Philadelphia sold him to Chicago, I went by train and left the car in Philadelphia. When the White Sox came into Philadelphia, I picked up the car — drove it to Detroit — traded cars and then brought it on to Chicago.

Back in those days, if the teams were on the road, and you were having a baby, they were not allowed to come home. I can't believe the way the players are treated today, and especially what they are making. But players back then loved to play ball — Lefty Archer and Herman Fink that went to Philadelphia from Landis and Kannapolis, and all the others just loved to play ball.

The winter before Buck was supposed to go to Little Rock, they were installing new knitting machines at the mill where he was working. They offered him a full-time job, and at his age, and with that arm operation, he decided he was better off staying home. We were in Milwaukee when he had his arm operated on. He went to St. Louis and Mike [son] and I packed up and met him there. Dr. Hyland did all the ballplayers. We drove on home from St. Louis.

Bob Johnson's check was $1000. We would get paid twice a month. And he was a star. Chubby Dean was Buck's roommate in Philadelphia before we got married. Chubby was from Mt. Airy and played some at Duke University.

Buck went up to the big leagues right after Connie Mack sold Jimmie Foxx, Pinky Higgins, and some others to the Red Sox. He needed the money. By the time Buck got there, there was nobody to score some runs. The Athletics ended up on the bottom of the league nearly every year. They just couldn't score any runs. Buck lost more games by one run. You can't win a ballgame without runs. Also the Yankees considered buying Buck, but nothing ever came of it. Buck was in the regular starting rotation, and he finished a lot of the games he started, not like today.

Mike was six years old in 1948 when Buck finished at Toledo. I came home early by myself, so he could start school. And then they had that polio problem and put off school for one month. Earlier, when we had those polio scares, I asked the doctor if he thought I should leave Toledo and go on home, and he said as far as they knew, Mike was as well off there as he would be in North Carolina. We were fortunate to escape it.

I never went to spring training with the A's, but I did go a couple years later on. When the A's went to spring training in Mexico City in 1937, nearly the whole team got sick, and all of them lost a lot of weight. Buck came by home on the way north, and after a few days, he went on to Philadelphia and joined the team.

It was an exciting life. You learned to pack in two hours. I remember Coca, Florida. After I got there, I picked up a newspaper, and by the time Buck got out of practice, I had found us a place to stay. What they allowed Buck to stay at the hotel, we could take the money, and all three of us: Buck, Mike and myself could stay together.

And any time your child had the measles or mumps, his daddy was always on the road. You learned to do everything all by yourself.

When the pension went into effect, if Buck could have gone back to the majors for eight days, he would have been eligible. He was in spring training with the Boston Braves, but he ended up in the minors.

When that Mexican League started up, they tried to get Buck to go down there. That was like the Carolina League; players jumped contracts to play there, but Buck wouldn't go down there. I know a lot of players did go. It was going big for a while.

When you started having children, it made a big difference, especially when they started school. Most wives would not join their husbands until school was out, and then they would have to leave the first of September when the big leagues still had a month to play. You would just pack up and leave the team. And that would cost extra money. Unless a player was a star, he was better off getting a job year-round and staying home, especially with children.

12

The Phenom: George Barley

Born: November 1914, New York, New York

While in high school on Long Island, George Barley spent his summers playing high level semi-pro baseball. Before he had graduated he had competed against the likes of Josh Gibson and Satchel Paige. He had also signed a clandestine contract with the New York Yankees, a contract that would pay him while he played and studied at Duke University and make him a kind of teenage baseball outlaw.

Barley, who had a good fastball and an even better changeup became a collegiate star while under the tutelage of Duke's legendary coach Jack Coombs. He spent his first couple of summers as a semi-pro pitcher in Greenville, NC. During the fall of 1935, he received a visit from a representative of the new Kannapolis Towelers, a Mr. Allen. Allen offered Barley an astounding $85 per week to pitch for his club the following summer.

Barley considered himself to be an experienced player at this point, but his collegiate days had not necessarily prepared him for the grizzled veteran players or the fast play that he would encounter in the outlaw Carolina League. The following interview provides a poignant first person account of a career that began with great promise but fell tragically short of expectations.

Barley was interviewed on May 31, 1995, in Southern Pines, NC, by R.G. "Hank" Utley.

> When I pitched in high school on Long Island, I used to pitch semi-pro ball with the Bushwicks. The Bushwicks were one of the top semi-pro baseball clubs in the United States.
>
> We played the New York Black Yankees, the Cuban All-Stars, Kansas City Monarchs, Satchel Paige, Josh Gibson — I pitched against those guys when I was in high school — 15, 16, 17 years old.
>
> After my sophomore year, Paul Krichell, Yankee scout, wanted me to sign and leave high school ball and play minor league ball. "No

George Barley at the 1941 New York Yankees spring training camp. Barley, who was a high school pitching phenom on Long Island, New York, was signed to a Yankees contract that paid him an annual stipend that helped pay his tuition at Duke University. Barley was already a college outlaw when he joined the Kannapolis Towelers of the outlaw Carolina League in 1936 (courtesy George Barley).

way, I'm going to college, Mr. Krichell," I said. "I won't play baseball all my life, and I want an education."

Krichell asked, "What college?"

I wanted to go to Duke University in Durham, NC, and play under Jack Coombs who I had read a lot about and understood to be a great pitching coach.

So that's when they signed me. He had a typewriter with him and typed out an agreement. My mother had to sign it because I was a minor. Actually, I became a college outlaw then, but there were others doing the same thing. So I played two more years in high school and then went to Duke University. My father wasn't making enough to send me there.

Editor's note: In effect, before his junior year of high school, George Barley became a professional baseball player. He was a high school phenom with a better than average fastball that became more effective because of his well-controlled changeup, a pitch that some professionals never master. Here is the agreement that his mother signed:

> For and in the consideration of the sum of $200 per year while I am in college payable as follows: $200 on September 10, 1933; $200 on September 10, 1934; $200 on September 10, 1935: or in lieu thereof of my unconditional release $200 on September 10, 1936, or in lieu thereof of my unconditional release I hereby agree to sign a contract with any minor league club the American League baseball club of New York may designate at the termination of my college career. If I should decide not to finish my college course, the above payments automatically cease, and I agree to enter organized baseball and sign with any club designated by said New York club. My salary shall be $200 per month for my first year, said salary to start when I report during the championship season.

> After my sophomore year at Duke, in 1935, I played semi-pro ball in the Coastal Plains League in eastern North Carolina. Greenville, Tarboro, Ayden, Snow Hill, Kinston and so forth. Each one of these little towns would go to the universities in NC and SC and try to hire the whole ball club. I don't know why we weren't supervised by the Southern Conference. I don't know why they didn't supervise us making money playing semi-pro ball. There was nothing illegal about it which surprised me. [College players lost their eligibility only after they were paid money after signing a contract with a professional baseball team. Barley was therefore ineligible because of his contract with the Yankees. Playing semi-pro baseball was like just another summer job for college players.]
> Nonetheless, the Greenville [NC] team was made up of Duke boys. Other teams were made up of UNC boys or NC State boys and so forth. So, we had a bunch of college kids playing for money.
> We played five or six games a week. I had a big year. I won fifteen games in a row down there in Greenville that year. We were paid $35 a week plus our room and board. That was damn good money; people in the mills were making $10 to $12 per week. We lived three or four in one house. And they fed us three meals a day. Our ball games were late in the afternoon. There was no night baseball in those days.
> That fall, it seems to me a Mr. Allen came down to Duke in my senior year. That was the fall of '35, and he induced me to come to Kannapolis the following year. He agreed to pay me $85 a week which was absolutely out of this world. My God, my father wasn't making much more than that in a month back on Long Island. Needless to say, I jumped at the chance. Plus the fact I was told it was a better league, and all ballplayers went to play in a better league. So that's the reason I went to Kannapolis in 1936 after my junior year — more money and a better league.

Anyway, I don't remember if I took a bus or a train to Kannapolis. I was met by this Mr. [George] Allen, evidently an executive with the Cannon Mills people [superintendent of Plant #1 in Kannapolis]. He took me over to a residential house and introduced me to the woman and man who lived there, and I do not remember their names. She took me upstairs in this mill house and showed me where my room would be and introduced me to my roommate, Bethel Rhem, who was also a pitcher with the Kannapolis club.

Then Rhem took me down town to Mr. Whitey's furniture store. Mr. Whitley evidently had some connection with the ball club [Henry Whitley was the business manager].

But I remember distinctly, on the sidewalks, of the main street of Kannapolis was printed with white paint — "Barley will pitch today." I will never forget that as long as I live. I was amazed that anybody would go to the trouble to write that on the sidewalk in white paint. I don't even remember if I won or lost that day. And I don't remember anything about my won and lost record. I do believe I pitched pretty good.

Note: The June 16, 1936, *Concord Tribune* carried an article about Barley's arrival. On June 17, 1936, the paper reported that Barley won 7–2 and hit a double and a home run in four trips to the plate, knocking in three runs. Barley ended up winning 8 and losing 5 with an additional loss in the playoffs.

Needless to say, Rhem took me to the ballpark, and I met the ballplayers. Now this was an entirely different group of ballplayers than I had played with before. I had played against the Cuban All-Stars, the Kansas City Monarchs and so forth, but I had never been on the same team, in the same dressing room with so many rough characters in comparison to the ballplayers I was used to in college. All these were adult grown men. Many of them had been out in the professional baseball world. I was a college junior.

I was intimidated, frankly, by their age, their experiences, and especially their social behavior. There was an awful lot of drinking going on amongst the ballplayers. Bethel Rhem, for example, who was my roommate, had a night table, and at night before he went to bed, he would place a bottle of gin and a package of cigarettes on it.

First thing he did when he woke up in the morning was to take a swig of gin and smoke a cigarette. Well, I had never had a beer in my life until that year in Kannapolis when I was initiated to my first drink. So you can imagine how different it was for me, living with those fellows as with college players and high school players and American Legion ball players that I had been used to all my life. But

12. The Phenom

it was a good season in that I was pitching against top flight ball players who were either on their way down from a higher level of baseball or who had left a professional team for more money. It gave me good experience for the following year which was 1937 [after graduating from Duke] when I went into pro ball.

We played ball six afternoons a week. It was really a traumatic experience. I was like a fish out of water. All my teammates were older men, at least a generation ahead of me. Of course most of them came from a different background than I did. I didn't have a real good social life in Kannapolis. I do remember meeting a girl who worked in the mill. She lived in a dormitory building the mill owned [note: Mary Ella Hall]. The women lived in one end of it, and the men lived in the other end, and all worked in the mill. She was a tall blonde girl — haven't the slightest idea of what her name was. That was only one summer nearly 60 years ago. I became friendly with her — not romantically at all, but friendly enough to sit in the park, around the lake and talk. That's the only social life I remember in Kannapolis.

I learned pitching in that league from hard knocks. I learned my pitching techniques from Jack Coombs at Duke.

All the guys in that league were there for the same reason I was — the main reason was money. Even though a lot of them had years of professional experience, they made more money in that league than they could in the pros.

Upon graduation from Duke in June 1937, Barley received a telegram telling him to report to the Newark Bears, the top Yankees farm club in the International League. "That was unexpected," Barley said. "Maybe I was naïve, but, nevertheless, I thought I would go to New York."

Reporting to Newark, Barley joined what may have been the greatest minor league team in history. Needless to say, he could not break in on such a team. He was soon sent down a level to the Class A Binghamton, NY, team in the New York–Penn League.

The 1937 Newark Bears won the International League championship by 25½ games. Its stars included future major league stars such as George McQuinn at first base, Merrill "Pinky" May at third base, Bob Seed, Jimmy Gleason, and Charley Keller in the outfield, and Buddy Rosar catching. Its pitching staff included Marcus Russo and Atley Donald. It was July 25, 1937, before Atley Donald, after winning fourteen consecutive games, suffered his first loss. There is little wonder that Barley was unable to break in to professional baseball on such a team.

Barley pitched his first game for Binghamton against Wilkes-Barre in Wilkes-Barre. It was a cold night, and Barley, throwing nothing but fastballs (curves would not break in the cold mountain air) hurt his arm and developed bursitis. "It was so painful that I couldn't raise my arm to comb my hair."

After being sent back to New York for therapy and heat treatment, Doc Painter, the Yankees' trainer, sent Barley to Johns Hopkins Hospital in Baltimore. Dizzy Dean was also receiving treatment from Dr. Bennett. With only a couple of weeks left in the season, Barley reported to the Norfolk team of the Class B Piedmont League, managed by Johnny Neun. In the warm weather of September, Barleys's arm began to feel pretty good, "and I had my fastball back."

During the winter of '37–'38, Barley kept his arm loose by throwing in a gymnasium near his home on Long Island. In 1938 he still couldn't break into that great Newark club that won the '38 championship by 18 games.

He reported to Binghamton, now in the Class A Eastern League, where he led the league with a 2.24 ERA. Binghamton won the championship that year by five games.

Barley had a good year at Newark in 1939 and a "very good year at Newark in 1940 when I won two games in the Little World Series against Louisville, champions of the American Association."

After his best year (1940) in the Yankees farm system, Barley's future looked good. But it was not to be. Even though he had two good outings against the Cardinals and Bill Dickey—the Yankees Hall of Fame catcher told him his fastball was as quick as Ruffings' and that his curve was as good as Monte Pearson's—Barley somehow got on the wrong side of McCarthy, the Yankees' manager.

Barley explains the situation.

> It was during an incident of picking a man off first base. We were all on the mound. Ruffing was there, Gomez, me and Chandler, and we were taking our position on the mound with a man on first base and making our pick-off move to first. I did what I had been doing for years in picking a man off first base, and McCarthy said to me loudly, so everybody could hear, "Whoever taught you to pick a man off first base like that?"
>
> I didn't say anything except, "That's the way I've always done it, and if I'm doing it wrong, I want to know how."
>
> McCarthy calls Ruffing over and says, "Red, show him how to pick a man off first base."
>
> So Ruffing took his position and did exactly the same thing I did. McCarthy never said a word. He just walked over to the bench and sat down, and that's the last spring training I attended with the Yankees.

So, it was not anything that I had done that I know of, but, nevertheless, they sent me down to Kansas City in the American Association.

Anyway, I reported to Kansas City, and when I reported, I told Billy Meyers, manager at Kansas City, "Billy, they've broken my spirit. I'm 26 years old, and I'm not going to play ball much longer. I'm in the wrong organization, but they won't release me, and they won't sell me, so I'll do the best I can for you, but I really don't give a damn whether I win or lose." When an athlete feels like that, you might as well wrap it up. So I played in '41 at Kansas City, had a fair year; I think I was 12–8 or something like that, but I wasn't the ballplayer I was before that.

Barley's voice quivered, and his eyes became watery as he continued, "My wife can tell you, it really busted me up. I'll never forget it."

One other event may help explain McCarthy's attitude toward Barley. It seems there was an unwritten rule that players in the Yankees training camp could not bring their wives with them to St. Petersburg, Florida. But the rookies, George Barley and Tommy Holmes, an outfielder, brought their wives along. Neither knew of the unwritten practice, and this undoubtedly had something to do with their cool reception. It is interesting to note that Tommy Holmes led the International League in hits (211) and runs scored (126) in 1940, and after being sent back to Newark in 1941, led the league in hits (190) once again.

In 1942 Barley was sold to Buffalo of the International League, and Tommy Holmes was sold to the Boston Braves, a perennial loser in the National League. Holmes had an eleven year career average of .302 in the National League.

After a year at Buffalo in 1942, Barley entered the U.S. Army for three and a half years. While in the service, the New York Giants purchased his contract. Barley reported to Leo Durocher, manager of the New York Giants, in April of 1946. He asked Durocher, "What the hell you want me for? I'm through. I haven't thrown a ball in three years, and I don't care to throw a ball."

Durocher explained that he wanted Barley to go to their International League farm team in Jersey City as a coach and help Jersey City manager Bruno Betzel, who could not always be with the team because of problems with ulcers.

"So that's what I did in Jersey City in 1946. I pitched some relief ball for Betzel. I don't recall my record, but I didn't have anything on the ball anymore. I was thirty-one years old at the time.

"Our season ended in Baltimore. I was so fed up with baseball. I had a bonfire in the Baltimore visiting team clubhouse. I burned everything I owned: my glove, my sweatshirt, my shoes, my jock strap, everything I owned and left the uniform. And that's the last ballgame I saw for seven years. I never saw another ballgame. I was so disillusioned with my whole life, especially when the Yankees wouldn't do anything with me at the end of that spring training in 1941. And that's my baseball career, wrapped up in a nutshell."

George Barley's refusal, as a high school sophomore, to join the Yankees farm system stood him well in later life. It is clear that baseball was George Barley's life, especially as a young man.

When Yankees scout Paul Krichell tried to sell him on joining the Yankees, few youngsters would have turned down such an opportunity, especially a Long Island, NY, youth who had pitched batting practice for the Yankees while he was still in high school. But the young Barley opted for an education and a chance to play for Jack Coombs at Duke.

The education apparently paid off. George Barley became a successful businessman. He joined the Emsheep Pen and Pencil Company as a salesman, covering Virginia, West Virginia, and North Carolina. Within five years, he was the Eastern regional sales manager. Years later he became regional sales manager for the National Homes Corporation, a prefabricated house manufacturer. Then for seventeen years, he was vice-president in charge of construction lending for a mortgage company in Washington, D.C.

After suffering a heart attack in 1978, Barley retired, and at the time of this interview, lived in a beautiful home on Fairway Drive in Pinehurst, NC, the golf capitol of the world.

13

The Truth: Ulmont Baker

Born: November 11, 1908, Portsmouth, Kentucky

Ulmont W. Baker was born November 11, 1908, in Portsmouth, Kentucky, and grew up across the Ohio River in Portsmouth, Ohio. As a youth, he discovered a talent for the game of baseball and in 1928 he signed his first professional contract with Greensboro, NC, of the Piedmont League. After two seasons with that club, he moved on to Alexandrea, LA, in the Cotton States League. At mid-season in 1930, that club folded, so Baker joined Shreveport of the Texas League. In 1931 he played for Fort Worth in the same league, and the 1932 season was split between Fort Worth and San Antonio. Next it was on to the Mid-Atlantic League where Baker wore the uniform of four different teams over two seasons: Huntington, Beckley, Dayton, and Charleston. In 1935 he played only 27 games for Fort Wayne in the Three I League, and was hitting .319, but decided to join a semi-pro industrial team in or around St. Augustine, FL, before playing 20 games for the St. Augustine pro team in the Florida State League. In 1937 he spent the entire season playing semi-pro ball in St. Augustine.

Lured by the offer of a high salary, Baker signed on with Concord, NC, of the Carolina League for the 1938 season. Not a member of the National Association, the governing body of minor league baseball, the league was considered professional in every sense of the word. Players came from around the country for the chance to make good money (more than they could for most minor league teams) and the opportunity to have a hard-to-come-by job during the off-season in the textile mills. The league folded after that season and Concord entered a new team in the Class D North Carolina State League. Baker signed on with that team and remained with them for three seasons, serving as manager in 1941. Baker's final games in professional baseball came in 1942 when he appeared in 22 games with Knoxville, TN, before being drafted and joining the Navy Seabees.

Ulmont Baker's career reflected the ups and downs of players in baseball's minor leagues during the Depression era. Players were forced to go where the money was, which is how Baker ended up in Concord, North Carolina, and became part of the story of the outlaw Carolina League.

The following interview was conducted by Hank Utley in 1991.

> I played baseball year after year with players all around me that went to the big leagues, and I didn't go. Another thing, I was feeling you're going backwards; you gotta get out of this. I should have played five years and got on out, but I loved it. I loved the game. I always thought, next year I'll go to the top.
>
> That fellow, Judge Bramham, president of the National Association of Professional Baseball Leagues—let me tell you about him — that damn Judge Bramham. You take 1928 to 1933, his ass weighed a ton. He would sit on you. Whatever he said, that was it. That ol' bastard ruled with a heavy hand. He wouldn't dicker with you. I finished the season of 1932 with San Antonio in the Texas League. It was during the Great Depression, and I didn't get paid at the end of the season. They owed me $500–600, and I wrote that damn Judge Bramham after I couldn't get the money. He wrote back and told me what to do, and I had already done everything he told me to do. I wrote and told him that. He wrote back and said, "If you know any other way to get it — get it." The ol' bastard, I didn't try to be ugly with him. I needed the money. But he ran the minor leagues. Whatever he said, that was it.
>
> And you know, I finally got the money. The St. Louis Browns took over the San Antonio team in 1933 and paid me just like that. I put it in the bank and four days later the bank busted — the Depression, you know. That was a lot of money then. Oh my, I hated to lose that. I finally got about a dime on the dollar. I've wondered

Ulmont Baker played third base for the 1938 Concord Weavers Carolina League team. He also played for the Concord Class D League team in 1939–41. This photo is from the 1941 Concord baseball program (courtesy Bernie H. Edwards).

about that money many times—how aggravated and worried I was, and then how pleased I was to get it, and then it was gone again. In a week's time, I had the money, and then I didn't have it.

I wish I had never pulled such a stunt as jumping that contract. I was in Indiana. I was mad at the owners, but I liked my teammates, and that wasn't treating 'em right pulling a stunt like that. Everybody was going broke during the Great Depression. There was 20 ballplayers trying for every position on the team. Things were tough. And those semi-pros were paying good money with a possible job. I begin to feel like I was going backwards. In my mind, I was saying, "You gotta get out of this," but I loved the game. Lord, how I loved the game. That's how I ended up jumping the contract. After I left, maybe the owners were glad to see me leave and just tuned in my outright release to that damn Judge Bramham. [*Note:* All of the players and family members I interviewed, every one of them, prefaced Judge Bramham's name with word "damn." I began to think that was part of his title.]

I first met Bill Steineke at Fort Worth in 1932 when I was playing ball in the Texas League. Then I would see him all over the country. I'll tell you one big thing, he never wanted a job. He was a hustler. He would play organized ball one year and then disappear and play in some semi-pro league, using a different name. Those semi-pros paid more money than some of the minor league teams, the Great Depression, you know. But now I wish I had never met him. [When Baker said that, his wife, Wilma, a high school teacher in Concord, NC, in 1941, shouted from the kitchen, "If you had never met Bill Steineke, you would have never met me." Baker quickly added, "Well, I guess some good did come out of that."]

Anyway, I came to Concord in that outlaw league in 1938. Bill Steineke was the manager. He had come to Concord in 1937 as Bill Selph after he had gotten suspended

Mrs. Wilma Wolfe Baker, Ulmont's wife, was a home economics teacher at Concord High School (Concord High School annual).

from the Sally League. He was still being called Selph when the season started in 1938, and then a few weeks in the season he went back to his real name—Steineke. He brought some good ballplayers to Concord. In fact, that whole league was loaded with good ballplayers in 1938. I didn't see any difference in organized ball and that league, except for the fighting. There was no joking around. There was no dogging it. A player put out everything he had, or he was sent on his way.

I played so many games I don't remember many specific incidents. I do remember when Virgil Trucks jumped a contract and showed up in Concord with Luke Gunnells. They came up from Andalusia in the Alabama-Florida League. Oh Lord, how that kid could throw a baseball. But he was pretty wild. He wasn't in Concord but one night and played under some fake name, and then he left. I think his dad came and got him. Nobody knew what happened to him. He could have ruined his career.

And then I remember Ken Chitwood. He had jumped a contract with Knoxville before I came to Concord. Ken was a tough pitcher. He would throw at some of those big hitters. I remember "Pick" Biggerstaff, manager of Valdese, cussed Ken when he was going down to first base. Now when you cussed Ken, he would "choose you" [colloquialism meaning he would pick you to fight]. Gosh, what a guy that Chit was. Chit was quick as a cat, and he popped Pick upside the head and brought blood. Well, Pick grabbed Chit around the neck, and they were rolling on the ground. It took a bunch of us to separate them. He nearly twisted Chit's head off. He couldn't pitch for a week. He walked around with his head practically over on his shoulder. The other guy he hit was Vince Barton of Kannapolis. He and Pick both were big enough to eat hay. Vince had to leave the game to get some stitches in his jaw. He came back into the game later. Neither one of the players were put out of the game. I really believe the umpires were afraid to take too much action against the players.

And the fans were mean as the players. When "Alabama" Pitts came to Concord to play, the fans ate him up about being an ex-convict. They were brutal. Pitts looked like a pretty good ballplayer to me. I heard he got killed in a fight in Valdese after he quit playing.

The fans would get on the umpires pretty good. Not just hollering at them but fighting them after the game. One night against Kannapolis—oh how the Concord fans hated Kannapolis—but the players didn't pay much attention except to look out for themselves. Anyway the ump made what the fans thought was a bad decision and a couple hundred came running out on the field after him.

13. The Truth

Ulmont Baker in June 1991 at age 85 in his Swannanoa, North Carolina, home (Hank Utley).

Hank Utley note: I was there. The fans chased him from the first base foul line all the way to left field and then up the 50 foot bank. The players were in the chase also. The players surrounded the umpire to protect him. By that time, my father took me out of the ballpark.

> We actually had to sit on top of that umpire with our bats to keep the fans off him. I was scared to death I was going to have to hit one of our fans with a bat. The police finally took the ump out of the ballpark. He was so scared he could hardly walk.
> And then there was that last game up at Hickory — the one they took away from us and gave Hickory the playoff. Their fans came out on the field. I didn't wait around to see if they were celebrating beating us in the playoff or coming after us. The umps had forfeited the game to Hickory because we would not take the field after an argument. When it came to baseball, the fans all over the league believed in it, and they would back their team with fists if need be. And when they would play those big rivalry games like Concord-Kannapolis and Hickory-Valdese, it was like a war. To the ballplayers it was just another game until we had to protect ourselves.
> One of the more likeable fellows in the league was a teammate — Lefty Witt Guise. He was just a big ol' country boy. All he would do was just get you out. He was very deceiving to me even when I was playing the infield behind him. I couldn't understand where the ball was coming from when he threw it.

You asked me what I thought made all those mill men and such put all that time and money into that outlaw league. For one thing those people knew baseball, and they loved it. And they saw a chance to have better baseball in that league than they had ever dreamed of. They lost some of their personal money. And they were doing it for the community. Things were tough, and they gave the people something to do. I think the fans took out a lot of their economic frustrations on the umpires and other teams.

Mr. L.C. Harmon at Gibson Mill in Concord was real nice to me. During the off-season, he tried to make a weaver out of me — that is, a real weaver, you know, making cloth, not a Concord Weavers ballplayer. They let me learn on something that was new. Woven glass. And they tried to make cloth out of it. Craziest thing I ever heard of. Anyway, those ends would keep breaking out, and I would keep tying 'em back in. I found out that I wasn't a textile man even though Art Hord (a former Concord infielder), who by then had a boss man's job, kept telling me I couldn't play ball forever and that Mr. Harmon would help me start another career.

After the outlaw league folded at the end of the 1938 season, Concord joined organized ball in the NC State Class D League. I didn't have any trouble getting back into organized ball in '39. I had jumped a contract, but maybe the owner just gave me an outright release later on. Some of the other players in that outlaw league were not so lucky. Anyway I was back in organized ball in '39, '40, and '41. I managed the Concord Weavers in 1941. I played a few games with Knoxville in 1942, then got drafted and joined the Navy Seabees.

14

Umpires

In the Carolina League there were many stories about fights not only between players but also between umpires and players and even fans and umpires. The line of protection for the arbiters of the game was not carefully drawn as in today's game. Several interviewees in this book describe situations where players, wielding bats for protection, surrounded umpires in order to protect them from agitated fans. A playoff game at College Field in Hickory, NC, which had ended in a forfeit, was punctuated by a scene which featured a sprint to the parking lot on the part of the umpires and the opposing team.

A June 20, 1935, *Sporting News* editorial commented on the umpires who worked in smaller leagues for "salaries that are not nearly commensurate with the grief they must endure." The same article defended the "enthusiastic fan who believes all the decisions should be favorable to the home team and against the visitors." The editorial noted that "the average fan above all is a sportsman and an upholder of fair play, but he often allows his partisanship to overcome his better judgment.... It is only when he steps over the bounds into rowdyism that he should be checked, and adequate police protection must be provided to see that fans with such tendencies are kept in check."

The editor saw the problem as rather one with club owners, too intent on winning at any cost, who allowed "violent umpire baiting." The editorialist maintained that the owner "is charged with maintaining order and enforcing respect for the umpire's decisions, just as the president of the National Association should have the authority to bring a recalcitrant club owner to a speedy sense of his duty through the imposition of an adequate penalty." He further noted that "it is a poor example to set before the public, whom they are trying to induce to attend games, if the owners themselves fail to perform their own duty first." Although this is a year before its inception, these words may as well have been written about the outlaw league. It is important to remember, however, that, in its case, an important part of the equation is missing. The Carolina League operated independently which means that there was no National Association with the authority to control the process. It was up to the league itself which at times did not prove to be enough.

We also include here an article that appeared on June 7, 1936, in the *Charlotte Observer*. Here, nationally recognized sportswriter Jake Wade comments about the umpires and the shenanigans that were taking place early in this first season. More than just a comment on the umpires, players and fans, this article is a testament to the quality of what was written about this league.

> Jack Wade's Sports Parade
>
> There is no finer fellow affiliated with the Carolina League than Chet Chapman, the umpire.
>
> Chapman is upstanding, forthright, clean cut in every way, and extremely conscientious in his work.
>
> But Chapman hasn't been umpiring very well. Or, at least that's what members of the Charlotte Hornets are saying. They've been on Chet's neck since the first day he donned the blue and started his chores in the league.
>
> Personally, I can't make sure. I've seen him miss some. Or at least I thought he missed them. But I've seen such veterans as the Messrs. Brandon, Hanna, and Mitchell miss them too.
>
> Chet, obviously hasn't had a lot of experience. There have been indications that he hasn't been quite sure of himself at times. The game hasn't been, at all times, under his control. And yet...
>
> This bureau hopes that Chet makes the grade. Baseball can use men like him. Maybe a few more games under his belt will give him the confidence needed and sharpen up his eyes if, as some claim, principally, the Hornets, he is suffering from acute astigmatism.
>
> This is, of course, a suspicion that umpires are born, not made. If that be true, Chapman must at the moment be a question mark.
>
> It is superfluous to point out that this is a tough league for umpires. The Piedmont League was never a cream puff for them, and goodness knows, last year the Piedmont certainly got some punk officiating.
>
> But the rivalry is uncommonly tense in the Carolina League. The fans are deeply loyal and are as biased as they come. Most of the players are veterans of organized baseball, old hands who know the game and who have toiled higher up where naturally they got first rate umpiring. They are apt to lose the perspective and forget that now they are in outlaw baseball, and it would be too much to expect this outlaw ball to have as capable umpiring as Class A, Class AA, and the Majors.
>
> Also, I have never seen a league in which there were as many complaints about the pitchers "cheating," that is pitching balls "out," "doctored" or "manhandled" so that they will cut capers as they fly through the air.
>
> And these complaints, of course, are well-founded. There are pitchers in several clubs, ours included, who have been given the assistance of "doctored" balls.

14. Umpires

Perhaps, considering so much shoddy pitching, there was never a league in which the mounds men so sorely needed this extra "lift." So one has the impulse to say that if "doctoring" the ball will improve the pitching, let the balls be 'doctored:' but this is against the rules, protests of the opposition can't be ignored, and it's a constant annoyance to the umpires, examining the balls and throwing them out.

These banned balls have been finding their way back into the game, that's certain.

Umpire Ben Mitchell, and, incidentally, there's an umpire for you, is planning a remedy for that. He proposes to mark these balls so that it will be impossible to put them back into the game without detection.

This "doctoring" of the ball is not only giving the umpires fits, it's growing gray hairs on the magnates, the club officials. They have to pay for the balls that are tossed out. And our league has enough overhead without piling it on.

Back to the umpiring. For all the squawking, I suspect the league is getting about as good officiating as any of the smaller organized ball circuits. League officials have certainly tried to round out a capable staff.

Brandon, Hanna, and Mitchell are seasoned and first rate officials. I mention them because I've seen them work over a long period of years. And it's a little surprising that they still aren't in organized ball, all of them.

But breaks count in an umpire's career, just as in a ball player's, a sportswriter's, a banker's. You may have plenty on the ball, but if you don't get the breaks, you don't move along.

Take Harry Warner. He didn't get the woods on fire in the Piedmont League, couldn't even make the grade. But he's in the Southern now. And Lou Kearney was fired from the Piedmont League, then went to the International and lost out there. Yet, the other day he hooked on in the American Association (one step below the Majors) at four and a quarter a month.

Clearly, the umpires were partially responsible for the uncertainty and volatility at the games. It could, however, be argued that their collective performance added excitement and helped create interest in the league. A legacy of slashed tires and games seething out of control is not necessarily a good one, but it is perhaps an appropriate one for an outlaw league.

15

The Canadian Tornado: Vince Barton

Born: February 1, 1908, Edmonton, Alberta, Canada; died: September 13, 1973, Toronto, Ontario, Canada

When Vince Barton arrived in Kannapolis to join the outlaw Carolina League, the Canadian-born outfielder had already made a significant mark in organized baseball. Barton first appears on the official record books as a twenty-year-old, playing for the AA International League Baltimore club, the top level farm club for the Chicago Cubs. Barton batted a respectable .285 in his debut season, driving in 34 runs and hitting four home runs. He began the following season a rung lower in single A ball with the Allentown, PA, team of the Eastern League. While there he batted .305 with 7 homers and 76 RBIs.

In 1930, at the age of twenty-two, Barton began to exhibit the power hitting that would be his trademark for the rest of his short career. His 1930 numbers reflected a sterling effort at the plate and earned him a chance at the big time in Chicago (.342, 26 HRs, 150 RBIs).

Barton began the 1931 season on the West Coast, playing in the outfield for the AA Los Angeles club of the Pacific Coast League. He had a fantastic season at the plate. By mid-July he was hitting .302 and had already slammed 17 HRs while driving in an impressive 67 runs. It was enough to catch the attention of the parent club, and the twenty-three-year-old made his major league debut on July 17. In Chicago, Barton continued his torrid pace as a power hitter, racking up 13 home runs and driving in 50 more runs. His .238 average, however, had to be a disappointment. Nevertheless, if you combine his output with the two teams, 1931 was one of his finest years.

One can only speculate as to why Barton failed to stick with the Cubs the following year or as to why he failed to get another chance at the big time. In 1932, in 36 games, he batted .224 with 3 HRs and 15 RBIs. He was

15. The Canadian Tornado

perfect on 67 chances in the field. Despite his efforts, Vince Barton played his last major league ballgame on July 24, 1932, just a year and a week after his promising debut. His time in Chicago was time spent with the legendary rowdy and later tragic Hack Wilson. Perhaps the rowdiness that won Barton infamy in the Carolina League drove him back to the minors and kept him there. For the next three years, he battled in the International League, in 1933–34 with Newark, and then 1935 back with Baltimore.

Barton's power hitting was again outstanding in both 1934 and 1935. Playing for Newark in 1934, he drove in 115 runs and hit a career-high 32 homers. It's hard to believe that he didn't get another opportunity in the majors the following year. But 1935 found Barton back in Baltimore where he cranked out another 28 round-trippers and boosted his average to a more respectable .286. The Canadian had to be disappointed when he was demoted early in the season to the A Birmingham club in the Southern Association.

Canadian slugger Vince Barton is seen here with the Kannapolis Towelers. Barton, who was a legendary carouser, came to the Carolina League after playing several seasons of major league ball. During the 1938 season, he hit five home runs in a nine inning game while playing for the Hickory Rebels (courtesy Bernie Edwards, Jr.).

There was already a buzz about the level and brand of ball being played in the Piedmont area of North Carolina. Word of mouth had spread the news of high salaries and winter jobs all over the country. Certainly, Vince had to view this new independent Carolina League as not just a good cash opportunity but also as a chance to revive his career.

William Henry Whitley, known as "Mr. Henry" or "Mr. Baseball" in Kannapolis, NC, had connections in Canada and knew that Barton might be available. Whitley and his organization brought Barton to town, and after winning a bidding war with Barron Hinson and the Charlotte Hornets, arranged for his housing.

Whitley, whose reputation had been made as a shrewd but ethical businessman and as a tireless church worker, became fast friends with the rambunctious ex-major leaguer. They remained close during the two years that Barton played for Kannapolis though as "Mr. Henry's" son Bill noted, Vince "really tested my Dad's faith in humanity."

It didn't take long to figure out what Barton was about away from the ball field. He soon had a violent row with his girlfriend who, after being treated at the hospital, headed back to Canada. Other instances of his misbehavior have been duly noted. The owner of the Wayside Grill in nearby Concord had kicked Barton out of his establishment for disorderly conduct. During the 1937 season, he lost several weeks of playing time when he was shot in the side at a Kannapolis poker house. In an interview, Bill Whitley confirmed the fact that his Dad would lock Barton and other rowdy players in a room over his furniture store on the nights before key games.

Despite all of Vince's shortcomings, Whitley continued their friendship and made sure that Barton's financial needs were met. Teammate Marvin Watts claimed that, including what he received under the table, Barton was making $385 a month, a salary competitive with major league pay at the time. Barton kept his own car and traveled to road games separately from the team, usually accompanied by a woman. On the field, he had star quality, often hitting his mammoth home runs in key game situations. He was also an excellent base runner and fielder. Barton was a tremendous physical presence on the field. He was six feet tall and weighed 180 pounds and was described by Ulmont Baker as "big enough to eat hay."

Vince helped lead a competitive Kannapolis team in 1936 that finished third with an outstanding record of 59–40. Final records for that season are not available, but Whitley, who kept copious individual records in his own journal gave Barton credit for a remarkable 29 home runs.

On January 4, 1937, the National Association of Professional Baseball Leagues officially branded the Carolina League an outlaw league and banned 27 of its players who were legally obligated to professional contracts. Barton, who had contractual obligations to the Chicago Cubs, was among five Kannapolis players to make the list.

In 1937, his second season, he rang up 27 home runs in just 300 at-bats, leading the league in that category. The Towelers finished the season in first by three games over rival Concord with a 57–42 record.

Under attack by the NAPBL, and with most of its teams suffering financial woes, the Carolina League struggled toward its third season. Many of the teams were forced to release high dollar players. Valdese released Alabama Pitts who signed with the Lenoir Finishers, and Kannapolis released Vince Barton who was picked up by the Hickory Rebels. This ended the often-strained but mostly amicable professional relationship between Vince Barton and Henry Whitley.

In its third year the Carolina League shrank by season's end to just four teams, and was mostly made up of dissatisfied veteran ballplayers. Fearing the wrath of Judge Bramham and the NAPBL, the college stars that had brightened the two previous seasons went elsewhere to play semi-pro ball. Even under these circumstances, Barton had another excellent year. He belted 26 home runs (second in the league) and knocked in 82 runs (also second). Behind Vince's bat and Tracey Hitchner and Tom Swayze's capable pitching, Hickory managed a winning record (52–44) and a second place finish.

Barton had many memorable moments during his time in the Carolina League, but he will always be remembered for what he did on Friday, August 26, 1938. In that late season match with his old pals from Kannapolis, Vince hit five home runs in a nine inning game. The Saturday *Hickory Daily Record* proclaimed in its sports headline: "Vince Barton Hits Five Homers to Set Record for Single Game." Wake Bridges began his coverage of the event with this opening paragraph:

> Vince Barton, right-field Hercules of the Hickory Rebels, today held the record for home runs in one game with five circuit drives in a Carolina League hitting melee against the Kannapolis Towelers here Friday night.

He went on to note that Lou Gehrig of the New York Yankees had set the previous record of four in a June 3, 1932, game. Bridges described the various homers with great flair:

Daniels of Kannapolis won in the fungo distance hitting contest.

Kannapolis	AB	R	H	O	A
Miller, cf	4	1	2	0	0
Daniels, 1b	4	2	1	10	0
McGill, ss	3	2	1	1	3
Tipton, lf	4	3	3	2	0
M. Watts, 3b	5	0	2	1	5
Suggs, rf	5	0	1	6	0
Redfern, 2b	4	0	1	3	4
H. Watts, c	3	0	2	1	0
Roscoe, p	3	0	0	0	0
Hart, p	1	0	0	0	0
Totals	36	8	13	24	12

Hickory	AB	R	H	O	A
Viau, ss	6	1	2	3	5
Scarborough, lf	6	1	2	4	0
Susko, 1b	6	1	3	5	0
Barton, rf	6	5	5	1	0
Randleman, cf	5	2	2	3	0
Tutaj, 3b	6	2	3	1	0
Shires, 2b	5	1	1	3	4
Murray, c	4	2	3	7	2
Mills, p	4	0	2	0	0
Totals	48	17	23	27	11

Kannapolis .. 303 011 000— 8 13 3
Hickory .... 022 018 22x—17 23 0

Runs batted in: M. Watts 2, Suggs 2, Tutaj 2, Tipton, Susko, Redfern, Barton 9, Daniels, Mills 2, Scarborough. Errors: McGill, M. Watts. Two base hits: Viau, Randleman, Mills. Three base hits: Susko. Home runs: Tutaj, Barton 5, Susko. Stolen bases: Redfern, Daniels. Sacrifices: Redfern. Double plays: Viau to Shires to Susko (2). Left on bases: Kannapolis 8, Hickory 1. Base on balls: off Roscoe 1, Hart 1, Mills 6. Struck out: by Roscoe 1, Mills 4. Hits: off Roscoe 11 in 5 innings. Hits: off Hart 13 in 4 innings. Wild pitches: Mills 3, Roscoe. Losing pitcher: Hart. Umpires: Burnette and Munday. Time of game: 2:25.

On August 26, 1938, Vince Barton hit five home runs in a nine inning game. This box score appeared in the *Hickory Daily Record.*

The longest hit of his phenomenal night at bat was estimated at 500 feet.

His screamer into the right field bleachers in the sixth with Scarborough and Viau on base put Hickory out in front 9 to 8, for the first time and the lead held for the rest of the game.

The right-fielder's seven league wallop in the eighth was preceded by a homer from the bat of Pete Susko, first baseman.

The Rebels eventually won the game 17–8 with 23 hits altogether.

It should be noted that one of the features of the Lenoir-Rhyne College baseball field where the Rebels played was a short right field fence. The baseball field shared space with the football field. The right field bleachers were actually the permanent home side seating for the football games. Halfway down these bleachers in right center field was the football press box. Harold Lail, batboy and clubhouse boy at the time, noted that several of Barton's home runs went over the press box.

Lail added this anecdote to the legend as well. He noted that Barton was late arriving for the game that day, and when he did arrive, he had obviously been drinking. Rebels' manager Stumpy Culbreath frantically instructed Lail to take him to the shower and get him ready to play. Lail said that he got him ready just before game time, and "He went out there and hit five home runs."

Much was made about Barton's home run record locally, and it has become a permanent part of baseball lore in the Hickory area. However, the Carolina League records are not official professional records and are left off of players' authorized professional documents.

Barton probably remained on the banned players' list. This would explain why a player of his ability would have seemingly disappeared from the scene. Christian Trudeau found a record of his play the following year for the Granby Red Sox of the Quebec Provincial League. Barton played right field and batted .286 with 7 home runs and 55 RBIs in 255 at bats over 73 games. Trudeau notes that there are "no accounts of his off-field behavior." He adds that "the QPL was an outlaw league that joined organized ball in 1940, and Barton didn't stay there for 1940." That is the last known playing record.

Bill Whitley has noted that his father made a number of attempts to contact Vince Barton over the years, that he even used his contacts with several major league clubs to try to track him down, but to no avail. Vince Barton, who had arrived on the Carolina League scene as a bigger than life character, chose to leave that impression as his final one.

16

Mr. Henry: William Henry Whitley

Born: June 4, 1890, Mecklenburg County, North Carolina; died: December 23, 1979, Albemarle, North Carolina

Mr. Henry Whitley's name is synonymous with Whitley's Funeral Home, the town of Kannapolis, and the sport of baseball. However, to him, his most important accomplishment was the work he did in the church when he was a young man. He began a Sunday school class for young men in 1918 that was identified as "Whitley's Sunday School Class" long after he stopped teaching it in 1928.

His son, Bill Whitley, present manager of Whitley's Funeral Home in Kannapolis, said his father's life revolved around his family and church first, his business second, and baseball third. In the summertime, "baseball became second and his business third. He was really a baseball fan. He loved the game from the time he was a child."

"Mr. Henry," as many of his friends called him, was born on June 4, 1890, in Mecklenburg County, in North Carolina just across the Cabarrus County line. He was a farm boy and never lost his love for the outdoors. In later life he was recognized as one of the best rabbit and possum hunters in North Carolina. In turn, he became a shrewd evaluator of farmland in the Piedmont section of North Carolina, buying and selling many farms. His personal favorite was a 200 acre tract along the Rocky River which he maintained and often visited till near the end of his life.

At the age of ten, his family moved to Concord where he went to work for Odell Mill. He also joined Forest Hill Methodist Church, a church next door to Odell Mill and known for years as Mr. Odell's church. Textile league baseball was king in those days, and Whitley soon became enamored with the game. His love for the outdoors was transferred to a love for the area's most popular outdoor sport.

At the age of 21 in 1911, he began to teach his first Sunday school class at Forest Hill Methodist Church. Because he realized there was a need for outdoor activities, and at the encouragement of Mr. Odell, he organized his first Sunday school baseball teams that played teams from other area churches.

Mr. Whitley was an eyewitness to history as he noted in a June 28, 1976, interview in the *Kannapolis Independent*. He remembered a day in 1905: "It was a Saturday afternoon in 1905 that I was standing on a street corner in Concord when the Rev. Thomas Smith came by in a buggy and asked me to ride up the road with him. I climbed in, and we rode about seven miles north, and we came up to what is now Kannapolis, and I went with him to contact three families about buying their property. The deal was closed that day, and the property he contracted for is what the town of Kannapolis was later built on."

The first Cannon Mills plant (#1) was built in 1907 in one of those fields, and shortly thereafter, Mr. James Cannon, founder of Cannon Mills, began to build houses and started a mill village owned entirely by Cannon Mills.

Five years later in 1907, Henry Whitley transferred to the Kannapolis plant where he wove the first Cannon "Name Towel" on a Jacquard loom. He never minded the then normal 10–12 hours a day in the mill. "I still found time for hunting, fishing, and playing baseball," but the day came when he just couldn't take being "penned in" any longer.

He worked for Life Insurance of Virginia, and then was circulation manager for the *Concord Tribune*. Finally, he moved from Concord to Kannapolis on November 19, 1918, and joined H.B. Wilkinson and Co. (Concord) as general manager of their Kannapolis operation in 1919. Wilkinson's was a furniture store with a funeral home next door.

In 1923, Whitley established his own China Grove Furniture and Undertaking Company in the nearby China Grove mill village. In 1925 he opened a company in Mooresville, about 15 miles away and in 1927 a third company in Lincolnton, NC, in the foothills of the Blue Ridge Mountains. In 1938 he purchased the Wilkinson operation in Kannapolis and incorporated it as W.H. Whitley and Sons. During these years, "Mr. Henry" established himself as the most noted and recognized civic, church, and business leader in Kannapolis outside of the Cannon Mills executives.

"Whitley's Sunday School Class" at Trinity Methodist Church established what proved to be a very good baseball team in 1921. Once again, Mr. Henry's love of church and baseball combined to face a new challenge. Whitley's team did so well that local citizens asked him to organize a town team to play against nearby towns, notably Concord, and to beat them. This was the beginning of the heated and sometimes violent rivalry between Kannapolis and Concord, two Cannon Mills towns, seven miles apart.

16. Mr. Henry

In 1923, the citizens of Kannapolis elected "Mr. Henry" president and general manager of the Kannapolis Baseball Club, a position he held through 1938, time that included the outlaw Carolina League of 1936–38. He quickly built one of the strongest semi-pro baseball teams in the Piedmont area of western North Carolina. The 1926 team was proclaimed semi-pro champions of North Carolina. This 1926 team included a University of North Carolina pitching star that had played with the New York Yankees after graduation in 1922—Clement Manley Llewellyn.

Llewellyn, who earned a law degree from UNC, had completed his professional baseball career the previous year with the Greenville, SC, team in the old Sally League (South Atlantic League). He appears in the 1926 Kannapolis team photo, wearing a Greenville uniform.

Mr. Whitley, an entrepreneur from Kannapolis, helped shape the baseball scene in that town for many years (courtesy Bill Whitley).

Llewellyn was a prominent figure in Concord area baseball for the next twenty years. Exactly how he ended up in Concord in 1927 is not clear. "Mr. Henry's" son Bill said that Concord, being the Cabarrus County seat, lured the young lawyer, as much for his baseball ability as for his legal prowess with the high expectations of organizing a team to beat Kannapolis, and to develop a lucrative law business near the county offices. Llewellyn's control of Concord baseball improved the town's ability to compete and helped to ramp up the fierce rivalry between the textile towns. This rivalry was truly the foundation that the outlaw league would be built upon during the decade of the Great Depression. The two teams had already begun to steal each others' players, and it was not that big a step to "steal" professional players to go along with the college stars that they imported to the area each summer.

After his purchase of Wilkinson's operations in Kannapolis in 1938 and the demise of the outlaw Carolina League during the winter of '38–39, "Mr. Henry" retired from being the leader of Kannapolis baseball. Kannapolis, like other outlaw baseball teams, joined the Class D NC State League, but "Mr. Henry" did not join in when organized professional baseball took over. Nevertheless, he was still known as "Mr. Baseball" in Kannapolis until the day he died.

Henry Whitley had spent 16 years making a name as one of the best procurers of college and professional baseball talent. He had honed his skills in the semi-pro ranks and perfected them in the outlaw professional league. Surely, he realized that he would never fit in with the tightly controlled hierarchy of organized ball where the executives were involved mostly for their own profit. His had been a successful venture as a volunteer baseball entrepreneur. He had turned all the income gained from the baseball fans to the task of buying "the best players our money can buy."

Besides, he was forty-eight years old and a successful businessman who was ready to turn his efforts toward the development of the Kannapolis Merchant Association, which he had helped organize. He became a charter member of the Kannapolis Rotary Club, a 32nd degree Mason as a member of the Cannon Memorial Lodge, a member of the Oasis Shrine Club, and the Independent Order of Odd Fellows Lodge.

As the town expanded, Mr. Whitley realized another opportunity. He purchased a cemetery on Cannon Blvd. and "established Carolina Memorial Park, recognized today as one of the most beautiful and best-kept cemeteries in the southeast." Mr. Whitley "laid walks, paved roads, planted gardens, built the Singing Tower, Veterans Memorial, and the mausoleum and crematory—the first in Cabarrus County" (*Kannapolis Independent*, October 19, 1981).

Kannapolis, a town built by Cannon Mills, was a better place to live because of Henry Whitley, and when baseball is discussed, "Mr. Henry" and the outlaw Carolina League command the most attention.

In 1976, at the age of 86, Mr. Whitley said, "Fletcher Heath, our second baseman, was by just a couple years ago, and Houston Hines and Eric Tipton (Duke football and baseball All-Americans in the '30s and later a major leaguer and a pro football player) always send Christmas cards. So do many others." The relationship he established with his players still endured nearly forty years later.

Even though Eric Tipton roomed and boarded at Mr. Henry's house free of charge (perks over and above the outlaw salaries) for two years, his favorite ballplayer was Vince Barton. To this day, old ball fans, and even his son, Bill, cannot fully explain the rapport and compassion these two men had for each other.

They were like the Alpha and Omega of the Kannapolis scene: one a recognized civic, business, and church leader, and the other a wild renegade professional baseball player from Toronto, Canada. Barton was gifted with major league talent and had played for two years with the Chicago Cubs (1931–32). After several years of struggling back toward the pinnacle of the game, Barton's penchant for fighting, baseball, drinking, and women (not necessarily in that order) and his awesome baseball ability led him to the outlaw Carolina League. His extraordinary relationship with the pious Mr. Whitley rested on one thing — baseball. One man truly loved the game, and the other could knock the ball out of the park quite frequently.

Mr. Whitley's son, Bill, talked about his father, Vince Barton, and others in an interview in April 1992. To say the least, Vince Barton was a character and one more hitter. In his second and last year in Kannapolis, he hit 29 home runs and drove in 94 runs. By that time he had worn out his welcome in Kannapolis and was released. The Hickory Rebels signed him for one last eventful year in the outlaw league.

Interview with Bill Whitley, son of Henry Whitley, by R.G. "Hank" Utley, April 27, 1992

> Vince Barton, age 28, came down here from Canada in 1936. He had played some in the big leagues, but he was almost shipped out of Kannapolis before he got settled in good. Mr. E. J. Sharpe, head of the Cannon YMCA, had a wife who was from Canada. He had heard of Barton's hitting. Mr. Sharpe talked to my father, and they arranged for Vince to come down here. They made arrangements for Vince to stay at Dr. M. L. Troutman's home. Vince brought a beautiful lady with him, everybody thought was his wife. They stayed over at Dr. Troutman's house, and everything was going fine until Vince and his "wife" had a little problem. The lady was beat up real bad and had to be taken to the doctor, and that's when we found out that Vince had a real drinking problem and also found out that the lady wasn't his wife. Now things like that were just not acceptable in society in Kannapolis in the "30s. So they had a big discussion, and Vince almost got the gate. The lady went back to Canada, and Vince stayed here. He played two years—1936 and 1937. During the two years he really tested my Dad's faith in humanity.
>
> Now back in '35 and '36 some of the players would not stay in very good shape. We played ball in the afternoons then, and the players, some of them, didn't take too good a care of themselves at night. My dad had a furniture store, and upstairs over the furniture store, we had what we called the rug and mattress room with a fireproof door that you could padlock. The night before a big game, such as Concord, or the playoff games, Dad would send us kids up there, and we'd pull out mattresses for all the players to sleep on, and a blanket or two. About eight o'clock, all the ballplayers would show up and go upstairs, and we would lock them in for the night. Dad always kept a fellow there on guard in case of a fire or something. Looking back,

it's a wonder they didn't burn the place down the way they smoked cigarettes back then. But they abided by the rules pretty well because they knew if they didn't, they'd get fired.

You might say Vince had some personality clashes with management. After Buck Redfern, a pretty straightlaced man, was named manager in 1938, Vince was released, and he signed with Hickory.

I remember my dad, my mother, and I went to Hickory with the team one night. Vince came over to our seats and said, "Mr. Henry, the wolves up here are on me pretty good, and I hate to do this to you folks because you were real good to me in Kannapolis, and there's no hard feelings, but I've got to help beat you tonight." And you know he hit five home runs, one of them over the center field fence that may still be going. That's the same way he hit them in Kannapolis. There's hundreds of people still living here that remember Vince hitting a home run over the center field fence on over the two story house on Bell Avenue. That had to be 450 feet, maybe 500 feet. He could hit the ball.

My dad really loved Vince Barton. Dad was a teetotaler all his life, and it was real odd they were such good friends. I really believe my dad thought he could turn Vince around. After World War II, he tried his best to find Vince. He may have been dead by then. [*Note:* Barton died in Toronto on September 13, 1973.] Dad knew a lot of big league scouts. He even called the offices of several big league teams trying to determine Vince's whereabouts. And finally he ran an ad in the New York Times asking if anyone knew the whereabouts of Vince Barton to contact him.

We had a lot of good players. On the other side of the coin, there was "Razz" Miller, a native of nearby Rockwell.

Vince Barton, in civilian clothes, recovering from a gun shot wound received in a poker game, reported as a pulled muscle.

16. Mr. Henry

Razz Miller was one of the fastest outfielders I ever saw. He was also a fine man. He graduated from Lenoir-Rhyne College and became a Lutheran minister. He loved to hunt possum with my dad. They even took Vince with them one night. Vince didn't like it. He would rather hunt women.

My dad was always trying to find better ballplayers. I remember one big league pitcher that was down in Georgia or South Carolina at his home on some kind of emergency visit. I just can't think of his name, but my dad drove down there one day, paid him a good bonus, and brought him back to pitch one game that night under another name and then took him back home the next day.

On another trip, he went to one of the Springs Mills plants in South Carolina to talk to a pitcher about coming to Kannapolis. He had to go on the mill property to talk to the player. Mr. Elliot Springs, himself, found out dad was there on mill property trying to get one of his better ballplayers, so he had a couple of other pretty big employees escort Dad off the property.

Dad helped pay some of the ballplayers out of his own pocket; one of them was Vince Barton. [*Note:* Marvin Watts, one of Vince's teammates, said Barton was making $385 a month counting Mr. Henry's money, and that was more than some big leaguers were making during the Depression.]

The ballplayers and my family were real close-knit. Eric Tipton, the All-American football and baseball player from Duke University and a professional big league baseball and football player after he graduated, stayed at our house—free, of course—that was one of their perks. He had a room upstairs and set down at the table with us every day. All the players and fans would hang out around our furniture store. A lot of the fans would come by. Some of the wolves would tell them how they could win, pitch, or hit better. It was like a village meeting place with everyone getting in his two cents worth.

One of the biggest problems we had in Kannapolis was raising money. The mill kept up the ballpark and lights—after all, they owned it, but as an organization, they didn't put up any money. Some of the executives did. And they did give jobs to the players that wanted to stay in Kannapolis during the winter. Considering that was the time of the Depression, the players had a good deal. Actually, they didn't work much. Most of them "worked" in Roy Propst's finishing department.

The way that worked, Mr. E.J. Sharpe, who was on the board of directors of the team and was the Cannon Mill man that managed the Cannon YMCA, would go to Mr. A.L. Brown, one of Mr. Charles

Mr. Whitley's 1935 Kannapolis Towelers in Carolina Textile League. Front row, from left, Bobby Hipps (1B, Manager), Harris (P), Buck Ross (P), Houston Hines (P), Rusty McCall (OF), Elrod (P); back row, Mr. W. Henry Whitley (General Manager), Tubby Bonds (C), Bob White (3B), Dennis (OF), Bethel Rhem (P), Gice Allen (P), Ellis Taylor (C), Tom Young (OF), Spencer Reynolds (2B), Woody Whitiak (SS) (courtesy Bill Whitley).

Cannon's most trusted executives and say, "Al, we have six or eight or whatever number of ballplayers that want to stay in Kannapolis this winter and play for us next year." You see, all the players signed only one year contracts and were free to leave, not like organized professional baseball where the team owned you.

Well, Mr. Brown would send word to Mr. Roy Propst, and then Roy would call up the player and invite him to work.

My dad was a very thorough man. I'd like to show you this small pocket sized notebook [sections included in appendix]. It looks like it's about 3½ by 5 inches. Dad kept the box scores of every game in 1937 in this little book. The newspapers very seldom printed team or player hitting, fielding, and pitching statistics.

At the end of the season, he figured out longhand all the averages that are calculated and printed by computers today. He even knew how many double plays each double play combination made during the season. He was probably the most knowledgeable executive in the outlaw Carolina League, and he did it all himself. Note: Mr. Whitley's personal team records can be found in Appendix B, page 169.

17

Home Boys

Who's on First?: Frank Hopkins
The Brother: Marvin Watts
The Sandlapper: Houston Hines

Who's on First?: Frank Hopkins

Born: October 3, 1911, Coddle Creek, North Carolina (Cabarrus County); died: March 28, 1994, Concord, North Carolina

Frank Hopkins played first base for the 1935 Landis Carolina Textile League team and first base as well for the 1936 Kannapolis outlaw Carolina League team. The beginning of the interview is a reference to the 1927 championship game between Kannapolis and Concord. The game was rained out when a torrential downpour interrupted a near riot between fans and players of the opposing teams. A few blocks from the ballpark there was no rain.

Hopkins was interviewed by R.G. "Hank" Utley on January 14, 1991.

> I was attending the game, but the way it started, they were making ground rules, and the fight started at home plate, making the ground rules.
> When it started, It rained as hard as I have ever seen it rain, and the water was shoe top deep on the ball field before it quit. I'm not sure about Concord, but Kannapolis had brought in Snag Almond and Mule Shirley to play first base. I was outside in a tree on the third base side. I was about seventeen years old.
> I was raised at Watts Cross Roads. We played in a pasture, and from there I went over to Rockwell, a good organized semi-pro team. I played with Rimertown the next year which turned out to be the telephone company team. Then with Mt. Pleasant I played in my first night game at Forest City. Pop Summers was a pitcher for Forest City,

and we wore him out. There were no leagues. We played other semi-pro teams. The Lancaster (SC) Red Roses claimed to be the best. We went down there and beat 'em, and they were supposed to come back up here and play us a week or two later, but they closed the mill, and we had the ballpark full of people, and they didn't show.

I played up at Landis with the Watts boys. Linn and Corriher Mills sponsored the team. They paid us through the mill, but when they joined the organized ranks, they couldn't pay us through the mill. When we did work in the mill, we went in in the morning and left about ten or eleven o'clock. We really didn't do any work.

In 1931 Ginger Watts left the Charlotte Hornets professional team and came to Concord. He brought Charley Horne, a pitcher, with him. I was at Hartsell Mill at that time, and we had Herman Fink as a pitcher. He went to the Philadelphia Athletics later. Every summer we would get a job in some mill that wanted us to play ball. In the winter we would go back to the farm. We worked on the farm early in the mornings during the summer.

In 1935 the Carolina Textile League started, and all the teams were run by the mills. Mr. Corriher at Landis, he furnished the money. The best pitcher I ever hit was Lanier at Lexington. He was a left hander and had good control for a youngster. He was from Denton, NC, and Branch Rickey signed him for the St. Louis Cardinals. Lefty Teague bothered me quite a bit at Mooresville. I hit left handed, but the only left hander I ever hit two home runs off of in one game was Lefty Robinson. He was at Mooresville too, but I could hit him.

Buck Ross was a good right handed pitcher. He went to Philadelphia. Wilt Guise was a left handed junk pitcher, and nobody hit him. He was slow, but nobody hit him. Ken Chitwood in Concord had a good curveball. Carl Doyles of Concord was the fastest pitcher I ever hit against. He hit me right there on the leg one time. I had hit one off him the time before. He hit me, and sometimes on a cold day, I think I can feel it yet. He could throw. He went on up to the Athletics pretty quick. This league would find those good ballplayers, and then the big leagues would come down and take 'em away. Freddie Chapman was another good ballplayer the big leagues took away. Broadus Culler was another one. Pro ball had threatened all those good young players in this league. Maybe that's why they signed and left. I played with Fred Archer, a left handed pitcher, on two different teams—Landis and Lexington—before he went to the A's, and then at Lexington in pro ball (Class D) when he came back. He got homesick like a lot of others that went up north. He was from the coal mines of Virginia but settled down around here. Archer finally married a girl from Landis.

Razz Miller was raised over at Rockwell. He went to school at Lenoir-Rhyne and finally went to the seminary and became a preacher. He was preaching in '35 when he played for us at Landis in the Textile League.

When Archer, Fink, and Coddle Creek Taylor pitched, you could expect to win.

Hopkins was offered a tryout with the Atlanta Crackers at the beginning of the 1935 season, but he elected to play with Landis in the Carolina Textile League because of the promise of year-round employment. The Landis club finished in first place by six games with a record of 49 wins and 24 losses. Hopkins, their first baseman, hit .285 with eleven doubles, three triples and ten home runs. Hopkins played first in 1936 for the outlaw league Kannapolis Towelers who finished third behind Concord and Charlotte. Hopkins was one of many outlaw league players who then made the jump back into Class D organized ball as minor league play expanded at the end of the Great Depression.

The Brother: Marvin Watts

Born: June 24, 1905, Watts Crossroads, North Carolina (Cabarrus County); died: August 11, 1997, Concord, North Carolina

Marvin Watts, the hard hitting shortstop and third baseman for the Kannapolis Towelers of the Carolina League, first made a name for himself in the Carolina Textile League where he played alongside his brother, Herman "Ginger" Watts. Watts batted .305 in 1935 and helped anchor the league champion Landis infield.

Watts established himself as a steady player both in the field and at the plate for the outlaw league Kannapolis Towelers. The club ran away with the league pennant in 1937, thanks in part to Watts' consistent hitting. He finished the season third in the league with 85 RBIs and hit 18 doubles and 11 home runs. He, Vince Barton, Razz Miller, and Fletcher Heath provided a lethal combination at the plate for the aggressive Kannapolis club.

Though the team was not as successful in the final season of the outlaw league, Watts continued to hit with power. He finished the season third in the league with 13 home runs, and his 70 RBIs placed him fifth.

Raised in the rural eastern Piedmont area of the textile belt, Marvin would be remembered as one of the legends of the fabled "outlaw" Carolina League.

Marvin Watts was interviewed January 14, 1991, by R.G. "Hank" Utley.

I started out in baseball when I was a young fellow out here at Watts Crossroads in the old pasture, and after a few years, I was at the old MPCI [Mount Pleasant Collegiate Institute], and I was there from '21 to '25. We'd play Oak Ridge, and we beat 'em so much they wouldn't play us at Mount Pleasant. We had to play in Albemarle.

One day I went to Professor McAlister. I wasn't too good in my books back then. I was thinking mostly about baseball. I asked him what he thought my future was, playing baseball or going to school. He said, "Boy, the way you can play ball, I'd go get that money." So, I started off with Red Irby. He was playing a bunch from South Carolina, and I was a pitcher then. I wasn't in too good a shape, and I started pitching — back then the pay was not too good, but I got $12 a game.

Then in 1926, I went to Clearwater, Florida, with a bunch from Red Springs, NC. We played all the teams around Orlando, and we beat all of 'em. That year they dug all the sewer lines down there, and people came up with the "Florida fever." We packed up before the last game in the playoff and got out of there as soon as the last out was made.

Brothers Herman "Ginger" Watts (left), a catcher, and Marvin, an infielder, are pictured. Hailing from the eastern Cabarrus County community of Watts Crossroads, they played for the Carolina League Kannapolis Towelers and for the 1943 Victory League Concord team (courtesy Bernie H. Edwards).

When we got back home, my brother, Ginger, was playing with Gibson Mill, and Sid Basinger was the manager. He gave me a tryout and put me in left field.

The first time up I hit a home run and the next time up I hit a home run, and the third time up I hit one against the right field fence. After the ballgame, Sid said, "Marvin, I want you on my ball club." After I played at Gibson for a year or two, I went to Landis at Corriher Mills.

I remember playing against John McInnis in the Concord ballpark, and John was a pretty good pitcher, but one day I hit one by his head and scared him to death.

Razz Miller and I were

on the same ball club. Razz lived in Rockwell, and he'd drive to my house, and then we'd go to the ballpark. Razz back then was studying for a preacher, and he was a good ballplayer. Razz was very fast. He could fly in that outfield.

I remember one night we were playing in Lexington, and Razz was in the ministry business, and the ballgame was tied in extra innings, and I patted Razz on the knee and said, "Preacher, I'm gonna end this ballgame," and lo and behold, the first pitch was in my alley, and I hit it out of the park.

After the outlaw league ended, I played for Winston-Salem. They were owned by the Giants, and the next year they wanted me to go to Bridgeport, CT, and so I was raising two daughters, and I didn't want to leave home. I asked for my release, and they gave it to me.

When Vince Barton came to Kannapolis, he belonged to the Chicago Cubs, and he told me he learned about the Carolina League, and he couldn't get along with the club and the ballplayers, so he decided to come to Kannapolis. Barton could really hit the ball. He was good, and he was tough. Nobody ran over him. He held his ground. He was a mean rascal. I remember one night he didn't show up for the ballgame, and everyone was wondering what was wrong. So everybody began to talk, and one fellow said, "He was in a poker game last night and got shot in the side." He was out of the game for about three weeks or a month, and the people said he had pulled a muscle in his side.

Bud Shaney was another one that could get mean. I remember one time I got two hits off Shaney the first two times up, and the next time I had to hit the dirt on the first pitch. On the second pitch, the catcher caught the ball, and my cap flew off my head. I finally walked. The next time up I walked again, but two of the pitches were behind my back. Bud was after my head.

I knew organized ball was after the Carolina League. I was in one game, and I was on second base when the shortstop came over to me. He was new, and I didn't remember his name, but he said, "I don't know you, but I've heard lots about you. I was sent in here by the commissioner of baseball to break up this league, me and Bill Steineke. I don't want you to get hurt, so you stay out of this mess. We're gonna fight and break this thing up."

Back in the ol' Carolina League, I went to Concord one evening. I was with Kannapolis. Gibson Drug Store in Concord was the hangout place for all the ballplayers, doctors, lawyers, and whatever. Ken Chitwood came up to me and said, "Come back here with me, behind the drug store and Dr. Ed Misenheimer's office."

I went back there with Ginger, my brother, and Razz, and he had a place fixed there like somebody had been buried there with flowers on it, and he said after the game tonight, "Here's where we're going to bury Kannapolis."

One year, the year I was playing in Landis, Mr. Corriher, who owned the mill and everything around there, came down to talk to us because we were in a slump. We were taking batting practice, and he came out there and said we gotta get out of this slump. We can't beat anybody playing like we are.

One of the players told Mr. Corriher, "Here's a bat. You go up there and show us how to hit."

So Mr. Corriher said OK, and he grabbed the bat. The old man was up in his years, but he hit the first pitch on a line drive over the shortstop. He laid the bat down and said, "Boys, that's the way to do it. If you hit like that, you can win."

One of the reasons a lot of the pro players came to this league was the type of ball we were playing here. There was good money if you were a good ballplayer, but ball players back then wanted to play in a good league. They loved the game and wanted to play with the best.

Branch Rickey, he was head of the [St. Louis] Cardinals, and he was up in Cooleemee looking over some ballplayers. After the game, Rickey came down to talk with some of the players, and I asked him how he found out about this league around here, and he said it was known all over the United States where baseball was played and that it was mighty good baseball, considering the size of the towns.

Mr. Roy Propst was after me to come to work in Kannapolis after the '36 season. I was a big quail hunter, and I told him I'd see him after hunting season. Later I decided to go up and see him, and he had a little office out in the mill, and I talked to him, and we talked about baseball a whole lot. Then he said he had a job for me in the sheet department. When he said he would pay me 35 cents an hour, I told him that wasn't any money. You know us ballplayers wanted plenty of money. He said that's all those people on the floor are making, and I know you don't want to work, and you ain't gonna do much work because you don't want to do anything anyway. That's all I can pay you.

Some days I would go in at nine or ten o'clock and throw up my hand to Mr. Roy, and would say, "OK, I'll take off you," and then I'd leave.

Some of the ballplayers didn't like what they heard Vince Barton was making. We heard he was making $125 a week — that was as much as some of those ballplayers were making sitting on the bench in the big leagues. Vince wouldn't ride on the bus with the rest of the players. He always drove his own car, and he usually had a woman with him. [*Note:* Barton left Kannapolis after the 1937 season, and played the final outlaw season for the Hickory Rebels, where batboy Harold Lail described him much as Watts does here.]

The Sandlapper: Houston Hines

By the time Houston Hines arrived in Kannapolis in 1934 at the invitation of Henry Whitley, he had already been playing baseball in the Greenville, SC, area since the late '20s. His rough and tumble diamond experience included pitching against an overweight Shoeless Joe Jackson. As the Depression set in, Hines realized the importance of playing mill ball so that he could maintain a winter job. He even turned down an opportunity to be a part of the New York Yankees organization because he feared he would be farmed down to a low paying level. Hines also knew that organized minor league ball held no guarantee of year-round employment. As a result, Hines, who pitched ball for over a decade, has an official professional record of 0–2 with the 1931 Greenville Spinners who played in the Depression-doomed Palmetto League.

Although a statistical record of Hines' play is difficult to locate, it is easy to imagine that he was a hard-nosed competitor. The 1935 Carolina Textile League records indicate that he absorbed 10 of second place Kannapolis's losses. However, a look at batting records reveals that he was capable of helping his own cause. In 56 at-bats he smacked two home runs, five doubles and racked up a .285 average.

Hines, like many players that passed through Kannapolis, became a big fan of general manager Henry Whitley. Whitley appreciated not only his pitching, but also his loyalty and mentioned him as a player that often came by to see him at his store. More recently, Hines returned to Kannapolis for a celebration of the outlaw days of baseball, one of the last living players from that era.

Hines was interviewed by R.G. "Hank" Utley on February 21, 1992.

> I signed up with the Greenville Spinners. They called them the Spinners then. That's when George Rhinehardt was playing with Greenville. I played with them till the end of that season. The next season they folded up. It was 1930, and the team went broke due to the Depression.
>
> Jersey City in the triple A International League had spring training down here. It was a Yankee farm team. I went out there and worked

out a few days with them, and when we got through, the manager said, "Come up to my room." That was in the old Franklin Hotel, but it's been torn down. I went up there and signed a contract. You see, when you sign a contract with the Yankees, you know how it was back then, they could send you anywhere they wanted to. But I signed a contract that I wouldn't be farmed out because I knew if they farmed me out below Jersey City, you don't make much money. I could make more money down here playing ball and have a winter job too. So we left Spartanburg to go to Greensboro, and I was going to pitch against some teams up there, but it rained every day we were up there. So at the end of the week, I asked them, "What are you going to do? I don't want to go up to Jersey City and then you release me."

He answered, "I tell you, I've got a bunch of these fellows coming up from these farm teams the Yankees have, and I have to play them." I knew what he was talking about, so I told him to go ahead and give me my release. A Mr. Kershaw was the business manager. I don't remember the manager's name. It was 1931, so I came back to Woodruff, SC, in the Western Carolina League. I had to look out for that winter job. There were thousands not working, and I had a job because I could pitch. A lot of times I pitched for more than one team. After pitching

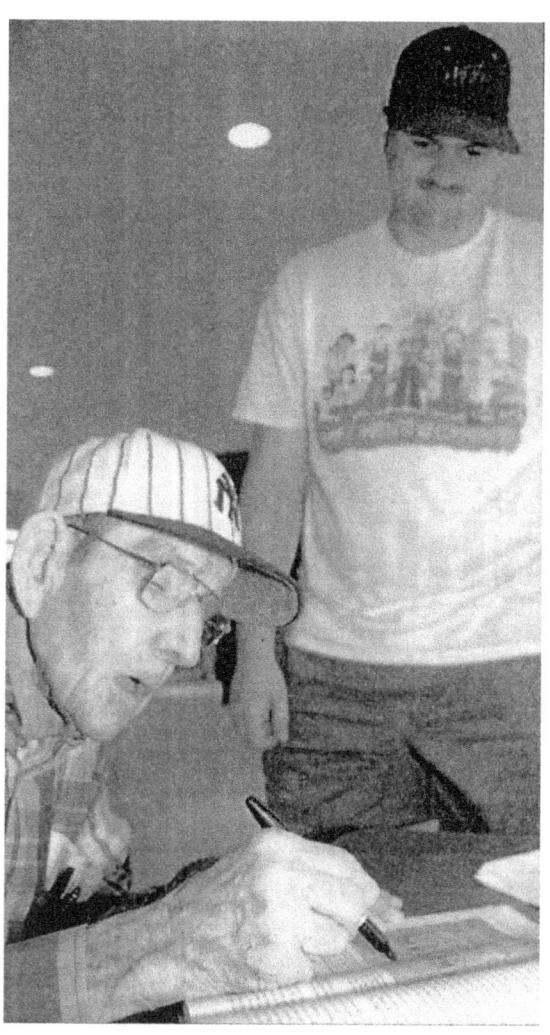

Houston Hines signs an autograph for a fan at a Piedmont Boll Weevils game. Hines came to Kannapolis in 1934 o play for Henry Whitley's Towelers (courtesy *Independent Tribune*).

in Woodruff on a Tuesday, I would go up to Lacy Mills in Gastonia and pitch on Saturday. I also pitched some at Forest City. Then when I pitched here at Monarch [Union, SC] I went down to Ninety-Six, SC, and pitched a playoff game down there. I went where the money was as long as it suited me and not them. I had to pitch steady at one mill, so I could have a winter job. I pitched two games for Ninety-Six one weekend and picked up $35 each game and then came back to Monarch Mills. Forest City would give you $20 or $25. It all depended on who they were playing and how bad they needed you. I played with Maurice Frees in Forest City. We always ate at Blanchard's Café in Forest City. We dressed in a place so small at Alexander Mills that we could barely get the players in there.

I went to Kannapolis in 1934 after Mr. Henry Whitley saw me pitch in Gastonia at Armstrong Park. I worked in the mill shop in Kannapolis in the wintertime. You remember Mr. A.L. Brown; he was a big shot up there. He had a big farm on the Charlotte Highway out of Concord, and he had some of us from the mill shop to come down there and put up a new silo. That silo was still there a few years ago, but I don't know what happened after the land was sold to Philip Morris for that new cigarette plant. Mr. Brown was a big ball fan and a good man. Of course, when we put up his silo, it was all on mill time.

They don't make 'em like Mr. Whitley anymore. Let me tell you; I had set up housekeeping in Gastonia, and I bought our furniture from Jacob's in Gastonia. Well, when I got ready to go to Kannapolis, I went to see Mr. Jacobs about moving my furniture. I was buying it on time. He told me he'd rather I not move it. He said I can't keep you from moving it. What he was saying was that he would make it hard on me. And you know what Mr. Whitley said? He told me to let Mr. Jacobs have his furniture, that he had a furniture store in Kannapolis with all the furniture I needed. He was a fine man.

I made what they called the All-Star team in Kannapolis in '34. Then in '35 when they started bringing in some better ballplayers, I made the All-Star team again. Some of those fellows were rough, but people like Tom Young that taught and coached at Lexington and Bethel Rhem were as fine a fellows as you could want. Nick Witeck from up in Pennsylvania was a good man. Spencer Reynolds had played in Charlotte, and Ellis Taylor had caught for Birmingham. All those guys could have kept playing pro ball, but they wanted that winter job. The Depression was rough. Probably the best man I ever knew was "Preacher" Miller. Some called him "Razz," and that man could run. He ran down many a long fly ball that I thought sure was gonna be a double or a triple. He saved me a couple times.

In the 1934 textile strike, the sheriff would use a lot of us bigger men out in front of the gate. They even deputized the boss men. Can you imagine that? Of course the mill owned everything in town and was paying the policemen anyway. Those were rough times. And the players were rough. They would keep baseballs in the refrigerator, and somebody in Charlotte was putting phonograph needles in the seams of the balls, making them top heavy. The teams even had a man on the bench that was in charge of those special balls.

After I came back to Monarch Mills, Johnny Walker put phonograph needles in the balls. He would only pitch at home like Bud Shaney did in Charlotte, and I had to pitch all the games on the road. We had a man on the bench that watched those balls better than the umpire. I never did any of that, but loved to get a roughed up ball. We played on dirt infields, and after it got scuffed up, I could make a ball go up or down or sideways. When that ball reached the plate, it moved so much that it was like it was exploding.

We had a lot of ballplayers coming into Kannapolis looking for work. One week I pitched nearly four whole ballgames. Those pitchers would come in and supposed to be so good; why some of them would give up three or four runs before we could get them out of the game. And then I would have to finish the game. There were two or three every week trying to get on the team. They came from everywhere, and you never knew whether they were using their real name or not. That Lefty Hart came up from Rome, Georgia, and he was good enough to stay.

You heard of Alabama Pitts? I played against him. He was tough. He had just got out of prison. I heard he got killed later on up at Valdese. The man that killed him must have been pretty tough.

The thing I remember most was Mr. Henry Whitley. That was one of the finest men I ever met, and boy did he love baseball.

At the time of this interview, Houston Hines still lived in Union, South Carolina. He shared a news article about pitching against Shoeless Joe Jackson, who had left the major leagues after the Black Sox scandal of 1919. Jackson played for several All-Star teams around Greenville, SC, in the '20 s and '30 s. The article quotes Hines as saying, "We always had a lot of respect for Shoeless Joe regardless of his age. When I pitched against him, he had put on some weight and had a big belly, but he still had those strong shoulders, and he could hit the ball. I walked him some to keep him from getting the big hit off us. It's a pity Shoeless Joe couldn't read or write. He probably would not have got in the trouble he did if he had some education."

17. Home Boys

Although Houston Hines was from Union, South Carolina, and returned to live there after his baseball career, he was certainly an adopted son of the baseball hotbed of Cabarrus County. Henry Whitley gave him the opportunity to work for him while he played and mentioned as well that Hines came around often to visit. Hines has returned over the years to the area to celebrate the days he spent pitching in the Piedmont area of North Carolina.

18

Rebels

The Pitcher: Tracey Hitchner
The Tramp Athlete: Robert Merritt "Pat" Shores
The Batboy: Harold Lail

The Pitcher: Tracey Hitchner

In 2004 Tim Peeler spent three hours in line waiting to vote in the presidential election. The line wound all the way around a local rural church and its adjacent buildings. What made that wait tolerable, however, was a conversation with the next man in line. He had worked for over twenty years at Century Furniture with Tracey Hitchner. We shared Hitchner stories. This man knew the outlaw ballplayer as an older gentleman, a friendly office worker who had built a business career on years of loyalty to the company president. Here was yet another example of how indelible a mark this New Jersey farm boy had left in Catawba County. Almost sixty years after his playing days ended, Hitchner is still the stuff of local legend. Nearly anyone who followed baseball in Hickory, NC, from 1936 to 1946 will produce memories of the fireballing pitcher.

Hitchner had signed to play ball for Albany in the International League in 1935. After a mediocre first year, he was not impressed with the amount offered by the club in 1936. Instead of signing he returned to his family farm in New Jersey. It was there that he received a phone call and an offer to play ball and work in Hickory, North Carolina, in the new Independent Carolina League. Hitchner arrived at night and thought he had reached the end of the world. He was not impressed with the facilities but was impressed with the caliber of baseball being played. In what was certainly a hitters league, Hitchner became the top hurler. Final records are not available for that season, but the local newspaper credits Hitchner with 21 wins.

Hitchner played two more successful seasons for the Rebels, one under a fake name. In 1937 the National Association of Professional Baseball Leagues declared the league to be an outlaw organization and produced a

18. Rebels

list of banned players. Hitchner suffered more than any other player as a result of this action. While most of the participants had their eligibility restored, he remained a banned player for ten years. It was only through the efforts of the ever-affable Sammy Bell in 1947 that Hitchner was allowed to return briefly to the organized game. Since he was not allowed to play during his peak years, we will never know how fine a pitcher he might have become.

Tracey Hitchner married and remained at the end of the world for the rest of his days.

The following interview was conducted in June 1991 by R.G. "Hank" Utley.

Tracey Hitchner in 1943 (courtesy Tracey Hitchner).

I was with Albany in the International League in 1935. I didn't sign a contract in 1936. They wanted to cut my salary, and I wouldn't accept it. It was the Depression, you know. So they suspended me, but after the season started, they sent a scout down home—it was a Washington scout. I can't remember his name. Anyway, he said they would pay me the same as in 1935 if I would report back. I told him I would accept it. So they sent me to Harrisburg, PA, for two weeks to get in shape, and then they took me back up to Albany, and when I got to Albany, they had one of the worst looking ball clubs I ever saw in my life. So I just told 'em I had a sore arm, just give me my release, I'm going home. They said, no, we're not going to do that, so they wanted to send me to Danville, VA, in a Class D League. I told 'em I wasn't a Class D ballplayer, and I wasn't going down there, so I tore the transfer up and threw it in the waste basket and told 'em I'd be on the family farm in New Jersey. So I went home to the farm.

One day I was planting potatoes, and this fellow called from Hickory, NC. His name was Ab Lutz. I asked him, How in the world did you get my name?" He said his manager, Stumpy Culbreth, got it from a man named Brown that was my roommate in Albany, NY.

I said, "Well, what do you pay down there?" He was going to pay me more money than I was making in Albany in the International League. I told him if he would send me transportation from Philadelphia to Hickory and from Hickory back to Philadelphia I'll come down there and see if I like it.

Note: Hitchner, when questioned about how much he was offered, said he wouldn't say, but it was more than Albany's offer.

They sent me the money. I came down and got off the train at the depot. This taxi driver came down there hollering, "I'm looking for a ballplayer. I'm looking for a ballplayer."

I said, "If you're looking for a ballplayer, it might be me." So he got me and took me to a boarding house, and he said he was supposed to take me out to the ballpark later.

When I did get to the ballpark and looked around, I was ready to catch the next train out of there. They had lights that didn't even light the outfield very good. And they had a dirt infield and cement bleachers that would hold 2 or 3,000 people. I wasn't used to playing ballparks like that. When the game started, there was a packed house, about 4,000 spectators. About the fourth inning, our pitcher got hit in the elbow and Stumpy Culbreth, our manager, was hollering, "Who can pitch on a short warmup?"

I said, "Gimme the ball," and we ended up winning 5 to 4 or 5 to 3. That was the first night I was here. I also found out that there were some pretty good ballplayers in the league, even if the ballpark didn't look so hot.

It was some time in June when I came down here, but I won 18 ballgames the rest of the summer and lost about 5. That year we played about a hundred game schedule, and we won 48 and we lost 49. I won 18 of those after missing over a month of the season. I was named to the league all-star team. I pitched about every second or third day and never had a sore arm. I was in good shape. For a little man, I could throw that ball through a brick wall. I had a good curveball too. I threw it off the end of my fingers.

The next season I changed my name. I knew a lot of the ballplayers down here that had changed their name, and I knew 'em by their right name. I remember one was Palmisano, Joe Palmisano, that caught for the Philadelphia Athletics a few years earlier. He played under the name Palm. And then there was Bill Steinecke that played under Bill Seph and then Steinecke in Concord.

I played under the name of John Davis in '37. They caught me at the end of the '36 season, and I got a letter from that damn Judge Bramham saying I was suspended.

18. Rebels

Note: On January 4, 1937, the National Association of Professional Baseball Leagues announced that they had blacklisted 27 players from the Carolina League because they had played in the outlaw league in 1936 while under contract to organized professional teams. The Hickory Rebels players included Hitchner, Russ Yeargren, and E.J. Porter.

The first ball game we played in Concord in '37 I was pitching against Chitwood, and that fellow Cassell that was running the Concord team sat down beside Ram Menzies, who was trying to run this ball club and said, "Ram, you know that fellow out there pitching looks a lot like that fellow Hitchner that pitched for you last year."

Ram said, "That's not Hitchner; that fellow's name is John Davis."

Anyway, I got suspended as Hitchner and Davis, and I was suspended from organized professional ball for ten years. [Hitchner did in fact get suspended a second time at the end of the 1937 season under the name of John Davis.] I guess I would still be suspended if it hadn't been for Carl Hubbell who was head of the New York Giant farm system in 1947. I was sitting down at the ballpark at that Class D League they brought in here, and I was already working with Harley Shuford at the Century Furniture Company when Hubbell asked me if I would help Sammy Bell, Hickory manager, with those young pitchers.

I said, "Carl, I can't go out there. I've been blacklisted from professional baseball."

A few innings later, Hubbell said he believed he saw my name on one of the Giants' farm team rosters. He was going to check it out.

A couple of weeks later, he called me on the phone and said he found my name on the roster of the Giants' farm team in Trenton, New Jersey.

I told him that I had never played for Trenton, and then he explained that the New York Giants had bought the Albany franchise and moved it to Trenton, and that I was on the Albany roster as an ineligible ballplayer. He told me what to do.

That damn Judge Bramham had died in Durham, and Troutman was then head of the National Association of Professional Baseball. I contacted Troutman, and in about a week, I got a letter that said I was now reinstated and in good standing and could sign with any ball club that I chose. So I signed with the Giants' Hickory team, and after ten years, I was no longer an outlaw.

From 1938 when the Carolina League ended, I played with a few mill teams until I signed to help the Giants' young pitchers in Hickory. I also won nine and lost two. I was 38 years old, and the only reason I did it was my wife was pregnant, and we needed the money. I was already working for Century Furniture that Harley Shuford started in 1947. After work, I went out there every night and ran until I could hardly stand up.

Note: When longtime Hickory Spinners scorekeeper Sam Duncan compiled his all-time best Hickory Spinners team, Hitchner made the list. The Spinners fielded powerhouse mill teams from 1925 to 1955 in Longview, a small town just west of Hickory.

During the winter I was a policeman in '36-'37, paid big money, $75 a month, twelve hours a day, six days a week. [One can hardly miss the irony of an outlaw ball player making his off season money as a man of the law.] The next winter I worked at Hotel Hickory seven days a week, eleven o'clock at night until seven o'clock in the morning for $75 a month. After the last season in '38, I went to work for Belk-Broome Department Store in the men's department. Stumpy Culbreth, our manager, worked for Shuford Hardware in the winter. Another one I worked for a ladies store up here, went out and collected bills.

One of the men that ran the ball club while I was playing was Ab Lutz. He was the one that called me in New Jersey. He ran a dry cleaning place. "Ram" Menzies was president of the ball club one year. He was also president of First Security Corporation Insurance. I think it was part of the Catawba National Bank. Others were Red Miller who was in the printing business, Major Lyerly in the hardware business, Hubert Lyerly in the hosiery mill business, "Rabbit" Hardin in furniture manufacturing, the Hardin and Suggs Furniture.

You know, those guys still owe me $596. They all lost money running the team. Hell, everybody running the teams in that outlaw league lost money. The only people making money were the players. Anyway, for several years, after we quit playing, I would see some of them in the bank and ask them, "When the hell you fellas gonna pay me that $596?" They answered, "We are in here still paying off a $5000 note."

That league was hard as nails, and the fans were just as hard. It was not unusual to see a fan use an umpire's head to open a bottle of Coca-Cola. Umpire Rube Brandon was an umpire the fans did not like. Rube did try control the game — maybe a little too much. I remember one game he missed a couple that I thought were strikes, and would just throw my head back like I couldn't believe it. He came out to the mound, and said, "If you do that again, you're out of here." I told him I could do anything I wanted to as long as I didn't say anything.

Towards the end of the 1938 season I came down with yellow

jaundice. They brought in Bryan Speese to replace me. He was an underhand, a submarine pitcher. He was supposed to be eligible for the playoffs because I got sick, but somehow the league ruled him ineligible against Kannapolis in the finals, and Kannapolis won the playoff championship with a forfeit. [Actually, Hickory, in protest of the decision, failed to show up for the last game.] That league was in a real mess when the '38 season ended. It looked like they made up rules as they went along.

The Tramp Athlete: Robert Merritt "Pat" Shores

Born: November 11, 1901, Prattville, Alabama; died: June, 1985, Hickory, North Carolina

Robert Merritt Pat Shores was born November 11, 1901, in Prattville, Alabama, about a hundred miles south of Birmingham. His father, James Wilson Shores, was a Methodist minister who also operated a furniture store. The father died when Shores was seven months old, leaving him to live with his mother, Emily Shores, off her family farmland. The mother died when Pat was eight years old, and he and his siblings were farmed out to various family members. Pat ended up with his father's widowed sister, Aunt Mary, in Birmingham. She was a severe woman who instilled discipline and order in the young man's life and also took an intense interest in his education, both mental and physical. Mary was a college educated public school teacher who eventually went on to become a stenographer and bookkeeper for a law firm. Despite her stern nature, she was a positive person and decisive when an action was required of her.

Because she was concerned about the track record of early deaths in the Shores family, she enrolled Pat in a YMCA program at a young age. There he learned and began to excel in many different sports.

Seen here in his earliest baseball picture, Robert Merritt "Pat" Shores would go on to become a high school and college coach as well as what he called a "tramp athlete" (courtesy Lenoir-Rhyne College)

When Shores finished elementary school, his aunt took him out of the public schools and enrolled him at Southern University Prep in Greensboro, Alabama. There he played in the three major sports and began his baseball career as a catcher, then moving to first base.

After spending the early part of 1918 working in a Birmingham bank because of family finances, Shores was able to enroll in the newly merged Birmingham-Southern that fall. There he again played all three major sports. The following year he was offered a full scholarship at Southern Military Academy where he lettered in three sports and even spent one season as the baseball coach when the school's coach, former major league pitcher Frank Allen, had a serious farm accident. Shores would attend two more colleges, Howard and Maryville, before completing his college work. He finally finished in 1925 and began his coaching career at Maryville High.

From there he moved to Hickory, North Carolina, where he coached the major sports at the local high school. He was incredibly successful in his five years there. His teams won a combined two hundred games while losing but forty-nine. He had eight conference champion teams and one state champion. Shores coined the team name "Red Tornadoes" while at Hickory and left an indelible mark on the lives of many of the area's young men. From Hickory High School he sidestepped to the local Lutheran college, Lenoir-Rhyne, where he coached many of the major sports up to the time of World War II. During his time as the Lenoir-Rhyne coach, Shores led twenty-nine teams to a composite record of 260 wins, 205 losses and 12 ties. He won one football, one basketball, and three baseball conference championships. His devotion to the school helped save its athletic program during the financially strapped Depression years. While Shores' teams at Lenoir-Rhyne were not quite as successful as the high school teams, there were many good ones, and he is a member of the school's sports hall of fame as well as a recently elected member of the county's sports hall of fame.

After he returned from World War II, Shores stepped down from his coaching career and embarked on a successful business career. All of his exploits are detailed in his very unique 1975 autobiography *Just Like It Was*. Shores' book, which received an endorsement from John Wooden, among others, includes a lengthy section about his years as a "tramp athlete," and more specifically his time as a summer baseball player. Beginning in 1919 Shores played for "fast" semi-pro teams for five years. These independent leagues in Mississippi and Alabama were stocked with top college players and ex-pro players in many cases. The small towns like Carterville and Selma appreciated their teams and kept them entertained with dances and "shindigs," which were infused with women from the local area. Shores enjoyed the experience, especially 1922 when he played most of the season in the South Alabama League where play was equivalent to Class B ball of the time.

18. Rebels

In 1924, he took his first pro job for Vicksburg in the Class D Cotton States League. He found the pitching tougher in pro ball, hitting .245 his first year, and the fans to be less accepting of the professional players. That did not stop him, however, from signing with Salisbury (NC) of the Class C Piedmont League the following year. He played for a month under the name "Pat Roberts" before ending his season with an independent league team in Alabama playing in the small town of Cullman. For some inexplicable reason, Shores blossomed into a home run hitter that summer, hitting somewhere between thirty and forty in his combined play with the two teams. While playing at Cullman, a Red Sox scout saw him hit two home runs, two doubles and a single in a doubleheader and signed him to a contract effective in May of the following year upon graduation from Maryville. His contract called for $400 a month and a $1000 signing bonus if he managed to stay with the team for thirty days.

Shores coached all the sports teams at Lenoir-Rhyne College in Hickory, North Carolina, during the Depression era. During the summers he played semi-pro and minor league baseball. He was also the business manager for the Carolina League Hickory Rebels team (courtesy Lenoir-Rhyne College).

Shores joined the Red Sox for a series in Chicago on May 23. I defer here to his description of that weekend:

> My adversary at first base was left handed throwing and hitting Phil Todt, who was such a fine fielder and long ball threat that he stayed with the second-division Red Sox for seven years with a career average of .250 or so. Until I saw Ferris Fain of the A's, I considered Phil the best fielder at that position I'd ever seen.

My major league "cup of coffee" consisted of that five-game series in the Windy City, and a like one in St. Louis. Each day Todt more than shared the fielding practice sessions with me, and I felt that with no comments to the contrary that I was doing okay, but I never replaced him during a game. I did get a couple pinch hits in the St. Louis series out of my only two appearances at bat. However, I have rarely mentioned this down through the years since both of them were credited to Wally Shaner, one of our utility men who quite often handled this role. The first was a medium, well-hit, line single directly over the third baseman off left hander Tom Zachary; and the other was a semi-Texas League single to right-center off right hander Elam Van Gilder. I died on first in both instances. The *Sporting News*, some years later, advised me they had no record of my ever having been with the Red Sox. I do remember, that on first reporting to the club in Chicago, this same paper listed me as Ted Shores. No doubt, I was reaping my reward then for using a fictitious name in the past in pro ball.

After the final game in the mound city, I was released outright when Manager Lee Fohl had a chance to sign experienced reliever, Lefty Gus Foreman.... Incidentally, Mr. Todt, a sort of silent type, almost talked me to distraction with his "Hello" when I arrived and "Good-bye" when I left. As to our team, we did have a miserable team by major league standards. Roy Carlisle, our big slugging right fielder from Georgia, once told me, "This club is only looking for two things. The end of the ball game and pay day." They more or less proved him correct in filling the bottom spot in the American League all season, with one of the poorest marks on the record. No sour grapes are intended by these remarks, for at the time I thought my very existence depended on me making good up there.

Pat Shores continued to play minor league and independent league ball during the summers each year after his coaching duties had been completed. In all he played for nineteen seasons, wore forty-one different uniforms, and played in twelve states. Much of his final three years, he enjoyed playing for the semi-pro Hickory Rebels team. He had become a fine pitcher in the second half of his career and had success on the mound in his adopted home town. Shores got the chance to play with not only some of his college players from Lenoir-Rhyne, but also with his greatest high school athlete, Norman "Pinkie" James, a Duke football player, who helped organize the '33 Rebels.

When his season batting average dipped below .300 in 1935, Shores decided to "hang up the spikes." The following season he began a six-year summer career as the business manager for the Rebels. It is important to remember that he was coaching all the major sports teams at Lenoir-Rhyne College during this time period and working as the manager for the Legion swimming pool. Here Shores describes his years as a business manager.

> Hanging up the spikes and glove after the 1935 season, I embarked on a six-year vocation with the same Hickory Rebels as

18. Rebels

business manager, along with the retention of my Legion Pool job. Along about that time baseball really picked up in our Western Piedmont area with the advent of what was often referred to as the outlaw league. The three prior years of night ball had whetted the fans' appetites and, despite the continuance of the Depression, area teams began paying big money for players. They attracted the cream of the college crop, and many contract jumpers from the high minors in organized professional ball.

In addition to Hickory, others to field teams during the 1936–38 era of super fast play were Lenoir, Valdese, Concord, Kannapolis, Forest City, Salisbury, and Shelby. Stumpy Culbreth ran the Rebel entry in 1936 and 1938 with Rube Wilson at the helm in 1937. Other standout holdovers from previous years were Country Boy Randleman and Chuck Nalbock, who were joined by the Scarborough brothers. The elder, Bill, a fleet, sharp-hitting outfielder, moved from the Valdese team after taking over the coaching duties at Hickory High in the fall of 1935. Brother Rae, then the star moundsman at Wake Forest College, pitched just the one season of 1936 for us before shortly making it to the majors. He spent thirteen years in the Big Top with the Washington Senators, New York Yankees, Chicago White Sox, and the Boston Red Sox, several of which he was a standout hurler.

Additional top-drawer players on our roster were Pete Susko, Vince Barton, Hawaiian Prince Henry Oano, Len Shires, major league Art's brother, and most colorful in his own right, and Fireball Tracey Hitchner, all of who had performed previously in the high minors, with two or three having had brief flings in the majors. Hitchner, upon retirement from the game, remained in Hickory.... Coming over from Valdese to play our shortfield was the exceedingly popular Louis "Babe-Papa" Vaiu. I had opposed him in 1926 when he and Joe Tinker, Jr. were the keystone combination for Sarasota in the Florida State League.

These stars gave our fans many thrills, one of the greatest being the night big slugger Vince Barton socked five home runs in a regular nine inning contest. Three opposing players of note made good in the big show. Kings Mountain native Jake Early had a long stay as the number one receiver for the Washington Senators. Duke's great punter in the 6–0 Wallace Wade victory over Jock Sutherland of Pitt on that snowy day in 1938, Eric Tipton, not only led our league in hitting one season, but continued his good stick work for a few years with Connie Mack's Athletics. Broadus Dickie Culler was Concord's stellar shortstop, and later held a regular job with the old Boston Braves for a few years. Mention of the latter performer illustrates just how difficult it is to make a prediction. Around our college circuit everyone felt that Culler of High Point College could make any basketball five in the whole country, but never figured he'd even turn pro in baseball. Durned if he didn't cross us up and stick it in the majors....

With not too many other places to go for entertainment during this era of high class baseball, going down to College Field to watch the Rebels got to be the in thing to do. Many of these fans were not satisfied with the three home games, and followed their favorites when they were on the road. Despite large crowds and good gate receipts, payday at times found us short of cash, and it was one of my duties as business manager to go begging on several occasions. We never would have made ends meet had it not been for true sportsmen and team backers such as Donald "Ram" Menzies, J.C. "Red" Miller, Ab Lutz, Walker and George Lyerly, Carl Dunklee, Frank Fox, and the like. As sound businessmen, every one of them would require proper justification for an outlay of extra funds in their various enterprises. However, they were usually a soft touch when our ball club was in financial straits....

When the high priced baseball practically broke the supporters of most clubs, we turned to the Class D professional type in 1939–41 before the war called a halt. The team nucleus in this was made up of raw youngsters primarily interested in a chance to play ball, and not so concerned with the pay....

R. M. "Pat" Shores may not have participated in the outlaw Carolina League as a player, but he certainly represented the independent spirit that so infused the operation. While his legacy is more likely to be his many coaching victories in multiple sports on both the high school and college level, what he did on the blazing hot summer baseball fields of Alabama, Mississippi and Florida should not be forgotten.

The Batboy: Harold Lail

Born: August 25, 1927, Hickory, North Carolina

Harold Lail is an exuberant athlete even at the age of seventy-nine. He is an avid golfer who still plays in tournaments with his sons and grandsons. A longtime resident of Longview, a small town on the western edge of Hickory, North Carolina, Lail is more than just an advocate for the golden days of sports in Catawba County. He is a remarkable living link to several legendary sports figures as well as to the outlaw league Hickory Rebels ball club.

18. Rebels

While serving as the batboy and clubhouse boy for the Hickory team, Lail became the personal custodian of Norman "Pinkie" James' equipment. James, a multi-sports star for many years in his native Hickory, had by this time founded his own business and traveled separately from the team. Lail also has the distinction of being Alabama Pitts' last batboy during the 1940 season. That year, perhaps the finest for the former celebrity ex-con, Lail befriended the Valdese resident who intervened when the other players picked on him. Lail also had brushes with other popular outlaw players such as Vince Barton, Bud Shaney, and Tracey Hitchner.

When Harold returned from World War II, he participated in each level as the popular sport shifted first from baseball to fast pitch and finally to slow pitch softball. He succeeded at each stop along the way. Newspaper coverage vouches for his ability as a power hitter and as a pitcher. Lail is a man who has lived through over sixty-five years of Catawba County sports and has some stories to tell.

Harold Lail (third from left, back row) was a fine ballplayer in his own right. As a youngster, Lail was the batboy and clubhouse boy for legendary outlaw players like Alabama Pitts and Vince Barton, as well as local heroes like Norman "Pinkie" James. Lail is pictured here with the Ivey Weavers team: (left to right, front row) Nolan Rozzelle, Buddy Giles, Hom Isaac, Howard Rowe, Pat Patterson, and Gary Teague; (left to right, back row) Ellis Cochran, Joel Rozzelle, Harold Lail, Howard Wright, ? Reep, and Bill Reep. Lail believes this photograph was taken in 1953 (courtesy Harold Lail).

Lail was interviewed by Tim Peeler in April 2004.

I'm Harold Lail, batboy and clubhouse boy for the Hickory Rebels. Two years in particular, we had Pete Susko; "Country Boy" Randleman, a pitcher; Bill Scarborough, he was in left field; and Stumpy Culbreth was manager and third baseman. Jack McWilliams was catching. "Pinkie" James, outfield. Vince Barton, a Canadian, was in the outfield. Jim Finger was a pitcher, about a six-foot-six-inch-tall pitcher, and "Alabama" Pitts was an outfielder. He went back over to Valdese and got stabbed to death. Hernandez was playing first base and the original Crawdad boys, Babe Viau and Len Shires, played second base and shortstop. Len would say, "You get a line." Babe would say "You get a pole." Then they'd both say, "Let's go down to the crawdad hole." They would sing these things the whole game, and it really stirred the crowd up, like a wave is what it amounted to.

Pete Susko had a Willis Night type car, and he was very proud of it, and he didn't want anybody sitting on it or leaning on it or anything like that so he rigged it with a shocker, and when anyone would lean against it or sat on his car, he'd mash a button, and they would move fast. It shocked 'em good. It was just like sticking a cattle prod to somebody. He was good at that.

Vince Barton was running late one night. And Stumpy Culbreth said to me, "Harold, when Vince gets here, I want you to get him dressed and get him on the field." Vince showed up about ten or fifteen minutes before the game, and I told Stumpy, but he's about half-drunk, and he said to get him in the shower, a cold shower. So I got him in and got him dressed, and he got to the field just as the game started, just barely made it. The game started and when it was over, Barton had five hits for six times at bat. All five were home runs. We played at the old Lenoir-Rhyne College Field. The right field line was a short line, and it had probably twenty rows of cement bleacher seats, and on top of that was a press box for football which was about thirty feet above the ground. Vince hit five home runs twenty to thirty feet over that press box. That's how strong he was. Vince Barton was a man of about 6' 2", and he weighed about 220 or 225. And it was known as Barton's Alley after that because those home runs were gigantic. They weren't little bloopers, but you can't tell that by reading it in the paper the next day.

George Bowman owned the city bus line in Hickory, and he furnished the bus transportation. I don't know the times that we'd probably be out on the road and coming back, the bus would break down. But we slept several nights on the bus or in somebody's yard. One night we were fortunate enough to stop on an overhead bridge that ran over a railroad, and we took the uniforms and laid 'em down on the concrete and slept on them till daylight till they could get a man down to take care of the bus. Charles Bowman, George's son was always the bus driver.

Bud Shaney was our groundskeeper. He was probably 5' 10" and weighed about 275 then. But he was the best at his job. When you went to play a ballgame after he had taken care of the field, no rocks, no pebbles, it was just like a carpet. It was dirt infield, but it was just like carpet. That's how well he kept it.

At that particular time, if we had a foul ball, whoever retrieved the foul ball could get a ticket for that night's game or the following night. They could turn the ball in and get it. A lot the times whoever got the ball would run. And we had some guys—we called them ball retrievers, and they'd chase these guys down and beat the tar out of 'em and get the ball back. We had one one night who took off and one of the boys that were chasing him, and the boy that had the ball, he didn't see the limb sticking out and it got him right under the chin.

We had some good times. This was some of the best ball that could be played. I would venture to say that if we took the best players from that outlaw league, there's not a team in the majors that could beat them. I really believe that. Because they knew how to hit, and they talk about these 90, 95 mile an hour pitchers, Jim Finger could throw that ball, I guarantee you, 90 to 95 miles an hour. It looked like an aspirin disintegrating. That's how hard he threw it. That's the truth.

Pinkie James, he was really my favorite player. He said to me one day, "Harold, I'm going to be taking my own car to the road games, and I want you to make sure my equipment gets to the game wherever we play." So that's the job that I took on. He said, "I'll give you a dollar for every game we play out of town to take care of my equipment." Back then, being a young man whose dad had just died two or three years before and had three sisters and my mom, an extra three or four dollars a week was a lot of money. Don't seem much today when kids come up and ask for a twenty dollar allowance. I never once let Pinkie James down on having his uniforms, his glove, his bats at the ball field where we were going to play. He was a super, super nice guy. Pinkie owned a wholesale house. When people had money back then, a lot of 'em didn't "know" people who had a lesser amount than they did. But never with him. You were the same to him if you had a million or if you had ten cents.

Note: Although Norman "Pinkie" James did not play for the outlaw Rebel teams for fear of being banned, he played an integral role in Hickory area sports, especially baseball. He organized the 1933 semi-pro Rebels team and convinced Lenoir-Rhyne College to relocate their football lights, introducing night baseball to the area. He was one of the greatest athletes to ever come from Catawba County. He held high school scoring records in basketball and football that stood for nearly forty years. He had the state high school pole vault record while at Hickory High School. He played football for Wallace Wade at Duke University, where he was also a champion diver. He held several swimming records, was a nationally ranked rifle marksman, and a state tennis champion. Later in life, he finished near the top in several national "lefty" golf tournaments. James was a successful businessman and civic leader who championed youth sports in the area as well.

> One night one of the Hickory players had his bat slip out of his hands and it went through the screen on the first base side of the ball field. A fellow by the name of Lindsay Deal got the bat and he refused to give it back. I went over to get it, and he said, "You're not getting this bat." So we kept trying to get it back. Finally, Cliff Teague, a policeman from over in Hickory, he walks over and says, "Mr. Deal, you've gotta give the bat back."
>
> And he said, "I'm not giving this bat back. It's mine." So they made about fifteen minutes of negotiations and finally gave him another bat and got the bat back. So the game went on then. But they did stop it while all this arguing was going on. It was a lot of things that happened that were never seen in the paper. It just happened, and nobody thought anything about it that day or the next day or the next day.
>
> On a given night, and this was what was really funny. You could see fifty, maybe sometimes a hundred people on the outside of the fence up in trees, perched on limbs, watching the ballgame. Or you could see fifteen or twenty, not just children, but grown men, looking through holes in the fence, or sneaking under or over the fence, being caught and escorted right back out the gate in front of everybody. In lot of cases, these people had the money to pay. They just wanted to see if they could get by with it.
>
> I enjoyed my years with them and some of the antics of some of the players. We would go to Shelby and go to Al's Drug Store with a dollar of meal money. You'd go in and the ballplayers would get a sandwich and a drink and something else. And a lot of the ballplayers would say they owe us a little something. And if you didn't watch them, they would pick up an extra pack of crackers or something and walk out the door eating it and not pay for it. But by and large, they

were all honest and good guys, just like a family. In the clubhouse, you always had a camaraderie like a perfect family, and Stumpy Culbreth was the daddy. As the manager, what he said went, and you may not like it, but you didn't disagree with him. He was a good manager, and he proved that by having winning teams the years that he was with the Rebels.

To me, I have to say these were the grand old days. I guess baseball took a backseat when fast pitch softball came in. I played baseball all my life until fast pitch came in and there were no longer any leagues. I played on semi-pro teams here with the Hickory Spinners and the Ivey Weaver West Hickory team and I played with Brockford. We played teams like Glen Alpine and Carpet City and Lenoir. Newton had a team, and a lot of these ballplayers that were on these semi-pro teams were guys that had been with the Rebels in the past, and they didn't want to move some other place.

Lail is pictured here with his bat collection in front of his Longview, North Carolina, house. During the summer of 1940, he played his sandlot baseball games in the Sing Sing Prison baseball uniform that Alabama Pitts gave him (courtesy Penny Peeler).

People don't realize that this was outlaw ball. These were outlaw players, and it wasn't that they couldn't play at a higher level. They just didn't care to be up there and to take the pressure. A lot of people really didn't know that.

One last thing — Alabama Pitts started his baseball career in Sing Sing Prison where they played one of the major league teams. And because he did so well, they managed to maneuver and work out details to get him out so he could play ball.

He played with several teams before he came to Hickory. He was a super guy — for what reason he was in prison I do not know. I think it was a grocery store robbery. Nevertheless, he got to play ball, and he came to Hickory. Anyway, I was the batboy, and one day he looked at me and said, "Harold, how would you like to have a baseball uniform?"

I said "I'd love it." He tosses me a uniform which says Sing Sing Prison across the front, and I wish I had it today. So I took it home, and I said "Mom, can you alter this uniform to fit me?" And she said, "It'll take some doing because he's a big man." So she altered it, instead of cutting it; she just seamed up and took darts where she had to. And we had a summer league, and I had my own little team, and we played at ten o'clock every Saturday morning in the summer. The Hickory Rebels gave me a used mask and chest protector, shin guards, and mitt. They gave me broken bats and balls that had been used for two or three practices. And I wore that Sing Sing Prison uniform for those ten o'clock games, and I was the only guy out there that had a uniform.

Appendix A: Pitts Family History

by Myrtice Ann Carr

The following is an addendum to the Alabama Pitts story. Myrtice Carr, second cousin to Edwin "Alabama" Pitts, shares her memories of her family and the events that surrounded her cousin's tragic death. Her knowledge of the family sheds some light on the mystery surrounding the man.

Edwin Collins Pitts was the son of Erma Mills Pitts and Edwin Pitts. Erma grew up in Opelika, Alabama, where her father was once a policeman and possibly chief of police. He had met and married her mother who had been married to a LaShea. Mrs. LaShea had one daughter, Vera, upon her marriage to Mr. Mills. Thus, Erma and Vera were half-sisters and grew up together with Mr. Mills as the head of the household. It is not known where or when Erma Mills met Mr. Pitts, but it was rumored that he was originally from Beulah community, off Highway 29 northeast of Opelika and near the Chattahoochee River separating Alabama and Georgia. It is located in Lee County, Alabama. There are still churches located there and at least one graveyard. I never knew that he was a cavalryman until I read this in newspapers years later. If this is true, he was likely stationed at Ft. Benning, Georgia, which is a few miles away from Opelika and on the Georgia-Alabama line. Would army records bear his name and further information? Being the older of the two, Vera married before Erma and lived in a house just off Highway 29, northeast of Opelika and a short "buggy ride" of the day from Beulah. She married William Rudd, oldest son of Will Rudd, farmer and son of the original settler on the land, his father having purchased said land in 1836 from an Indian whose "X" is still visible on the abstract to the deed. They had three children, Will, Edna, and Albert, but Will did not survive to adulthood. When pregnant with Albert, the father died of blood poisoning before the age of antibiotics. Edna was my mother, and she was born on February 1, 1910, and once informed me that Edwin and she were born in the same year. It is my understanding that Erma stayed with this Rudd family after her husband, Mr. Pitts died. This is where she met and married her second husband, Robert E. Rudd, the second son of Will Rudd. Thus, brothers married sisters.

On February 4, 1914, Mildred Aileen Rudd was born to Erma and Bobby Rudd. This provided Edwin Pitts with a half-sister whom he always adored, but seldom had an opportunity to see after she was about two years old. At that time Uncle Bobby was working as an overseer on a farm just outside of what was then the city limits of Opelika. Exactly what caused a divorce is not known, but records may still be available in the Lee County Court House where the decree was filed. I do recall hearing that Erma desired to work as a secretary, and this did not set well with her husband or his father. The grandfather became involved in the custody hearing process and demanded custody of Mildred. The judge (who knew him well) awarded said custody of Mildred to William Rudd or possibly to Uncle Bobby. But, he awarded custody of Edwin Pitts to the mother, Erma Pitts Rudd. It is most likely that my great-grandfather refused to take him since he was not "of his blood." There was certainly such an incident of this occurring a few years later when Vera married again, moved to Peoria, Illinois, and was most unhappy there as were her children. Yet another uncle brought them home, but she was already pregnant with her new husband's child. When the child was born, she died 3 days later, and the grandfather refused to take him in, instead allowing the attending physician to adopt him. His reasoning was that he would take care of his "own blood," but no others. Thus the reason for the separation of the siblings. Please note that Uncle Bobby Rudd, the stepfather, did not die until 1977 or 1978 after marrying again and fathering about 9 children by his second wife. Many of these children still live on the same farmland as do their children. The farmhouses of William and of Will still stand as does the church the original Rudd started and the cemetery he provided the land to establish. Mildred Rudd Gillespie Oliver is buried in this cemetery next to her first husband, Dan C. Gillespie. She died in February of 1996.

The grandfather, William, now had several grandchildren in his home to rear. These included Mildred, little Will, Edna, Albert, and later David Martin Harris, son of his daughter. These children were a hand full for the elder Rudds to care for, some of whom could be rather wild. Fortunately, there were numerous aunts and uncles around to help out. This did make for a very close relationship among the grandchildren who became closer than brothers or sisters would normally become. My mother, Edna, the oldest of the group, left home to work in Opelika first, and married first. Subsequently, she and my father opened their home to the younger ones as they flew the coop. All lived with them in their home on Avenue E at one time or another. That same open door was given to Edwin, and this could account for his providing their address in Opelika as his home. Because rural schools did not always go through the 12 grade, William and his wife purchased a house in town and lived there during the school years to allow these grandchildren the opportunity to get an education. They returned to the farmhouse during the summers and holidays as he turned over much of the farming to the sons who were all of age, except two who chose to work outside of farming. When all were through school, one son purchased the house after his marriage and another purchased one around the corner. Mildred and Edna moved in with them, alternating between homes until my mother, Edna married my father, Lewis C. Greene. He was a motorcycle cop, the first of such in Opelika, under his father, the chief of police during the late 1920s and early to mid-1930s. They married in 1928 and moved into a house on the corner of 8th Street and Avenue E in Opelika. Mildred followed them by moving into a room there and enrolled in school at Troy State Teachers College (now Troy University). One of the uncles paid for her education beginning around 1932, but she made this address as her home for summers and holidays. She later transferred to Alabama Polytech Institute (now Auburn University) to complete her degree in elementary education. She continued living with my parents after completing her schooling and beginning to work as a first grade teacher at Smith Station (now Smiths, Alabama). She commuted with several other teachers daily.

In 1935 or possibly 1936, Edwin Pitts came to stay for a while and lived in our home as well. Mildred's schooling was drawing to a close, and Edwin purchased her a car to possibly use commuting to school. I was born on December 29, 1933, but have a vague memory of him as a large body in and out of the house. Mildred was a quiet and self-contained person who rarely showed emotion, but was very sentimental. During Edwin's stay with us, he took her to a ballgame in Montgomery and bought her a corsage with a small football attached. The remnants of this corsage hung on her dresser in her room until she married in 1946. I suspect she took it with her.

During the early years of growing up, the Rudd family lived in their ancestral home in the country near what is now called the Shady Grove Church community on Highway 29, north. All was not easy for Mildred during these years since her mother had been granted visitation rights. Erma would show up, unannounced, apparently out of nowhere as she had no buggy or car to transport her. It was a good 3 miles to the house from the main highway. It was assumed that she caught a ride, then walked the rest of the way. As soon as she arrived, she would pick Mildred up, take her inside, bathe her completely, then dress her in garments she brought with her. This was not a pleasant experience for Mildred. Next, she actually kidnapped her from the school grounds. She was hunted down and caught, and Mildred was returned to her grandparents' custody. A watch was then placed on her, both at school and at home. Yet, a second time Erma attempted to kidnap the child, but was thwarted. From then on, an adult watched her constantly for fear of another kidnapping. This caused her to fear her mother, and she was overly protected to her dismay. These incidents apparently caused Edna to fear Erma greatly. No one ever knew how Erma earned a living for herself or for Edwin. No one was able to determine how she was able to travel about the country, alone, so much. Nor, did she reveal where Edwin was during these visits. Some thought she was living and working in Birmingham where her father was a police officer in the old Southside area. Mr. Mills lived in a large, old home on Highland Avenue in Southside until his death in the 1940s. Yet, he did not associate with his grandfather there. This is still a mystery.

Erma did discover that Mildred was living with Edna on Avenue E in Opelika and came to town to locate her. She did this several times and Mildred was always thankful to have been away in college when she came. Mother was not so thankful as she was very afraid of Erma, her aunt. My father was in a situation to know when she arrived, somehow, and always called Mother ahead of time, so she could lock her doors and not answer her knocks. He would then get on his motorcycle and come to her rescue. He was excellent at handling difficult situations. I have often wondered if she was also looking for Edwin since these visits appeared to have coincided around his visits. Since she lost Mildred, she appeared to try too hard to hang onto Edwin, thus some of his problems. Upon hearing of his arrest and incarceration, she went to New York and sought out a law library where she studied ways to get him out of prison. She may have even teamed up with the warden as I have seen a film of her speaking outside of the prison on the day of his release. I have heard that she was an excellent typist, and this may account for how she supported herself. She was reputed to have been a brilliant person. Mildred was an "A" student in college. High intelligence appears to run in the family on their mother's side (Mrs. Mills). Somehow, I got a little of that myself, thankfully. From all that I heard from the Methodist Children's Home, Edwin's daughter, Patsy, was very intelligent. Edwin never returned to Opelika after the visit when he bought Mildred a car. As a child, I heard constant talk about him in the family and hoped he would show up again. My father was killed while working on the Central of Georgia Railroad in Columbus, Georgia, on October 12, 1940. Mildred was still living with us and commuting to Smith's Station to teach with little 5 year old me tagging along and being taught by her in the first grade. One of the uncles also moved in to help Mother with bills, etc.

In June of 1941, Mother; Albert; his wife, Mary; daughter, Shirley; Mildred; and this writer were to take our annual vacation together with a trip to North Carolina to visit with Edwin; his wife, Mary; and little daughter, Patrician Ann (Patsy). He had given her the name Ann after my name, Myrtice Ann. I was so excited to get to meet her and see Edwin. We were to leave on Sunday driving to Valdese, and Edwin had reserved rooms for us in the local hotel. On Saturday morning I was busy getting my little things packed for the trip when the phone rang. Mildred was not only my school teacher, but was my baby sitter as well. She answered the phone, and her world turned upside down as someone in Valdese had called to tell her about Edwin's death during the early hours of the day.

Plans immediately changed, and we quickly completed our packing and called Albert who lived in Manchester, Georgia. We left as soon as Mother got off work at the local department store and drove to Manchester where we picked up Albert, Mary, and Shirley. We drove all night and reached Valdese in the very early morning. In my memory, everything appeared to be in disarray. Mary, Edwin's wife, did not feel she could plan the funeral. Albert ended up doing this at the funeral home. I met Patsy for the first time and fell in love with the little thing. Albert spent his time attempting to learn the details of his murder. During that time, he apparently developed contacts with people in the area who later fed him information about Mary. The funeral is hazy in my memory, but I do recall a large volume of people in that small funeral home. What I do recall most vividly, however, was the funeral procession to Fallston and the cemetery. Please remember that I was only seven years old, and Shirley was only six. Yet, we both have some memory of the event. We were traveling just behind the hearse, and I looked back at the procession following and could never make out an end to it. We were all impressed. I later read that there were 50 cars in the procession. We drove up to this little white Methodist church and parked on a slight incline facing the church. For some reason, Mother and Albert would not allow Shirley and me to depart from the car during this service. We watched from a distance. In 2003, I ventured to Fallston to locate the cemetery and Edwin's grave. My son was with me along with his wife, but I could not remember the name of the church. Tim drove up to the Methodist church there and stopped the car. I looked around and knew I had been there before even though the church had expanded and was now a brick one. The cemetery was located to the left as before. It took some time to confirm the location to be correct because I was asking about a Walker Memorial Church (wrong name). When asking the funeral home director if he knew the location of a famous baseball player's grave, he immediately knew where Edwin was buried, but informed me there was no tombstone to direct us. Much to our surprise, we did find a tombstone on the grave.

The object of my search for the grave was to locate clues as to where

I could find Patsy, the daughter. I figured that whoever placed the stone on the grave would know where to locate her. The secretary at the Baptist church across the street provided me names and phone numbers of the most elderly Walkers in the area since Mary was a Walker. I contacted them and no one remembered her parents or knew of her. It was interesting to note the secretary of the Methodist church's reaction to my request for information as to who purchased the stone. She asked me why so many people came looking for that tombstone. She knew he had been a famous baseball player, but stated that everyone thought he was visiting the area and became sick and died there. That is when I left my name and phone number with her in case other people came asking questions. The Baptist secretary stated that about 20 years ago they and the Methodists cleaned up and organized that cemetery, and recalled the tombstone was likely purchased then. While at the funeral, Albert inquired of Mary as to where Erma was and had she been informed of Edwin's death. She directed him to Morganton's Mental Institution and stated that Erma had threatened her and Patsy requiring Edwin to have her committed there. After the funeral, we drove to this facility and Albert asked for Erma Rudd since this was her legal name. They had no such person there. Needless to say, this puzzled all of us, but figured if she was out, then she could be wandering around and would eventually show up in Opelika. We went searching for her and for Mary and Patsy in December of 1946. Albert maintained contact with someone in Valdese who suggested that we search for Erma under the last name of Pitts and search for Mary at a specific hotel in Greensboro.

Albert; his wife, Mary; Shirley; Edna and this writer went to Morganton first and located Erma there under the name Erma Pitts. It was learned that Edwin used this name to make it a legal commitment. Shirley and I were not allowed to visit with Erma, but Albert, Mother, and Mary did have a long visit. Apparently, Mother had lost some of her fear or felt it safe to visit where there were guards to protect her. She reported that Erma recognized her immediately, and instead of a greeting said, "Edna, why are you wearing camouflage?" She assumed this was because she was wearing modern type makeup. Her specialty at Hagedorn's department store was cosmetics. Mildred had married Dan Gillespie the July previous to this trip and was residing in Spencer, Iowa, where he worked as a jeweler and she taught school. None of the group ever suggested bringing Erma to Alabama or any other alternative. She died about 4 years later in the facility and was buried on the grounds. Mildred had been notified of her location and had sent her mother money monthly. She paid for the burial, but did not elect to have the body brought to Opelika. No one ever knew the exact diagnosis of her mental problem, but she was obsessive compulsive.

After locating Erma, we drove to Greensboro and obtained rooms in the hotel where Albert had been told Mary worked in the restaurant as a waitress. We managed to procure a table that evening that she was in charge of and reintroduced ourselves to her, much to her surprise. There we learned that Patsy had been placed in the Methodist children's home in Winston-Salem as she did not have the funds to pay for child care and work odd hours as well. We asked permission to visit Patsy and were granted same. It was odd to us that Mother and Albert had to strongly reassure Mary that we did not intend to kidnap Patsy or remove her from the home. I still wonder if Erma had expressed her own experience with Mildred when she was awarded to the grandparents and had instilled this thought with Mary. For some reason, she was under the impression that Edwin's Alabama relatives were rich. We were not at that time, but were hard working people with much extended family support.

The following day we drove to Winston-Salem and located the children's home. I had to choke back tears when Patsy was brought out to see us. She was dirty and had on a dress with the skirt half torn from the waist. We were able to take her for a drive around the campus, but dared not try going further with her. She sat in my lap the entire time and was thrilled to learn that part of her name was from my name. She clung to me, and I cried when we had to leave her. Before we left, Albert and Mother established a bank account through the home for her to purchase clothing and school supplies. We subsequently replenished the fund constantly, even until 1950 or 1951. Since she was in the first grade, I arranged to correspond with her and continued to do so on a monthly basis for 4 or 5 years.

My mother, Edna, married my stepfather in May of 1950 in Opelika. C.G. "Son" Littleton was from an old family there and had introduced my parents to each other. He was a veteran of the 8th Air Corps in England and had a severe drinking problem upon his return, but would not discuss anything about his flying experience. Mother encouraged him in his efforts to stop the drinking and promised she would marry him if he quit. He did so, and they were married. He immediately purchased a cattle farm and moved us to a rural area where we had not only cattle, but horses to ride, too. This was a sideline for him as he owned a real estate and insurance agency. Truthfully, it was a teenager's paradise, and I had a very happy environment where all the kids from my school enjoyed the farm and horses with me.

Years later I learned I was the envy of the girls in my class at school. My stepfather bought me a car, so I could continue schooling in the city system with my friends. The only restriction placed on riding and enjoying the farm was that we had to attend our denomination's youth services on Sunday evenings if we played on Sunday afternoons. No one complained about this, and my stepfather became a surrogate father for several of the boys. They all became highly successful businessmen or bankers. I tell this to end my story, for "Son," my stepfather came to me one day as I was writing to Patsy and suggested that he and Mother would like to adopt her as I had wanted to bring her for a summer visit. We got together with Mother, and I typed up a letter to the administrator of the children's home requesting guidance on what action to take to adopt Patsy. They took this under advisement, then contacted Mary regarding the request. We received a letter from the home stating that after making the request to her, Mary came to the home, jerked Patsy out, and disappeared with her. That was the last contact any of us have had with Patsy. In 1956, Albert contacted me while I was living in Atlanta and said he had received word that Mary had married again and was living and working in a hotel in Atlanta. Without her new name, I was not able to locate her for him. Several years passed; then Albert informed me he had heard that Mary had moved to Louisiana. He heard no more after that.

Albert died in June of 1975 with "Son" passing away in February of 1976. Mildred died in February of 1996, and my mother in April of 1999. Albert's wife, Mary, is still living, but is in a nursing home in Auburn. Shirley married Martin Dorman, former safety director at the Marshall Space Center in Huntsville, and in his retirement he set up and serviced the electronics system for West Point Stevens. They reside in Opelika, but help their son manage the Auburn Furniture Store in Auburn. I married Thomas (Tom) Carr, a Methodist minister in the Alabama West-Florida Conference. He was killed in a car wreck in Pensacola in 1975. I returned to Opelika for several years or until I completed my master's in vocational rehabilitation counseling and moved to Birmingham for my first job in the private rehabilitation field in 1979. I have been here ever since. Mildred's husband died, and she married again to Percy Oliver, and they retired to Pensacola. He died in 1984, and I moved her to Birmingham to look after her as she had no children. She was like my second mother.

Appendix B:
Henry Whitley's Team Record

Henry Whitley, the business manager and general manager of the Kannapolis Towelers, kept copious records of game statistics. Included here is an example of part of the 1937 season record. An example of Whitley's fastidious effort would be his inclusion of how many double-plays were turned by various team combinations. One gets a better idea of the player volume as well. Whitley lists 17 pitchers in his "Won-lost" section ad 17 again in the "Struck-out-by" section.

The hitting figures here are slightly inflated from those published previously. Barton has two extra home runs, and Marvin Watts, Razz Miller, and Barton all have higher RBI totals. One must speculate that either non-league or playoff games were included in the totals.

Appendix B

Home Runs

Barton	29
Suggs	20
Heath	13
Tipton	12
M. Watts	10
E. Taylor	7
H. Watts	6
Morris	4
Miller	3
Dunbar	3
parks	3
Hart	1
Jones	1
Cairus	1
Total	113

	Won	Lost
Rhem	3	2
V. Taylor	10	7
Wilson	10	6
Dakus	3	3
parker	7	4
Hayes	6	2
White	9	5
Mobley	1	2
Hart	6	6
Grisdale	2	1
Dennis	0	1
spencer	1	0
Strickland	1	3
Shelton	0	1
Shaney	1	3
Coleman	1	2

Runs Batted in

M. Watts	97
Barton	94
Miller	87
Suggs	70
Heath	64
H. Watts	53
E. Taylor	46
Tipton	51
parks	37
Morris	26
Harris	15
Dunbar	14
Jones	13
Cairus	8
V. Taylor	4
sten Hart	2

Struck out By

White	93
parker	63
Hayes	58
Wilson	54
Hart	53
V. Taylor	49
Dakus	30
Mobley	22
Rhem	18
Dennis	14
Shaney	14
Strickland	12
shelton	6
Coleman	6
Grisdale	5
porter	2
spencer	1

Total 490

Appendix C: Selected Batting and Pitching Statistics

Key to Teams and Leagues: Alb/New, Albany/Newark; Am. As., American Association; Bi. St., Bi-State League; Cape B, Cape Breton League; Car-Tx, Carolina Textile League; Cot. St., Cotton State League; Ft. W/SA, Fort Worth/San Antonio; Gast./Vald., Gastonia/Valdese; Gboro, Greensboro; Hunt.Dayt., Huntington/Daytona; Int., International League; Mid-Atl., Mid-Atlantic League; Mil./Tol., Milwaukee/Toledo; New E, New England League; NY-PN, New York-Penn League; N.C. St., North Carolina State League; P. Coast, Pacific Coast League; W. Car., Western Carolina League

Selected Batting Statistics

ULMONT BAKER

Year	Team	League	G	AB	R	H	2B	3B	HR	RBI	BA	SB
1928	Gboro	Piedmont	115	401	55	98	21	1	12	56	.244	2
1929	Gboro	Piedmont	130	466	78	142	22	9	20	80	.305	8
1930	Alexandria	Cot. St.	56	231	47	77	11	2	10	42	.333	9
	Shreveport	Texas	46	149	23	50	11	0	3	30	.314	1
1931	Ft. Worth	Texas	111	395	38	104	15	2	4	57	.263	1
1932	Ft. W/SA	Texas	129	468	45	117	18	4	3	45	.250	6
1933	Htgtn-Dayton	Mid-Atl.	132	523	80	149	23	6	14	93	.285	1
1934	Dayton	Mid-Atl.	123	482	62	143	35	4	5	58	.297	3
1935	Ft. Wayne		27	113	19	36	10	2	3	19	.319	14
1937	Concord	Carolina		258	39	68	18	1	3	35	.264	2
1938	Concord	Carolina		356	57	104	25	5	6	48	.279	4
1939	Concord	N.C. St.	108	418	83	139	44	3	3	76	.333	8
1940	Concord	N.C. St.	110	460	75	154	48	7	10	103	.335	13
1941	Concord	N.C. St.	98	375	65	125	42	0	7	78	.333	16
1942	Knoxville		22	94	15	29	5	0	1		.309	6

Vince Barton

Year	Team	League	G	AB	R	H	2B	3B	HR	RBI	BA	SB
1928	Baltimore	Int.	63	155	26	47	10	0	4	34	.285	1
1929	Allen, NH	Int.	106	446	70	136	37	10	7	76	.305	11
	Baltimore	Int.										
1930	Baltimore	Int.	150	589	143	201	38	13	32	133	.341	8
1931	Chicago	National	66	239	45	57	10	1	13	50	.238	1
	LA	P. Coast	83	334	60	101	21	6	17	67	.302	4
1932	Albany	Int.	105	384	57	113	18	4	18	70	.294	8
	Chicago	National	36	134	19	30	2	3	3	15	.224	0
1933	Alb/New	Int.	118	427	55	105	18	2	12	69	.246	1
1934	Newark	Int.	146	544	97	142	32	5	32	115	.261	3
1935	Baltimore	Int.	114	381	69	109	15	7	27	85	.286	8
1936	Syracuse	Int.	44	155	20	37	5	8	1	18	.239	4
	Birmingham	Southern	16	61	7	14	3	0	1	7	.230	1
	Kannapolis	Carolina	NA									
1937	Kannapolis	Carolina		300	74	96	15	5	27	77	.320	6
1938	Hickory	Carolina		361	97	117	19	8	26	82	.324	3
1939	Granby	Canadian	73	255	46	73	19	2	7	55	.286	6

Lawrence Davis

Year	Team	League	G	AB	R	H	2B	3B	HR	RBI	BA	SB
1937	Gastonia	Carolina		270	46	72	9	5	5	46	.267	2
1940	Philadelphia	American	23	67	4	18	1		0	9	.269	
1941	Philadelphia	American	39	105	6	23	3		0	8	.219	
1942	Philadelphia	American	86	272	31	61	8		2	26	.224	
1946	Lawrence	New E	113	440	78	131	23		19	94	.298	
1947	Lawrence/L/P	New E	118	420	71	128	23		2	79	.300	
1948	Durham	Carolina	143	540	106	171	50		10	80	.317	
1949	Raleigh	Carolina	124	453	59	134	34		7	60	.296	
1950	Raleigh/Reids.	Carolina	133	497	60	130	29		4	46	.262	
1951	Raleigh	Carolina	140	480	69	124	28		2	66	.258	
1952	Raleigh	Carolina	116	416	55	96	15		1	41	.231	

Bobby Hipps

Year	Team	League	G	AB	R	H	2B	3B	HR	RBI	BA
1926	Hartford	Eastern	126	16	34	8	1	1	0		.270
	Chattanooga	Southern	39	124	21	42	4	3	2		.339
1927	Chattanooga	Southern	69	258	33	54	9	4	1	29	.248
	Asheville	South Atlantic	84	312	31	79	15	6	2		.253
1928	Durham	Piedmont	46	164	17	42	5	2	0	15	.257
1929	Asheville	South Atlantic	140	501	68	162	25	7	5	72	.323
1930	Asheville	South Atlantic	134	534	105	184	26	11	3	78	.345
1931	Asheville	Piedmont	130	481	104	173	36	17	11	106	.360
1932	Tulsa	Western	143	592	147	171	26	10	9	75	.289

Selected Batting and Pitching Statistics

Year	Team	League	G	AB	R	H	2B	3B	HR	RBI	BA
1933	Knoxville	Southern	126	470	73	136	17	4	7	81	.289
1934	Asheville	Piedmont	18	56	4	10	2	1	0	5	.179
	Williamsport	NY-Penn	96	354	47	92	22	1	6	59	.260
1935	Cooleemee	Car-Tex.									
	Kannapolis	Car-Tex.		144	26	39	8	3	4		.342
1936	Concord	Carolina		180	42	58	15	2	8	42	.322
1937	Concord	Carolina		300	71	95	12	7	12	56	.317
1938	Lenoir	Carolina		338	79	122	20	7	8	50	.361

GLENN MILLER

Year	Team	League	G	AB	R	H	2B	3B	HR	RBI	BA	SB
1935	Landis	Car-Tx		278	76	82	11	3	4		.295	
1936	Kannapolis	Carolina		203	45	69	9	2	5	39	.340	5
1937	Kannapolis	Carolina		334	47	104	16	2	5	74	.311	14
1938	Kannapolis	Carolina		410	76	133	23	7	6	48	.324	7
1939	Martinsville	Bi-State	85	317	65	98	18	3	6	61	.309	10
1940	Kannapolis	N.C. St.	50	177	21	47	12	1	1	16	.266	3
1942	Concord	N.C. St.	87	297	31	40	18	3	1	40	.303	1

EDWIN PITTS

Year	Team	League	G	AB	R	H	2B	3B	HR	RBI	BA	SB
1935	Albany	Int.	43	116	14	27	3	0	0	9	.233	2
1936	York/Trenton	NY-PN	41	156	26	35	6	0	2	11	.228	2
1937	Winston-Sal.	Piedmont	23	71	13	20	2	1	4	17	.278	0
	Gast./Vald.	Carolina		321	96	107	21	6	14	73	.333	7
1938	Lenoir	Carolina		336	68	90	16	1	10	58	.268	4
1940	Hickory	Tar Heel	64	245	48	74	14	1	0	39	.302	5

NORMAN SMALL

Year	Team	League	G	AB	R	H	2B	3B	HR	RBI	BA
1934	Martinsville	Bi. St.	40	123	24	37	12	3	2	Ng	.301
1935	Asheville	Piedmont	15	58	14	11	2	0	0	3	.190
	Greenwood	E. Dixie	16	49	2	8	2	0	0	3	.163
	Martinsville	Bi. St.	47	135	12	33	5	1	1	Ng	.244
1936	York	NYP	2	7	1	1	0	0	0	0	.143
1937	Mooresville	N.C. St.	35	148	44	58	12	2	12	51	.392
	Durham	Piedmont	38	318	49	87	18	7	2	42	.274
1938	Durham	Piedmont	69	276	40	76	9	9	5	43	.275
	Waterloo	Three I	9	29	3	2	0	0	0	2	.070
	Columbia	South At.	21	78	10	32	6	1	2	16	.410
1939	Columbia	South At.	111	455	60	123	24	10	6	54	.270
	Meridian	So. East.	11	39	9	11	2	0	4	7	.282
1940	Mooresville	N.C. St.	103	437	95	151	41	6	25	115	.346
1941	Mooresville	N.C. St.	95	386	75	128	22	8	18	73	.332

Year	Team	League	G	AB	R	H	2B	3B	HR	RBI	BA
1942	Mooresville	N.C. St.	100	383	91	144	35	6	32	107	.376
1943	Jersey City	Int.	53	168	21	42	10	1	4	19	.250
1946	Mooresville	N.C. St.	99	388	100	135	31	10	18	69	.348
1947	Mooresville	N.C. St.	104	398	106	143	36	2	31	102	.359
1948	Mooresville	N.C. St.	110	431	103	154	32	4	33	130	.357
1949	Mooresville	N.C. St.	124	456	115	157	20	4	41	152	.344
1950	Mooresville	N.C. St.	98	350	73	103	23	0	32	104	.294
1951	Hickory	N.C. St.	126	485	106	165	35	6	37	127	.340
1952	Hickory	W. Car.	20	32	15	28	10	2	2	13	.341
	Raleigh	Carolina	112	419	59	113	25	4	12	68	.270
1953	Mooresville	Tar Heel	95	385	75	131	31	1	14	87	.340

Marvin Watts

Year	Team	League	G	AB	R	H	2B	3B	HR	RBI	BA	SB
1937	Kannapolis	Carolina		391	79	125	18	3	11	85	.320	1
1938	Kannapolis	Carolina		260	43	72	13	4	6	40	.277	0
1940	Concord	N.C. St.	95	352	65	95	24	4	7	60	.270	2
1941	Mooresville	N.C. St.	94	349	60	95	26	1	10	65	.272	4
1942	Concord	N.C. St.	98	366	51	116	30	4	6	64	.317	3

Selected Pitching Statistics

George Barley

Year	Team	League	G	IP	W	L	H	R	BB	SO	ERA
1936	Kannapolis	Carolina	Inc.	45	4	1	41	24	14	23	
1937	Binghamton	Int.	No	Dec.							
1938	Binghamton	Int.	23	189	15	5	153	63	53	113	2.24
1939	Newark	Int.	40	174	10	10	189	89	76	71	4.09
1940	Newark	Int.	27	135	15	9	196	105	47	92	4.43
1941	Kansas City	Am. As.	30	167	11	13	174	80	68	77	3.50
1946	Jersey City	Int.	22	70	3	3	73	38	31	20	3.99

Tracey Hitchner

Year	Team	League	G	IP	W	L	H	R	BB	SO	ERA
1935	Albany	Int.	17	43	1	3	48	33	20	10	5.44
1936	Hickory	Carolina	NA								
1937	Hickory	Carolina		123	9	6	123	73	75	85	
1938	Hickory	Carolina	21	142	10	4	132	80	83	117	
1947	Hickory	N.C. St.	15	79	6	2	82	47	45	86	4.67

Selected Batting and Pitching Statistics

Lee Ross

Year	Team	League	G	IP	W	L	H	R	BB	SO	ERA
1935	Kannapolis	CarTex.			16	6					
1936	Philadelphia	American	30	201	9	14	253	146	83	47	5.82
1937	Philadelphia	American	28	147	5	10	183	102	63	35	4.90
1938	Philadelphia	American	29	184	9	16	218	132	80	54	5.33
1939	Philadelphia	American	29	174	6	14	216	143	95	43	6.00
1940	Philadelphia	American	24	156	5	10	160	91	60	43	4.38
1941	Philadelphia	American	1	4	0	1	10	9	2	0	18.00
	Chicago	American	20	108	3	8	99	51	43	30	3.16
1942	Chicago	American	22	113	5	7	118	63	39	37	5.02
1943	Chicago	American	21	149	11	7	140	61	56	41	3.20
1944	Chicago	American	20	90	2	7	97	56	35	20	5.20
1945	Chicago	American	13	37	1	1	51	28	17	8	5.79
1946	Milwaukee	Am. As.	21	110	9	6	121	48	31	43	3.27
1947	Milwaukee	Am. As.	30	159	10	13	200	102	69	64	5.09
1948	Mil/Tol.	Am. As.	29	76	3	6	97	55	33	34	6.28

Bud Shaney

Year	Team	League	G	IP	W	L	H	R	BB	SO	ERA
1922	Independence	S West	32	233	19	8	195	90	61	152	2.59
1923	Independence	S West	42	312	18	18	317	150	60	168	
	Milwaukee	Am. As.	8	47	4	2	63	26	11	9	4.21
1924	Milwaukee	Am. As.	24	85	2	6	113	60	26	25	5.51
	Mobile	S Atl.	12	65	2	6	100	52	17	23	5.68
1925	Mobile	S Atl.	4	4	0	1	16	13	5	0	
	Asheville	S Atl.	38	233	13	10	271	126	54	86	3.86
1926	Asheville	S Atl	40	262	19	14	315	156	56	90	4.33
1927	Asheville	S Atl	41	273	15	14	271	110	46	95	2.74
1928	Asheville	S Atl	42	257	21	11	270	104	55	93	2.59
1929	Asheville	S Atl.	37	255	17	12	295	128	62	92	3.67
1930	Williamsport	NY/PN	35	224	14	14	219	92	49	72	3.38
1931	Charlotte	Piedmont	39	280	24	10	258	126	67	161	
1932	Charlotte	Piedmont	37	235	14	13	288	146	52	129	4.79
1933	W-B/Scrant.	NY/PN	38	199	7	15	238	112	47	60	4.48
1934	Columbia	Piedmont	12	44	3	3	59	44	17	16	
1935	Portsmouth	Piedmont	19	98	6	5	127	70	35	28	5.42
1936	Charlotte mid-season only	Carolina		125	13	0	131	51	15	101	
1937	Trenton	NY/PN	17	100	5	5	105	49	15	36	3.15
	Sydney	Cape B	5	31	3	1	19	4	5	23	0.29
1938	Spartanburg	Sally	15	84	3	6	100	54	8	42	4.29
1940	Hickory	Tar Heel	33	194	12	10	202	98	25	111	3.71
1941	Asheville	Piedmont	1	8	0	1	9	4	0	0	4.50

Appendix C

Year	Team	League	G	IP	W	L	H	R	BB	SO	ERA
1942	Hickory	N.C. St.	30	179	8	9	199	94	16	88	2.92
1953	Asheville	Tri-St.	1	5	0	0	9	3	0	2	5.40
1954	Asheville	Tri-St.	1	5	1	0	4	0	1	0	0.00
1955	Asheville	Tri-St.	1	2	0	1	7	7	2	2	31.50

Appendix D: The Carolina Victory League

As summer approached in 1943, the second full year of World War II, the American home front was beginning to feel the full brunt of all-out war. Rationing of everyday needs was commonplace. But most important, more and more men were being drafted into the armed forces and more casualty and death notices were being received by the parents and wives of the men already fighting.

America was taking the offensive. U.S. and Australian forces took Buna, New Guinea. U.S. bombs fell in the first U.S. air attack on Germany. U.S. troops secured Guadalcanal. Sicily was invaded. Anglo-U.S. Headquarters, to plan the invasion of Europe, was set up in Britain on March 23, 1943.

Professional baseball, like all other non-essential work, began to feel the pinch. In 1941 there were 41 professional minor leagues. In 1942, 31 leagues started the season, but only 26 leagues completed the season. Able bodied athletes were being drafted into the armed forces by the hundreds. In 1943 only 10 professional baseball leagues started the season. Among the casualties from the 1942 season was the Class D N.C. State league composed of mostly textile towns with team names such as the Concord Weavers, Mooresville Moors, Thomasville Tommies, Landis Senators, Lexington Indians, Statesville Owls, Salisbury Giants, and the Hickory Rebels. Only two of these teams were affiliated with major league teams—the Thomasville Tommies, who were associated with the Cleveland Indians, and the Salisbury Giants, working with the New York Giants. The remainder were independently owned and operated by local businessmen. It appeared that if these textile towns in piedmont North Carolina were to have any baseball in 1943 it would be semi-pro mill teams playing each other within one town's geographical area.

However, one man, C. Manley Llewellyn (respected lawyer and former judge), who had been president of the N.C. State League for four years, stepped forth to give guidance and leadership to this historical hotbed of baseball. (Later Llewellyn would be president of the Class D N.C. State

1943 Victory League Champion Concord Weavers — Front row, left to right: Richard Mauney, pitcher; Bob Boger; Billy Goodman, infield; Ginger Watts, catcher/manager; Harold McAnulty; Ralph Ritchie; Johnny Talent, catcher; second row: Chaver Allred; Troy Furr, infield; Boots Fletcher, 1st base; Archie White, pitcher; Bill Kluttz; Leroy Stewart; third row: "Toots" Rogers; Slim Ingram, 1st base; Virgil (Coddle Creek) Taylor, pitcher; Don Harwood; Marvin Watts, infield; Shade Honeycutt. This team included many former Carolina League stars as well as seventeen-year-old Billy Goodman who went on to have a sixteen year major league career. Ten years later, in 1953, he led the American League in hitting with a .354 average. Richard Mauney also went on to pitch for the wartime Philadelphia Phillies in 1945 where he posted a 6–10 record. In 1946 he won 6 and lost 4, and in 1947 he made nine appearances with no decisions and one save (Hank Utley).

League two more years, 1945–46, and president of the Class B Tri-State League five years—1946–50) As president of the now defunct N.C. State League, he encouraged these small textile towns to organize town semi-pro teams that would play close-by neighboring towns. Thus was born the Carolina Victory League — semi-pro baseball at its best during wartime restrictions but also at its worst with the typical textile town intrigue, fighting, gambling and plain ol' baseball cheatin.' It would be no easy task to make this league a success.

Organization

By March 25, 1943, just a few days into spring, N.C. State League president C. Manley Llewellyn said, "I want to see baseball continue in the communities of our N.C. State League this season despite the fact that we were forced to close shop. It was impossible for our clubs to continue this year due mainly to the player shortage. But that doesn't mean necessarily that baseball in our cities must cease for the duration. Up and down streets these days, even on the golf course, I find people discussing what will be done about baseball on the local front. They want baseball this year, probably more than ever because a few hours of relaxation and recreation come in handy after a hard day's work."

In Concord, NC, the home of the Concord Weavers, Claude Weddington, who organized two local semi-pro leagues in 1942, was elected president, and Roy Christenbury, *Concord Tribune* writer, was elected secretary-treasurer of an organization that would pursue a town semi-pro team and an inter-city semi-pro league. Llewellyn praised these men and their work on the local baseball front. "They are doing exactly what should be accomplished in every town of the N.C. State League. It has been a hard job because most of the boys (semi-pro and professional) who played last year are now in the service of our country. This will mean much to the smaller cities during wartime. It will keep alive the sport for both the players and spectators, and the use of the lights at Webb Field for night games will tend to elevate the game to professional league style. It means a lot to a player to play night ball. It just seems more like organized (professional) ball. I hope baseball leaders in our N.C. State League cities can organize semi-pros for regular league baseball this season. Some of our boys who get started this year may develop into stars of tomorrow, but more than that, it's our job to keep some form of recreation at home." Little did C. Manley Llewellyn know that Billy Goodman, a seventeen-year-old, Concord native and future (1950) American League batting champ, would get his start in the 1943 Carolina Victory League.

With those words, Llewellyn initiated a compact semi-pro league (made up of aged professional veterans and youngsters) that would provide the piedmont North Carolina home front needed recreation in the midst of ever increasing casualty and death notices from the fighting front.

Within one day, Bill Peeler, sports editor of the *Salisbury Post* (home of the 1942 Salisbury Giants) added his voice to the plans for a semi-pro league in the textile towns of North Carolina's piedmont. He said, "Thanks to the efforts of Robert (Red) Ennis [who pitched for the Landis Senators in 1942 and eventually had a ten year professional baseball career] and the ready cooperation of men who played leading parts in the now-suspended

N.C. State League, it looks as though semi-pro baseball will be revived in this section for the duration. Ennis has been contacting baseball enthusiasts in several nearby towns in the attempt to organize a wartime semi-pro circuit to partially take the place of the N.C. State loop."

Five neighboring towns — Mooresville, Kannapolis, Concord, Landis and Salisbury — indicated interest. A sixth team would be needed to balance the league. An organizational meeting was called for Friday, April 2, at the Landis school. It was noted that players could be secured for the ranks of Class D professionals and other minor leaguers now working in the local textile plants and up and coming local amateurs. It was hoped that a four games per week schedule, two at home and two away, could be maintained. Some of the interested civic leaders indicated they had buses at their disposal while other teams would be able to travel by public transportation if necessary. This question of the mode of travel was responsible for the first name the league selected — the Gold Highway League, referring to U.S. Highway 29 that ran from Salisbury in the north through Landis, Kannapolis, Concord, Charlotte and Gastonia. The players would get no salaries but would agree to split any profits — playing mainly for the fun of it.

The *Concord Tribune* praised the organization. Plans for the league included "numerous benefit games to be played throughout the season to aid in the sale of war bonds, help for the Red Cross, and in general give the fans a chance for the recreation and assistance in the war effort at the same time. This means the league is for recreation and keeping the sport alive while our boys are on the battle fronts. They will return some better day after they have made this country and the world a safer and saner place in which to live."

Because of the wartime restrictions, every effort would be made to use the uniforms, equipment and ballparks of the suspended N.C. State League. All games would take place at night because the players would be working at their regular jobs during the day. On April 9, 1943, the *Concord Tribune* reported that the Gold Highway League had been organized with C. Manley Llewellyn president and Gordon "Chubby" Kirkland vice-president (Kirkland was a coach at Catawba College, Salisbury). The board of directors was Bobby Hipps, a long time minor league professional from Kannapolis; Boyd B. Horton, businessman from Concord; George Wright from Landis; Max Brockman from Salisbury and A.S. Jarrett from Highland Park Mills in Charlotte. Llewellyn, as he accepted the president's position, said, "The man in the street has spoken. He wants the Gold Highway League."

During the next few days there was considerable discussion of the league's name — Gold Highway League — and the necessary commercial or public transportation that would have to be used due to gas rationing. Very few agreed that Gold Highway League reflected the conditions for this wartime ration league. Bill Peeler suggested "The Worker's League." By April 25 the "Carolina Victory League" was permanently adopted, referring to North Carolina and the war victory for which the entire nation was praying.

On April 25, Kannapolis dropped out of league consideration. Representing Kannapolis at the league meeting was Mack McKa, *Kannapolis Independent* writer, and Joe Palmisano, a Kannapolis resident who had a "cup of coffee" with the Philadelphia Athletics in 1931, and was for many years a minor league catcher. Joe made the following statement, "Officials in Kannapolis are interested more in winning the war than in baseball." It was also added that Cannon Mills, which owned the entire town, was to begin a campaign to enlarge and upgrade the local YMCA which had nearly 8,000 people participating, compared to a daily attendance of 800 at the N.C. State baseball games in 1942. League baseball leaders argued in vain, and the Kannapolis attitude persisted. Thereafter, the league was finalized with Salisbury, Landis, Concord and Highland Park Mills in Charlotte. Salisbury was somewhat of a puzzle. John Heving, who had spent part of eight years in the majors and had been the manager of the 1942 Salisbury Giants, was lining up some good ballplayers but had not been able to get the small monetary backing needed. Finally, Sam Swartz, an avid baseball fan for years and a local junk and salvage dealer, agreed to back the team financially. It was reported that the Highland Park players, who included a number of former professionals, were more interested in playing in the Carolina Victory League than in the Twilight League of the Charlotte area. The schedule was finalized with 55 games, with the season to begin May 14 and end on August 14, to be followed by a playoff. Four games per week would be played on Tuesday, Wednesday, Friday and Saturday nights. Baseball (on a ration basis) was back, but the league president, C. Manley Llewellyn, would experience more trials and tribulations in this semi-pro league during the summer of 1943 than he would in his six years of organized baseball's Class D N.C. State League and five years as president of the Class B Tri-State League.

The Season

The Landis Millers opened the season on May 14 by defeating the Concord Weavers 7–1 behind the 3-hit pitching of Robert "Red" Ennis. Ennis, a native of Salisbury, would have a ten year career in organized professional baseball, ending in 1953, after six years with the Richmond Colts of the Class B Piedmont League. His lifetime record in professional baseball was 131 wins and 94 losses. Concord's losing pitcher was Virgil "Coddle Creek" Taylor, a native of Cabarrus County and a well known hurler in the N.C. State League. Taylor had also pitched in the outlaw Carolina League for the talent-laden Kannapolis Towelers team.

Because of rain, the Highland Park Mills Highlanders of Charlotte could not open their season with the Salisbury Aggies until May 16. However, the second game between the Landis Millers and the Concord Weavers in Landis on May 15 indicated just what a wild and wooly baseball season was in store for the baseball hungry fans in these piedmont North Carolina textile towns. In the fourth inning Landis was winning 5–0 behind the pitching of former Philadelphia Athletics pitcher Herman Fink, a native of piedmont North Carolina. That is when all hell broke loose. Concord scored eight runs on five hits, one walk, three errors and according to the subsequent actions, some very questionable umpire decisions. Herman Fink, (former major league pitcher) after questioning ball and strike decisions by umpire "Chock" Ross (a native of Concord), backed off and hurled a baseball at the head of umpire Ross. His control did not improve — the ball missed Ross's head. At that point Reid Gowan, Landis pitcher, a professional baseball veteran (as well as a former professional umpire) charged home plate from the Landis bench and became embroiled in a slugging match with umpire Ross. Other Landis players said they had a difficult time parting the two men. George Wright, a Landis team official and a member of the league's board of directors, said that he saw an open knife in Ross's hand during the scrap. Ross, a highly respected semi-pro umpire, was known to carry a knife in case he needed it for protection. Landis won the game 9–8.

League president C. Manley Llewellyn suspended Fink and Gowan for the remainder of the season. Llewellyn handled the dispute just as he would have in organized professional baseball. Llewellyn said, "We just can't have anything like that happening in the league. Therefore, I have suspended Fink and Gowan for the season." That left Landis with only two quality starting pitchers—Robert "Red" Ennis and Lacey "Lefty" James. (Three years later in 1946, James, pitching for the Concord Weavers in Class D N.C. State League, would lead the league with 22 wins and an earned run average of 2.47.)

Finally, after this brouhaha, the Highland Park Mills Highlanders and the Salisbury Aggies opened their season on Sunday afternoon, May 16, at Griffith Park in Charlotte. The Highlanders won 2–1 behind lefty Dwight Wilkerson's six-hit pitching. The losing pitcher was Ray Blair, a youngster from Catawba College who allowed eight hits.

As the month of June approached, professional baseball scouts (both major and minor leagues) were beginning to comb the Carolina Victory League. Everyone was losing baseball players to the military draft. Ira Thomas, long time Philadelphia Athletics scout, compared the league to wartime Class C baseball or peacetime Class D baseball. He invited "Red" Ennis to Philadelphia for a workout with Connie Mack's Philadelphia Athletics. Ennis, after refusing the invitation, later signed with the Boston Red

Sox for delivery in the 1944 season. Claude Dietrich, a scout for the Atlanta Crackers of the Class A1 Southern Association, was also active in the Carolina Victory League area. His prize catch was Billy Goodman, a seventeen year old that would report to the Atlanta Crackers in 1944 and six years later would be playing for the Boston Red Sox and lead the American League in hitting with a .354 average. These scouts began to make quite a few enemies among the leaders of the Victory League. Dietrich, trying to sign Bob Wilkens, Catawba College player and shortstop of the Salisbury Aggies, incurred the wrath of Catawba College coach and league director "Chubby" Kirkland. Kirkland minced no words in the subsequent dispute.

Don Harwood, American Legion star from Albemarle, NC, was pitching a no-hitter for the Concord Weavers against the Salisbury Aggies when Dietrich called him aside during the fourth inning and tried to persuade him to sign then and there. After returning to the mound, Jim Mallory, Salisbury outfielder (and former University of North Carolina star and Washington Senator player, presently a Catawba College coach) homered to start a five run rally for Salisbury that won the game. Concord's manager, Ginger Watts (a former outlaw league player with four years' experience managing in the N.C. State League), was furious over the bloodhound's inopportune tactics. Sam Swartz, general manager of the Salisbury Aggies, also hit the ceiling when Dietrich tried to talk to his players while a game was being played. Swartz called Atlanta and told the Atlanta Crackers officials how their scout was operating, and they promised to correct the situation.

During June, the fans and sportswriters thought the quality of the umpiring had become intolerable. Good umpires, like good players, were hard to find during the war. Llewellyn, league president, was having his own troubles keeping umpires at the game. Irregular wartime working hours at the umpire's primary job plus gas rationing sometimes prevented an ump from appearing at a scheduled game. Bill Peeler, sports writer for the *Salisbury Post* wrote:

> It shouldn't be new to Victory League Prexy Llewellyn that fans are more than a little dissatisfied at the handling of the umpire situation and are demanding that something should be done ... for some time now games at Salisbury have been run by one league umpire, with a player or two from the competing teams filling in where there should be another "blue suit" with eyes ... it always makes players serving as umps look bad when they have to call a close play against their own team ... Bill Ridenhour, veteran umpire from Cooleemee hasn't turned up for so long that you'd think the prexy would realize that he'd quit ... Charlotte and Salisbury have both protested vigorously and repeatedly over the work of the Dingler brothers, who call all or practically all of the games in Landis and Concord. Sam Swartz and John Heving [Salisbury team] are going to turn up with stomach ulcers one of these days

from just thinking of the Dinglers, but Lew won't get rid of them or split up the combination. [It did not take much imagination on the part of the fans to change their name to "Dingbats."] And, of course, there was some criticism earlier in the season when Ed Cross [former professional and outlaw league player], with a son on the Landis team, umpired a lot of games which Landis played. Later he quit as arbiter and signed as a player with Landis. Of course, Ed had been in the game a long time and no doubt was calling 'em like he saw 'em regardless of who was affected, but that didn't keep the bleacher wags from saying Ed had turned over a new leaf and decided to be honest about the whole thing—any honest fan will admit that the outcomes of a few games here have been affected by decisions called by players acting as umpires—players trying to do their best in an unfamiliar role. Those decisions have gone both ways—we don't want to see anybody go on relief and we know that rotation of umpires is impractical now, but if we were prexy we'd break up the Dingler combine, in which one of the partners declares that he makes his own rules, and we'd dig up a couple more experienced guessers—it's not that anybody's getting robbed or anything like that, but lousy umpiring, which usually evens up over the long stretch, just irritates the customers so much they can't enjoy the game and they finally get in the habit of staying at home and reading the papers, where they can get just as mad at John L. Lewis [Labor leader] and Hitler without buying a ticket or burning gas.

With problems like this, why would C. Manley Llewellyn love this game? It could be that the Victory League was doing just was Lew wanted it to do—it was supplying good family entertainment with a lot of hullabaloo that temporarily diverted their attention from the war and gave the folks something to talk about away from the ballpark.

In addition to the extra-curricular activities, there were baseball games being played. Here are the league standings as of June 22, 1943:

Team	Won	Lost	Pct.
Landis Millers	12	9	.571
Highland Park Mills	12	10	.545
Concord Weavers	11	10	.524
Salisbury Aggies	7	13	.350

On July 1 President Llewellyn called a league meeting. After the meeting, Lew said, "Everybody seemed to feel better when he got everything off his chest. We believe the league will operate more satisfactorily and more harmoniously in the future. We believe now we are on an even keel." President Llewellyn announced that A.F. Dinger, an umpire from Kannapolis whose umpiring had caused some dissatisfaction in the league, had resigned and accepted a position in Akron, Ohio. He was replaced by a Mr. Vickers, formerly an N.C. State League umpire. Officials believed that all the past turmoil would be removed under the new setup. The league also increased the monthly club dues from $27.50 to $30.00 and boosted the umpire traveling expenses. The other news was that ballots were being distributed to the teams and voting would start immediately on a league All-Star team that would play the Navy Pre-Flight team from the University of North Carolina in Greensboro on July 17 and in Chapel Hill on August 1. The Pre-Flight team was loaded with former major leaguers such as Ted Williams and Johnny Pesky from the Boston Red Sox.

By July 11 the Concord Weavers had taken over the league lead with a 17–14 record, followed by the Highland Park Highlanders with 18 wins and 16 losses. Landis was third with a 15–16 record, and the Salisbury Aggies were still on the bottom with a 14–18 record. But the Aggie fans may have been having more fun than any other fans in the league. The Aggie general manager, Sam Swartz, was keeping everybody loose with his antics. Fred Severance wrote in the *Concord Tribune* that Sam, with his manager, Johnny Heving, out with a case of lumbago, was acting manager and good-will ambassador for the Aggies. Severance wrote:

> The first thing that impressed us about Sam Swartz was that when his players ran to the Salisbury dugout to take their turn at bat, that swarthy Swartz would proceed as though wound up like a mechanical toy in the other direction and take his place alongside our own affable "Slim" Ingram [Concord first baseman and former professional] at first. Then, as his team cavorted to their playing positions, he would decide to warm the bench during Concord's brief interval at bat.... His face reminded us of Charlie Chaplin with a mustache to match the inimitable movie star's ... he would return to the bench with a walk suggestive of Donald Duck ... if he faced a Concord lawyer, his mustache would lift almost imperceptibly and a word or two of greeting would follow ... we could see that his fellow Sam had scored a bull's eye with the bleacherites. As he passed by, one of them would say, "Get in there and pitch, Sam. You can hypnotize the sluggers with your mustache" ... if his flinger [pitcher] shows signs of falling apart, Sir Samuel with a shifty glance at the umpire, will enter the sacred precincts of the infield like a dancer leading the grand march. A hush descends over the ball park as the First Citizen of Salisbury approaches his luckless pitcher, gesticulating and waving his arms like Don Quixote's wind mill. He evidently wants to relieve the hapless pitcher in the box, but the southpaw won't surrender the ball and grips it tightly midst the howls of delight from the stands. The one-man comedy is a hit with all except the umpires who eye the star performer icily from afar ... then the malice aforethought gives the pitcher a Red Grange push as he is edged away ... he is somewhat allergic to the umpire's decisions—if they are against his team. His temperature also mounts when one of his men is called out on a very close decision. Sam has very emphatic ideas about aerial runways over which "strikes" operate, and their boundary limitations. When the umps spot Sam coming their way, they reach for their gas masks as though they had served in World War I.... Not getting any affirmative action from the arbiter, Sam led the charge-minus his bayonet-to the box seat of Prexy Llewellyn. For another ten

minutes, the Rowan ball magnate conversed with quivering impatience with the Victory League chieftain, who eyed the stratosphere, waiting for the all clear signal. Sill no satisfaction and the game continued much to Sam's annoyance. If Sam faces the umpire with his fingers registering a V for Victory sign, the fans know that he has "just begun to fight."

On July 11 the Victory League announced the All-Star team that would play the Navy Pre-flight team from UNC at Chapel Hill in Greensboro on July 17.

First Team	Position	Second Team
John Little-Sal.	1B	None Selected
Nig Lipscomb-H.P.	2B	Bob Beal-H.P.
Holy Cross-Landis	3B	Marvin Watts-Con.
Bob Wilkens-Sal.	SS	Homer Trexler-Landis
Cecil Lawing-Landis	LF	Bill Goodman-Con.
Glenn Short-H.P.	CF	Bill Carter-Sal.
Jim Mallory-Sal.	RF	Chuck Lentz-Landis
Ginger Watts-Con. (Manager)	C	Boley Todd-H.P.
Dwight Wilkinson-H.P.	P	Don Harwood-Con.
Dick Mauney-Con.	P	Red Crocker-Sal.

It is interesting to note that Salisbury, with the worst record in the league, had five players on the two teams, the same as Highland Park and Concord. Landis had only four.

The nine leading hitters in the Victory League were: Glenn Short, Highland Park—.350; Dub Johnson, Concord—.333; Chuck Lentz, Landis—.333; Homer Trexler, Landis—.333; Boley Todd, Highland Park—.327; Bill Carter, Salisbury—.324; Queen, Highland Park—.310; Harry (Slim) Ingram, Concord—.301; and "Toots" Rogers, Concord—.301. Four of the top ten leading hitters of the league were not chosen for the All-Star team.

Sam Eaton, Salisbury; Chick Suggs, Landis; and Nig Lipscomb were tied for the home run lead with four each. Jim Mallory, Salisbury, and Chuck Lentz had three home runs each. Vernon Benson had two home runs. John Little, Salisbury; Hack Wilson, Highland Park; Marvin Watts, Concord; and Holy Cross, Landis, had one home run each.

Pitching records at the All-Star break were: CONCORD—Aldridge 4–0; Mauney 7–2; Harwood 4–4; Taylor 1–3; Ferguson 0–2 and White 0–3. HIGHLAND PARK—Short 1–0; Spain 2–0; Wilkinson 9–1; Cozart 3–1; Jenkins 2–1; Cooper 0–2; Little 1–2; Monteith 0–2; Stone 0–5. LANDIS—Spencer 0–1; Ennis 6–4; James 4–4; Gowan 1–1; Thompson 2–4; Lemly 1–2; Lowder 0–1. SALISBURY—Peirce 2–0; Blair 4–3; Lentz 2–2; Fesperman 1–1; Creason 2–3; Crocker 2–4; Eaton 1–2; Swanner 0–1; Bigger 0–1.

As expected, the Navy Pre-flight team mauled the Victory League All-Stars 11–3. The Pre-flight team included Harry Craft CF, Cincinnati Reds; Johnny Pesky SS, Boston Red Sox; Buddy Hassett 1B, N.Y. Yankees; Ted Williams LF, Boston Red Sox; and second baseman Moriarity, Boston Red Sox. Craft, Pesky and Williams all had three hits each. Glenn Short, league leading hitter for the All-Stars, also led the team in the All-Star game with two hits. There is no doubt that the Victory League players would remember playing against the major leaguers as long as they lived. However, the thrill and excitement of this game on July 17 was somewhat diminished by a league meeting on Friday, July 16.

The meeting was enormously contentious. In its wake, league President C. Manley Llewellyn read the following statement: "I am suspending Sam Swartz for the remainder of the season from the operation, ownership or management of the Salisbury team of the Carolina Victory League on account of conduct and attitude detrimental to baseball. I am leaving the suspension open to the league board of directors should Mr. Swartz decide to take an appeal. If they disapprove of my action, it will be allowed." The conduct detrimental to baseball referred to in Llewellyn's statement was the "Cardinal Sin" of baseball — gambling on the outcome of games. Swartz immediately appealed. Because Mr. McEwen was representing Highland Park Mills in place of the regular director, A.S. Jarrett, the directors decided to put off the appeal until no later than 2 p.m. Saturday afternoon so that the Charlotte director could be there. The already precarious life of this wartime semi-pro league had taken another dangerous turn.

At the Saturday meeting Concord and Charlotte voted in favor of upholding the suspension. Robert "Red" Ennis, Landis director and player, said, "I thought the announcement of the action of the other directors today [Saturday] was made rather early and that a new meeting of the directors should be called." Sam Swartz was ready to play his ace card. The Salisbury players stated they would not play for anyone else. Swartz added that he had an ironclad lease on Newman Park at Catawba College, home ground of the Aggies, until September 15, and that no other team sponsor could have the right to use the field. After this news, Llewellyn stated, "I don't know just what will happen to this league. Other towns will be contacted, and we hope to have an announcement within the next day. However, if the league should fold up, I think it would be better for baseball to have the league fold up than to continue having such action as has been that of the Salisbury owner and acting manager."

In a public relations defense Swartz said he had lost about $1,000 of his own money but that he had split the winnings with his players because the gate receipts were not enough to pay the players any kind of salary. Swartz said he had been "railroaded" because the suspension came several weeks after Ray Howe, writer for the *Charlotte News,* wrote that he had been betting on the games. It was also noted that Swartz had worked up the anger of Gordon "Chubby" Kirkland, Catawba College coach, when Kirkland learned that Swartz was planning a trip to Philadelphia for a tryout of several Catawba College players (Bob Wilkins, Vernon Benson and Jake Almond) with Connie Mack's Athletics. Swartz even planned to cancel several league games while they were gone.

The Mooresville Moors, under manager Johnnie Hicks, joined the Victory League on July 20, just three days after the league board of directors upheld Sam Swartz' suspension for gambling. It is ironic that Mooresville would be playing against Norman Small, a member of the Concord Weavers. Before his professional career ended in 1953, Small established himself as one of the greatest home run hitters in minor league history. Today, he is still a legend in Mooresville where he played 10 years of his 18 year career in professional baseball. Small was drafted after playing 53 games with the Jersey City Giants of the International League. He returned home to Mooresville and joined the Concord Weavers on July 10. On July 20 he would be playing against his adopted home town and the town where he became a legend. He literally destroyed the pitching of the Victory League before he left in August to join the army. After one game, the *Tribune* reported: "Lost: one baseball. Last seen over the left field fence at Webb Field Thursday night, the destination appeared to be North Union or Church Street. P.S. It was the homer hit by Norman Small" (approximately three city blocks away).

With the league approaching the end of the season and more and more players being called up in the draft or taking their normal summer vacations, teams scrambled to field a team. After Mooresville was in the league only two days, they had to forfeit a victory over Landis for using ineligible players. Earlier in the summer, Mooresville residents Russ Morrow and Forrest Thompson had signed contracts with Landis and had played several games for the Millers. After not having the gasoline to get to games, they had quit playing. Now that Mooresville had a team, they started playing with Mooresville, even though they were ineligible to play for anyone but Landis—so Mooresville had to forfeit a 5–4 victory over Landis.

On August 1, the Carolina League All-Stars suffered their second defeat at the hands of the Navy Pre-flight team in Chapel Hill 7–4. Ginger Watts, Nig Lipscomb and Billy Goodman got two hits each in a losing effort. Ted Williams, Red Sox star, went hitless in four times at the bat. The pitchers that held the Splendid Splinter hitless were Dick Mauney, four innings; Virgil "Coddle Creek" Taylor, three innings; and Robert "Red" Ennis, one inning. Dick Mauney would later have a 12–14 record with the Philadelphia Phillies, 1945–47. "Coddle Creek" Taylor was a native of the Coddle Creek

This partial team photograph of the 1943 Concord Weavers incudes slugger Norman Small who joined the team late in the season. Left to right: first row, Billy Goodman, Norman Small, Leroy Stewart; second row, Marvin Watts, "Shade" Huneycutt, Bill Kluttz, Manager Herman (Ginger) Watts; third row, Richard (Dick) Mauney, Harry (Slim) Ingram, Don Harwood, "Toots" Rogers. Absent: "Buck" McAnulty, "Coddle Creek" Taylor, Arch White, Ralph Ritchie, Hoyle Boger (Hank Utley).

area near Concord and had many years in the Class D leagues. Robert "Red" Ennis had a ten year minor league career, six years with the Richmond Colts in the Class B Piedmont League. Shutting down Ted Williams was something to remember.

The 1943 season of the Carolina Victory League ended on August 14 with the Concord Weavers in first place with a 34–20 record, followed by Highland Park Mills at 29–25. Third place was claimed by Landis with a 26–27 record and Mooresville (Salisbury) was on the bottom with 18 wins and 35 losses.

The fireworks were not over yet. In the first round of the playoffs between Concord and Landis, Concord protested after the fourth game, claiming that Landis had been using an ineligible player, (Roy Pinkston who had jumped a contract with Rochester, N.Y., in the International League). The time element was all important in this protest. Pinkston claimed he did not know he had been placed on the ineligible list. After the

Victory League inquired, Judge W.G. Bramham, czar of organized professional baseball, replied that Pinkston had not been notified of his ineligibility until Saturday, August 21, so he was eligible to play for Landis up to that date. President Llewellyn said, "If Pinkston didn't know he was placed on the ineligible list on Friday, August 20 and received notification on Saturday, August 21, it would seem he was within his rights signing with Landis. It's not certain games in which he played prior to Friday, August 20 should be tossed out." To further complicate the matter, Landis filed a counterprotest that Concord had also been using ineligible players, Norman Small and Dub Johnson.

Bill Peeler of the *Salisbury Post* summed up the situation with this statement from the Landis representatives:

> 1. Pinkston was informed that he had been placed on the ineligible list of professional baseball only after the fourth game of the playoff series with Concord had been played. (Concord was down 3 games to 1 and then lost the fourth game later)
> 2. Pinkston participated in the fifth and final game, (giving Landis the series 4 games to 1) but this fact is nullified by the fact that Concord used two unsigned players, Norman Small and Dub Johnson, in the fifth game. The two men had played with the Weavers before, but after entering the army they were temporarily released (furloughed). But they had not been resigned by the Weavers before the playoffs began.
> 3. The Weavers were over the player limit of 18 men during the regular season and playoffs. During the season the Weavers had 21 men in uniform for three games and in the playoffs they had at least 19 men in uniform. A picture of the Weavers on August 23 showed 19 men in uniform.

President Llewellyn decided to drop this hot potato in the laps of the league's board of directors. At the meeting were Llewellyn, Vice-president Gordon "Chubby" Kirkland of Salisbury, I.B. McKeown and Luck Brackett of Highland Park Mills, Byron Hager and Johnnie Hicks of Mooresville. Highland Park told the group that unless an amiable agreement could be worked out that they would end the season immediately, and the finals would not be played. (Highland Park had eliminated the Mooresville Moors from the playoffs.) After reading the charges and countercharges from Concord and Landis, President Llewellyn and Bill Peeler, Salisbury reporter, attending the meeting for the press, retired from the meeting.

Much later, Llewellyn was called back into the meeting to count the votes. There was some sentiment that both teams had broken the rules, but since Landis had won the series decisively, 4 games to 1, the games would stand as played.

Roy Christenbury, sportswriter of the *Concord Tribune,* summed up the season to date when he wrote: "It looks like Prexy Llewellyn has had a hard job from the opening of the season to the present date. Lew, in our estimation, has handled matters well. He has had to smooth out matter to the satisfaction of all several times. We must say, 'He's done O.K.'"

The Highland Park Highlanders won the Victory League Championship on September 2 by defeating the Landis Millers 4 games to 3. On September 8 the Italian government surrendered to the Allies, but there would be many months of bloody fighting and many deaths before the world would return to peace and textile town baseball could once more join the peaceful ranks of the National Association of Professional Baseball Leagues.

Bibliography

Newspapers

Asheville Citizen-Times
1953: September 6
1954: September 5
1970: March 20
1970: April 2

Atlanta Constitution
1940: August 20

Atlanta Journal
1940: August 19

Charlotte News
1936: June 30

Charlotte Observer
1935: June 7, 8, 11, 12, 18
1936: July 7, 19, 22

Concord Tribune
1936: June 16, 17, 20
1943: April 9; July 11

Durham Herald
1937: August 27
1993: May 11

Hickory Daily Record
1938: August 27
1941: June 7, 10

1951: April 11, 27; June 21; August 8; September 15

Kannapolis Independent
1976: June 28

Morganton News Herald
1941: June 7

New York Times
1932: September 8
1933: September 15
1935: September 4, 11
1937: April 15
1941: June 7

Salisbury Post
1943: June 1

The Sporting News
1935: June 13, 20; July 25; August 1, 8, 29; September 12
1936: May 14
1939: April 27
1941: June 12

Winston-Salem Journal
1948: February

Internet Articles

Clark, Michael. "The Sad Tale of Alabama Pitts." *Philadelphia Athletics Historical Society*. 2002. Accessed 07 Feb. 2005. http://www.philadelphiaathletics.org.

Densa, Steve. "Minor League Baseball 50 Years Ago." *Minor League Baseball.com*. 21 April 2004. Accessed 25 April 2004. http://minorleaguebaseball.com/articles.

Journal Articles

Overfield, Joseph. "Product of Sing Sing Won Public's Support." *Baseball Research Journal.* October 1985, 19–22.

Books

Shores, R.M. *Just Like It Was.* New York: Carlson, 1975.
Utley, R.G., and Scott Verner. *The Independent Carolina Baseball League, 1936–1938: Baseball Outlaws.* Jefferson, N.C.: McFarland, 1999.

Index

Agnew, Troy 28
Albany, NY 16, 22
Albany Senators 36
Allen, George 105, 106
Allen, Gile 132
Allred, Chaver 178
Appling, Luke 78
Asheville, NC 22, 53, 54
Atlanta Crackers 9
Autograph Ball Co. 80

Baker, Ulmont 43, 72, 111–116, 171
Barley, George 1, 103–110, 174
Barton, Vince 1, 120–124, 128–130, 153, 156, 172
Battle of the Bulge 81
Becker, Heinz 78
Biggerstaff, "Pick" 114
Binks, George 78
Bi-State League 17
Boger, Hoyle "Bob" 178, 189
Boken, Bob 76
Bolick, Mark v
Boston Red Sox 151
Bramham, Judge W.G. 4, 37–40
Broughton, Gov. 50
Broughton Hospital 52
Brown, A.L. 131
Buffalo Bisons 9
Bush, Joe 8

Calvary Lutheran Church 16
Cambria, Joe 22, 36
Cannon Mills 126
Carolina League 17
Carolina Victory League 12, 19, 177–191
Carr, Johnny 47, 48,
Carr, Myrtice 51
Carrier, Bill 84, 85
Carrier, Edna 84, 85

Catawba College 18
Cavaretta, Phil 80
Chapman, Chet 118
Chapman, Fred 5, 16, 42, 44
Charlotte, NC 19, 45, 84, 85
Charlotte Hornets 45
Chicago Cubs 120
Chicago White Sox 68, 97, 98
Chitwood, Ken 114
Church, John 52, 57
Cicotte, Eddie 56
Clark, Michael 49
Clarke, Grey 66–68
Coastal Plains League 82
Columbia, SC 28
Concord, NC 19
Concord Weavers 12, 18
Cooleemee, NC 2
Corriher Mill 23
Coveleski, Stan 9
Culbreth, Stumpy 124
Culler, Richard Broadus 2, 14, 71–80

Dallas, Texas 68
Davis (Hitchner), John 146, 147
Davis, Lawrence "Crash" 5, 86–96, 172
Deal, Mildred 49
Dean, Dizzy 37
Dobson, NC 7
Duke University 86, 89, 90, 91, 104, 105
Durham Bulls 26, 27
Durham *Herald Sun* 26, 32
Durocher, Leo 77, 109
Dyer, Eddie 76–78
Dykes, Jimmie 78

Elrod 132
Evers, Johnny 38

Fallston, NC 47, 50
Fernandez, Nanny 79

196 Index

Fink, Herman 134
Fisher, C.P. 16
Fletcher "Boots" 178
Forest City, NC Owls 55
Foster, Evelyn Williams Culler 71, 73
French, Oliver 24
Furr, Troy 178

Gibson, Josh 109
Gilbert, Larry 74, 75
Glen Cove, NY 21
Glock, Charley 75
Glover, "Buck" 15
Goodman, Billy 178, 181
Greenville Spinners 9
Griffith, Cal 13
Griggs, Hal 30
Guise, Witt "Lefty" 115
Gunnells, Luke 114
Gurley, Dick 15

Hager, Cloyd 15
Harman, L.C. 116
Harris 132
Harrisburg-York, PA 23
Harwood, Don 178, 189
Hemphill, Jim 56
Hickory, NC 29, 30, 32, 144–149
Hickory *Daily Record* 30, 31
Hickory Rebels 153
High Point College 73
Hines, Houston 133, 139–143
Hipps, Bobby 56, 60–65, 132, 172, 173
Hitchner, Tracey 56, 123, 144–149, 174, 175
Hollis, Ruth 17, 18
Hopkins, Frank 20, 133–135
Horan, James D. 3
Hot Springs, AR 22
Hoyt, Waite 8, 9
Huggins, Miller 9
Huneycutt, Shade 178, 189

Ingram, Harry "Slim" 178, 189

James, Norman "Pinkie" 152, 158
Japan 29
Jenkins, Jay 13
Jersey City, NJ 28
Jones, Sam 8

Kannapolis, NC 7, 10, 82
Kannapolis team records 169, 170
Kannapolis Towelers 18

Kansas City Monarchs 103
Kinston, NC 81
Kiser, Jack 15
Kluttz, Bill 178, 189
Knapp, Charles H. 41
Krichell, Paul 103, 104
Krist, Howard 76, 77

Lail, Harold 48, 154–160
Lamesa, Texas 30
Landis, Judge K. M. 37, 38, 40
Landis, NC 2, 19, 22, 23
Landis Cardinals 17
Lawes, Lewis E. 35
LeFevers, Newland 49
LeFevers, Roy 49
Lehman, Hubert H. (Gov.) 39
Lenoir-Rhyne College 14, 26
Lentz, Marvin 22
Lexington, NC 17
Little, Lloyd 15
Llewellyn, Clement Manley 7–13, 127, 177–191
Llewellyn, Robert C. 8
Lochbaum, Emil 75
Lutheran Theological Seminary 16
Lutz, Ab 145, 148

Mack, Connie 5
Macon, GA 67
Mamaux, Al 22, 23, 38, 43
Marianna Islands 29
Marshall, Willard 75
Martin, Hersh 78
Martinsville Manufacturers, VA 17, 22, 28
Mauldin, Nell 68
Mauney, Richard "Dick" 178, 189
McAnulty, Harold "Buck" 178, 189
McCall, Rusty 132
McCarthy, Joe 108
Means, Tony 83
Menzies, Donald "Ram" 147, 148, 154
Meyers, Billy 109
Mihalic, John 76
Miller, Cal 14
Miller, D.C. "Pud" 29, 30, 31, 32
Miller, Glenn "Razz" 2, 14–20, 173
Miller, Hollis 14, 16, 18, 19
Milwaukee, WI 68
Les Miserables 39
Mooresville, NC 21, 23, 24, 25, 29
Murray, George 8
Murtaugh, Danny 76

Index 197

Nagel, Bill 78
Narron, Sam 28
National Association of Professional Baseball Leagues (NAPBL) 12, 17, 37, 84, 112, 122, 144, 147
NC State League 12, 18, 29
Neville, Eddie 32
Newark Bears 107, 108
Ninety-Seventh Army Division 29
Normandy Beach 81

Oak Ridge Military Academy 7
Oano, Prince Henry 153
O'Doul, Lefty 8
Opelika, AL 33

Packard, Frank "What-A-Man" 46
Paige, Satchel 103
Palmisano, Joe 146
Peck, Hal 78
Peeler, Ethel Sloop v
Philadelphia Eagles 35, 44
Philippine Islands 29
Pilsen, Czechoslovakia 28
Pinehurst, NC 110
Pitchford, Ruth 9
Pitts, Edwin Collins "Alabama" 33–52, 114, 173
Pitts, Erma Mills 33, 52
Pitts, Mary Walker 47
Pitts, Mildred 44
Pitts, Patricia Ann 47
Pitts family history (Myrtice Carr) 161–168
Poole, Jim 24
Prague, Czechoslovakia 28
Priddy, Gerald 27
Propst, Roy 131, 132, 138

Ray Doan's Baseball School 22
Reidsville, NC 72
Reynolds, Spencer 132
Rhem, Bethel 106, 132
Richmond, Earl 32
Rickey, Branch 22
Ritchie, Ralph 178, 189
Rizzuto, Phil 77
Rocco, Mickey 76
Rockwell, NC 2, 14
Rogers, "Toots" 178, 189
Ross, Buck 1, 5, 97–102, 132
Rudd, Robert E. 33
Rumple, Shine 15
Russian Army 29
Ruth, Babe 7

St. Louis Cardinals (Chain Gang) 68
St. Peters Lutheran Church 19
St. Stephens–Mount Olive Lutheran Church 19
Salisbury, NC 19, 69
Scott, Everette 77
Secory, Frank 78
Shaney, Charles M. "Bud" 1, 46, 53–59, 175, 176
Shaney, Charles R. 57, 58
Sharpe, E.J. 131
Shawkey, Bob 8
Sherer, Al 28
Sherrill, Sara 25, 26, 27
Shires, Len 153
Shirley, Ernest "Mule" 8
Shores, Pat 149–154
Short, Clyde 13
Sing Sing Prison 34
Sisti, Sibby 79
Small, Harry 21
Small, Norman 1, 21–32, 173, 174, 178, 181
Snow Hill, NC 82
Southern University Prep 150
Southmont High School 17, 18
Southworth, Billy 80
Stanky, Eddie 79
Statistics, batting and pitching 171–176
Steineke, Bill 113, 114
Stewart, C.E. 10
Stewart, Leroy 178, 189
Susko, Pete 153
Suttle, Reid 49

Tallent, Johnny 178
Taylor, Ellis 132
Taylor, Virgil "Coddle Creek" 81–83, 178, 179
Taylor, Winnie 81, 83
Thomasville, NC, Tommies 18
Tipton, Eric 128
Trinity Lutheran Church 19
Tri-State League 12
Tron, Horace 49

University of North Carolina 7, 10
Utley, Jack v
Utley, Jean v
Utley, Ruby v

Valdese, NC Textiles 46
Vale, NC 19
Verner, Scott 1, 3

Wade, Jake 4, 39, 118, 119
Walker, Frank 10
Washington Senators 16
Waterloo, IA 28
Watkins, Mrs. G.C. 81, 83
Watts, Herman "Ginger" 136, 178, 189
Watts, Marvin 11, 135–139, 174, 178, 189
Watts Crossroads 2, 133
White, Archie 178, 189
White, Bob 132
Whitiak, Woody 132

Whitley, Henry 10, 106, 121, 125–132, 141
Whitley, William "Bill" 122, 124, 132
Wichita Falls, Texas 30
Wilks, Ted 76, 77, 78
Williams, Edwin "Cy" 69, 70
Wilson, Hack 42, 121
Wilson, Rube 11
Wolfe, Wilma 113

Young, Tom 132

www.ingramcontent.com/pod-product-compliance
Ingram Content Group UK Ltd.
Pitfield, Milton Keynes, MK11 3LW, UK
UKHW042007140426
5217IPUK00015B/1028